GOVERNING AI

Governing AI is about getting AI right. Building upon AI scholarship in science and technology studies, technology law, business ethics, and computer science, it documents potential risks and actual harms associated with AI, lists proposed solutions to AI-related problems around the world, and assesses their impact. This book presents a vast range of theoretical debates and empirical evidence to document how and how well technical solutions, business self-regulation, and legal regulation work. It is a call to think inside *and* outside the box. Technical solutions, business self-regulation, and especially legal regulation can mitigate and even eliminate some of the potential risks and actual harms arising from the development and use of AI. However, the long-term health of the relationship between technology and society depends on whether ordinary people are empowered to participate in making informed decisions to govern the future of technology – AI included.

Onur Bakiner is Professor of Political Science and Director of the Technology Ethics Initiative at Seattle University.

Governing AI

A PRIMER

ONUR BAKINER
Seattle University

CAMBRIDGE
UNIVERSITY PRESS

CAMBRIDGE
UNIVERSITY PRESS

Shaftesbury Road, Cambridge CB2 8EA, United Kingdom

One Liberty Plaza, 20th Floor, New York, NY 10006, USA

477 Williamstown Road, Port Melbourne, VIC 3207, Australia

314–321, 3rd Floor, Plot 3, Splendor Forum, Jasola District Centre, New Delhi – 110025, India

103 Penang Road, #05–06/07, Visioncrest Commercial, Singapore 238467

Cambridge University Press is part of Cambridge University Press & Assessment, a department of the University of Cambridge.

We share the University's mission to contribute to society through the pursuit of education, learning and research at the highest international levels of excellence.

www.cambridge.org
Information on this title: www.cambridge.org/9781009738309

DOI: 10.1017/9781009738347

When citing this work, please include a reference to the DOI 10.1017/9781009738347

First published 2026

A catalogue record for this publication is available from the British Library

A Cataloging-in-Publication data record for this book is available from the Library of Congress

ISBN 978-1-009-73830-9 Hardback
ISBN 978-1-009-73833-0 Paperback

Contents

Acknowledgments

Matt Gallaway is an amazingly quick, thorough, and encouraging editor. Thank you for everything, Matt. I would like to thank Stephen Ceccoli, Robin Jacobson, Maroussia Lévesque, Amit Ron, Amy Semet, the participants of the Value and Responsibility in AI Technologies Conference at Gonzaga University (April 3–4, 2025), and the anonymous reviewers for their useful comments on earlier drafts of this book's chapters. I would also like to thank Sarah Cate, Mark Chinen, Julie Homchick Crowe, Pejman Khadivi, Erik Moore, Juan Carlos Reyes, Sara-Jo Swiatek, and Dongsheng Zang for their feedback on earlier versions of this book. Special thanks to Maggie Chon and Nate Kremer-Herman, who gave this book the most meticulous and rich read-through imaginable. I have benefited from many conversations with Caitlin Carlson Ring, Jeffery Smith, and Randy Souza over the years, for which I am grateful.

I would like to thank Sevdiye Bakıner, Kemal Bakıner, Egenur Bakıner Yücebilgiç, Çağlar Yücebilgiç, Alp Yücebilgiç, Eylem Sönmez, Ayşe Kurşun, and Maya Alev for giving me love and support through the years. *Hep aklımdasınız.*

This book is dedicated to my wife Ece. *İyi ki varsın.*

Introduction

Thinking Outside and Inside the Box to Govern AI

Artificial intelligence (AI) will cure cancer. AI will destroy humanity. AI is the *ichor* of humanoid robots. AI is Big Data. AI is the new oil, the new electricity, the new Industrial Revolution, the new atomic bomb. AI is like tobacco. AI is like junk food. AI is a parrot.[1] AI is a mirror.[2] AI is marketing hype – snake oil.[3]

I am sure you have read or heard these statements about AI.[4] Depending on which opinion leader you follow, you might think that it is the most transformative technology of our times, a hyped-up technology that has not given humanity reliably useful products yet, or something in between. In popular imagination, AI is at once magical and dangerous. Crowd-pleasing movies portray it as a soulless destroyer (*The Terminator*), a soulless seducer (*Her*), or a misunderstood, curious humanoid on the verge of developing consciousness – and, who knows, a soul (*Atlas*). Novels like Kazuo Ishiguro's *Klara and the Sun* and Ian McEwan's *Machines Like Me* interrogate what it means to be human when machine intelligence is so close to our minds, hearts, and perhaps supermarket shelves. Documentaries like *Coded Bias* and *The Social Dilemma* take issue with the social ills associated with software and platforms powered by algorithms. It seems like we are at the precipice of something great if we get AI right. And if not … well.

This book is about efforts to get AI right. Building upon AI scholarship in science and technology studies, technology law, business ethics, and computer science, it documents potential risks and actual harms associated with AI, lists proposed solutions to AI-related problems around the world, and assesses their impact. This book presents as many theoretical debates and as much empirical evidence as possible to

[1] Bender et al., "On the Dangers of Stochastic Parrots."

[2] Vallor, *The AI Mirror: How to Reclaim Our Humanity in an Age of Machine Thinking.*

[3] Narayanan and Kapoor, *AI Snake Oil: What Artificial Intelligence Can Do, What It Can't, and How to Tell the Difference.*

[4] A note on term usage: Throughout this book, *AI* refers to the underlying science and technology. Qualifiers, such as *generative* or *symbolic*, are used where appropriate. *AI tools* are software, services, or platforms available to customers. *AI systems* denote the combination of hardware and software systems with AI and non-AI components. Specific definitions are provided in Chapter 1.

document how and how well *technical solutions*, *business self-regulation*, and *legal regulation*, which stand out as AI governance toolkits, work.

Governance refers to coordinating and steering a society with a multiactor, multilevel, and networked framework.[5] Whereas standard theories of government focus on the state as the organized actor ruling over society, governance models argue that international organizations, nation-states, local governments, businesses, and nongovernmental organizations coordinate and decide in harmony. Thus, governance acknowledges multiple levels of jurisdiction and a networked decision-making process rather than top-down decision-making by government.[6] *AI governance* is about collective decisions about people, and the artifacts they develop and use with an AI component.[7] Such decisions come from businesses developing and using AI systems, regional, national, and subnational governments and, to a lesser extent, international bodies. As it will become obvious, AI governance has not emerged as a result of conscious coordination by multiple actors; to the contrary, a combination of technical fixes, business practices, and government regulation has coalesced in an unplanned and imperfect way. Throughout this book, *AI governance* is used as a descriptive, not normative, term. In other words, governance does not a priori mean that the technical, business, and government solutions to AI risks and harms are always useful and effective. Rather, the objective in this book is to hold this governance model to critical scrutiny.

AI can be governed partially through a combination of scientific and technological improvements in accuracy, reliability, safety, data protection, and fairness; in-house or external boards, councils, and teams that oversee adherence to ethical business principles in the AI sector; laws and policies regulating AI products (e.g., chatbots and automated decision-making software) and techniques (e.g., deep learning and generative AI) specifically; and laws and policies addressing issues adjacent, but not exclusive, to AI, such as data privacy, data protection, antitrust, and content moderation. In the ideal scenario, technical solutions propel AI models and resulting products to successful implementation of ethical norms, while self-regulatory bodies commit businesses to ethical conduct, and laws and policies set binding parameters around private-sector practices to ensure respect for fundamental rights. This idealized governance scheme is likely to produce some desirable results in part because AI-centric and AI-relevant laws and policies build upon established legal systems with a history of regulating the negative impact of scientific and technological developments, and in part because business incentives are at times aligned with the deployment of accurate, reliable, safe, and fair AI products.

5 Bevir, *The SAGE Handbook of Governance*; Rhodes, "The New Governance: Governing without Government."

6 Kooiman, "Social-Political Governance: Overview, Reflections and Design."

7 For recent scholarship on AI governance, see: Bullock et al., *The Oxford Handbook of AI Governance (Oxford Handbooks)*; Batool, Zowghi, and Bano, "AI Governance"; Veale, Matus, and Gorwa, "AI and Global Governance: Modalities, Rationales, Tensions."

The idealized governance model will not work seamlessly, however. Each component of this governance scheme has weaknesses – some more than others. Technical solutions are often found in proof-of-concept papers, with little evidence of business adoption. Even when they are implemented, there is no evidence that they offset the magnitude of the problems they claim to address. Ethical AI boards, councils and teams, at arm's length from the core money-making endeavors they oversee, have been fighting for relevance and impact, if not survival, since their origins in the mid-2010s. In other words, technical solutions and business self-regulation have limited leverage vis-à-vis the business incentives, models, and practices they want to reform. Disciplining businesses through binding laws and policies remains an untapped potential: There are numerous bills but few actual laws regulating AI. Legal regulation is not without its shortcomings, though. Lawmakers in major AI-producing countries are all too happy to seek advice from the same corporations they are supposed to regulate; thus, the risk of what legal scholars call "regulatory capture" by industry is all too real. The systemic negative impact of AI on the environment, workers' rights, and market competition has received almost no legal attention. Furthermore, some of the worst risks of AI – for example, lethal autonomous weapons systems – keep concerned activists, journalists, academics, and international lawyers up at night, but politicians have averted serious regulatory proposals in national or international law.

The shortcomings of techno-solutionism, business self-regulation, and legal regulation are only part of the story. Getting AI governance right cannot be disentangled from local and global struggles for justice and equality. A racist society cannot but develop racist AI. A sexist society cannot but develop sexist AI. A society in which a significant part of the population denies basic facts and scientific findings cannot get content moderation right. A society in which technological progress empowers only a small number of corporations – and a few startups in their orbit – cannot build fair AI. Critical decisions around AI governance (e.g., decisions on what constitutes hate speech, who deserves to be hired, what to do when an algorithm flags the wrong person for arrest, or even what is true and what is false) are almost entirely made by the companies developing AI products or government and private-sector actors using them. The people who are negatively affected by those decisions are denied a seat at the table. It is true that AI creates new problems and amplifies existing ones, but deep down, where AI fails is where human societies fail.

Data-driven, machine learning-based AI was born into a planet facing an ecological crisis, declining trust in political institutions and severely challenged information ecosystems in democracies, not to mention deepening national and global inequality. Most people, including citizens of technologically advanced countries, feel alienated from the decisions shaping their lives. The gap between citizens and the politicians who are supposed to represent them is widening. At any rate, a small number of unelected corporate leaders have been making decisions that shape people's lives as much as, if not more than, governments. People enjoy the convenience and fun brought by contemporary technologies but cannot stop asking why supposedly transformative technologies come with a baggage of bias, discrimination, surveillance, disappearance of data privacy, disinformation, rumors of massive unemployment, and the specter of even more inhumane warfare than ever before.

That is why this book is a call to think inside *and* outside the box. Pragmatically, existing AI governance models are too important not to advocate for. Technical solutions, business self-regulation, and – especially – legal regulation can mitigate and even eliminate some of the potential risks and actual harms arising from the development and use of AI, and no other short-term solution is realistic. However, the long-term health of the relationship between technology and society depends on whether ordinary people are empowered to participate in making informed decisions to govern the future of technology – AI included. Put simply, the problem is disempowerment and alienation, and the solution is people's informed participation.

Reflecting on decades-long critical discussions on modern technology, I argue that the development of today's AI is at once a cause and consequence of most people's disempowerment and alienation. Academic and journalistic evidence of AI risks and harms refutes the naïve assumption that all technologies benefit everyone without qualifiers. Misalignment between the profit motive and human interests, the presentation of artificial intelligence as an expert field, the market concentration of a few companies, research and development gaps that threaten to deepen access inequality within and across countries and the hierarchies of the capitalist workplace all contribute to disempowerment and alienation. Politicians and political parties have so far done little to close the gap between the interests of most people and decisions made by AI industry leaders. Academia, suffering its own crisis of alienation from the public, faces stiff competition from industry in research infrastructure and recruitment of top talent. Nongovernmental organizations, academics, journalists and a few politicians advocating for the defense of rights in the context of technological change appear to be the only actors bringing ordinary people's struggles to public debates, but their economic and political power is limited.

Anyone interested in the development of AI as a technology in the service of the common good, in whatever way defined, should therefore take the call for the expansion of citizens' agency in making collective decisions seriously. The technical intricacies involved in technological decision-making cannot be ignored, but the academic and journalistic evidence compiled in this book leaves no doubt that decisions that go into the research, design, development, deployment, and use of AI are about the distribution of benefits and risks among people – in a word, politics. Thus, I argue that everyone has an interest in, and skills for, shaping the future of AI.

This analysis of technical, corporate, and legal governance should acknowledge the true heroes in this story: Journalists, researchers, social movement activists, whistleblowers, lawyers, conscientious corporate workers, and (a few) politicians who have raised awareness around AI risks and harms. Every single case of course correction described in this book was made possible thanks to someone who sounded the alarm after meticulous research on an AI system that affected someone negatively. Without them, we would have lived in a world of illusions in which we would accept without evidence that every technological product is good and anyone raising objections is a hopeless technophobe.

I believe AI can still be reimagined and developed as a technology that serves humanity while causing minimal or no harm. Humans can live in harmony with technology. It requires a robust governance model that leverages technical, business, and government solutions to detect and mitigate risks and harms. A genuinely successful governance model that goes beyond avoiding the worst harms to actually reconstruct AI as a public good necessitates a radical rethink of technology, and through it, society. Citizens cannot allow themselves to be passive recipients of technology in the age of AI. We need to reclaim our agency to build a better world.

DATA AND METHODS

This book draws upon a study of online media archives, which cover (1) newspapers (e.g., *The New York Times*, *The Washington Post*, *The Boston Globe*, *The Globe and Mail*, *The Guardian*, *The Economic Times*), (2) technology magazines (e.g., *Wired*, *TechCrunch*, *MIT Technology Review*); (3) online technology blogs; (4) academic publications in the social sciences and humanities, law, journalism, and computer science; and (5) company blogs and reports.

News articles about the following are selected:

- AI and AI-related concepts, such as machine learning, deep learning, algorithms, automated decision-making systems, and generative AI;
- Potential risks and concrete harms arising from AI, such as bias and discrimination, disinformation, surveillance, data privacy violations, and labor exploitation;
- Terms associated with socially desirable AI, such as accuracy, ethics, fairness, responsibility, safety, and transparency;
- Proposed technological solutions, such as AI for social good, de-biasing, AI detection, and red-teaming;
- Business oversight boards, councils, and teams, such as Meta's Oversight Board and Microsoft's Responsible AI Council;
- Bills and laws that aim to regulate AI or AI-related concerns, such as privacy and consumer protection, around the world; and
- Opinion pieces that offer a bird's-eye view of the relationship between AI and society.

The collected information is analyzed using quantitative and qualitative content analysis. The quantitative analysis relies on a comparison of term counts over time (e.g., the use of *AI ethics* over time), term co-occurrences (e.g., *de-biasing* used in the same sentence as *discrimination*) and in comparison to similar terms (e.g., *AI ethics* vs. *responsible* AI). These comparisons present a picture of the evolution of ideas and practices around AI governance. The qualitative component of analysis identifies common patterns, themes, and meanings, and instances of scholarly agreement and disagreement across texts. Every piece of academic and journalistic evidence that a proposed solution has worked or failed is documented, and analyzed in light of available information. If the explanation for an event or decision has generated disagreement among academics, journalists, social movements and industry spokespersons, multiple evidence-based viewpoints are reported.

BOOK OUTLINE

Chapter 1 introduces basic terminology. Terms such as *artificial intelligence*; *data*; *algorithm*; *machine learning*; *neural networks*; *deep learning*; *large language models*; *generative* AI and *symbolic* AI are presented to develop a sense of what AI is, how it has evolved and what it does. This chapter also introduces some of the major conceptual disagreements in the field. Different ideas about how to develop AI in the best way drive disagreements, as well as philosophical differences over what intelligence means and whether machines can develop human-like intelligence.

Chapter 2 is devoted to AI ethics, broadly defined. It provides an overview of *ethical*; *responsible*; *safe*; *trustworthy*; *transparent* and *explainable*; *accurate*; *just* and *fair*; *accountable*; *sustainable*; *robust*; *accessible* and *inclusive* AI. Just as the definition of AI itself is fraught with disagreement, words with a connotation of "good" AI have generated considerable controversy among academics, social movement activists, journalists, business leaders, and lawmakers. This chapter aims to represent the plurality of positions. Furthermore, the adjectives associated with getting AI right are mutually supportive, but tensions between desirable goals are mentioned as well.

Chapter 3 presents the other side of the coin, namely AI risks and harms. Automated decision systems, chatbots, recommender systems and other AI-powered software and platforms have been found to cause potential risks or actual harms to affected persons and communities. Such risks and harms include *bias and discrimination*; *surveillance*; *inaccurate, incorrect, and unreliable output*; *disinformation, misinformation, or manipulation*; *harm to life, livelihood and wellbeing*; *privacy violations*; *decline in product and service quality*; *political polarization, online radicalization and algorithmic censorship*; and *job replacement*. Some of these harms, like bias and discrimination, have already been experienced frequently, while others, like job replacement, point to future risks. It is also worth noting that AI risks and harms often aggravate existing social and political problems. For example, political polarization and radicalization, while exacerbated by algorithmic curation, appear to have origins in societal divisions. Finally, AI is criticized for causing system-level harm in the form of *environmental degradation*; *exploitation of labor*; and *market concentration*.

Chapter 4 is devoted to technical solutions to rectify AI risks and harms. *AI for social good projects*; *human-in-the-loop solutions*; *de-biasing*; *AI-generated text, image and voice detection*; and *testing* are presented as potential technical fixes. Detecting AI-generated content remains a major challenge. Human-in-the-loop solutions and testing have proven to be such commonsense practices that they are promoted by AI-producing or -using businesses themselves as well as by laws. AI for social good projects and de-biasing produce positive impact, but there seems to be a gap between expectations and reality. As is documented throughout this book, the roots of AI risks and harms are not technical; therefore, technical solutions cannot bring about transformative change in the face of AI risks and harms.

Chapter 5 addresses business self-regulation as an AI governance model. Voluntary AI principles and codes of conduct have risen to prominence in the absence of AI laws since the mid-2010s. Numerous large companies have established internal or external advisory boards or councils and responsible AI teams to hold themselves accountable. The evidence on these self-regulatory bodies is mixed: Journalistic reports suggest improvements in business conduct in a number of cases, but one cannot ignore the fact that none of the boards, councils, or teams can force businesses to respect their decisions or suggestions. What is worse, some powerful AI companies have ignored calls to create self-regulatory institutions or disbanded them at first sight of friction.

Chapter 6 is about laws as binding mechanisms to eliminate or mitigate AI risks and harms. Most countries have AI-promotion strategies that devote little or no attention to potential problems. The number of bills proposed in national legislatures to address those problems has been increasing since the late 2010s, but only the European Union and South Korea have thus far legislated laws regulating AI. Despite the absence of AI-centric lawmaking, however, some trends are emerging. First, AI regulation has been taking place, to a limited extent, in AI-adjacent realms such as data privacy and protection, consumer rights, antitrust, and children's protection. Second, the European Union's AI Act has set the trend for risk-based, future-proof, and technology-neutral legislation that will likely be followed by other countries. Third, the absence of national legislation in the United States, home to most cutting-edge AI technologies from the 1990s to the early 2020s, has led states and cities to take initiative. And finally, even the successful passage of a law does not address all AI risks and harms – lawmakers' omission of military AI as an area of regulation is a case in point.

Chapter 7 zooms out of conceptual and empirical studies of AI governance to ask if we can build a better future with AI. The technical, corporate, and legal governance models presented in this book are necessary but insufficient to endow ordinary people with the power to push back against risks and harms, and chart a course for AI for the common good. Thinking together with philosophers and social scientists in the Critical Theory, Science and Technology Studies, and Democratic Theory traditions, I argue that most people's experience with AI is one of fear as a result of their long-standing disempowerment and alienation from the technologies shaping their lives. Attributing disempowerment and alienation to technical aspects of AI is wrongheaded: It is the evolution of modern capitalism that has widened the gap between people and the technologies that are supposed to make their lives better. Reorienting the relationship between people and AI requires a radical-democratic politics that questions hierarchy in government and in the workplace. Technology can serve as a force for the social good only if informed citizens participate in the decisions shaping their lives in the design, development, deployment, and use of modern technology, AI included.

The prologue fleshes out the lessons drawn from this book. It offers best practices for a workable AI governance model that uses technical solutions, business self-regulation and legal regulation. Then, it delves into some of the shortcomings of that model. The radical-democratic perspective I advocate makes five general, practical suggestions for everyone concerned with AI risks and harms. (1) *Organize*: Build networks of support and civic organizations around technology-specific concerns as well as conventional rights considerations; (2) *Learn*: Acquire cross-disciplinary capabilities on the uses, practical applications, potential risks, and governance models associated with technologies like AI; (3) *Participate*: Push politicians and businesses to expand the boundaries of decision-making in the public and private sectors; (4) *Care*: Approach technological change from the perspective of vulnerable populations, and with an ethic of non-domination that refuses to treat nature and other people as instruments; and (5) *Resist*: Maintain an openness to contention with the producers and users of technologies that generate risks and harms.

1

What's in an Abbreviation? Defining and Understanding AI

The term *artificial intelligence* (AI) was first used by mathematician, computer scientist, and cognitive scientist John McCarthy in his letter of application to conduct a workshop on machine simulation of intelligence funded by the Rockefeller Institute in 1955.[1] The attribution of intelligence was in reference to getting computers to accurately, quickly, and efficiently complete tasks generally associated with human logical, mathematical, strategic, and sensory capabilities. McCarthy's application, which culminated in the Dartmouth Summer Research Project on Artificial Intelligence of 1956, is often portrayed as a founding moment in AI research. Interestingly, McCarthy coined the term as a placeholder. He did not mean the term to invite direct mind–machine comparisons; he simply wanted to avoid the conceptual baggage accompanying similar terms at the time, like *automata* and *cybernetics*.[2]

Despite the term's humble origins, a machine's ability to mimic human cognitive behavior has captured the imagination of generations of AI researchers. AI is deceptively hard to define. This chapter offers a conceptual background on AI and AI-related terms to set the context for the rest of this book. What is more, definitions demystify: The science of AI is admittedly complex, but its underlying intuition should be made understandable to lay audiences. Portraying it as some kind of magic is not only scientifically wrong but also serves to give undue power to a small group of AI developers and the companies employing them.

This short chapter is structured as follows: "Defining Artificial Intelligence and Related Terminology" offers nontechnical definitions for *AI*, *data*, *algorithms*, *machine learning (ML)*, *neural networks*, *deep learning*, *large language models (LLMs)*, *generative AI*, and *symbolic AI* – leading concepts in the contemporary AI discourse. Closely related technical terms, such as *supervised learning*, *unsupervised learning*, *reinforcement learning*, *hidden layers*, *weights*, *attention*, *self-attention*,

[1] Ball, *The Book of Minds: How to Understand Ourselves and Other Beings, from Animals to AI to Aliens*: 276.

[2] Nilsson, *The Quest for Artificial Intelligence: A History of Ideas and Achievements*: 78.

context window, *statistical error*, *false positives*, *false negatives*, and *benchmarks*, are introduced as well.

The section called "Definitional Controversies" delves deeper into the causes underlying conceptual disagreements. Three sets of disagreements in the scholarly literature and practitioner discourses deserve mention:

(1) Rule-based, data-driven, and hybrid AI: Nowadays, most AI applications are based on complex algorithms that learn from large quantities of data. An earlier conception of AI, one that relied on building rules and facts into computer systems, is widely regarded as obsolete, but its defenders claim that combining the strengths of rule-based AI with those of data-driven AI in a hybrid format can address the inaccuracies and safety failures of the data-driven version.
(2) AI and human-like qualities: The language around AI, starting with the word *intelligence* itself, reflects a choice by the field's pioneers to describe their work as giving computer systems human-like capabilities. The tendency to anthropomorphize AI lives on, but not everyone thinks that this is an honest description of reality.
(3) AI as hype: AI has become as much a marketing and sales term as one that describes the underlying science and technology. Critics question whether some companies that claim to use AI actually do so, how much value the AI component adds to their business, and how realistic speculations of general or superhuman intelligence are.

This chapter concludes with some observations on why definitions and definitional disagreements matter for AI governance. For all the hype around machine intelligence, learning, reasoning, and perception, today's AI is not endowed with human-like contextual awareness, cultural nuance, and meaning-making. Lawmakers, nonprofit leaders, industry professionals, journalists, and the broader public should treat AI as what it is – an impressive yet inherently limited application of statistics, calculus, linear algebra, and social network theory to large quantities of data. The more we all are aware of what AI can and cannot do, the better we can harness its power to help us solve real problems.

DEFINING ARTIFICIAL INTELLIGENCE AND RELATED TERMINOLOGY

Artificial Intelligence

The Organisation for Economic Co-operation and Development's (OECD) definition of an AI system, which has been imitated verbatim or with minor adjustments by other official bodies worldwide, reads: "a machine-based system that, for explicit or implicit objectives, infers, from the input it receives, how to generate outputs such as predictions, content, recommendations, or decisions that can influence physical or virtual environments."[3] Stuart Russell and Peter Norvig's authoritative textbook on the subject defines AI as "the study of agents that receive percepts from the environment and perform actions."[4] This rather broad definition leads the authors to break down different philosophies of agency: Artificial agents can be said to behave (i.e., perform certain tasks) or think (i.e., perform cognitive processes). The yardstick against which to measure computers, in a maximalist sense, is human behavior and thought. Instead, Russell and Norvig choose to focus on rational action, which they define as delivering the expected outcome. This way, they hope to avoid controversies surrounding the use of words like thought and behavior to refer to machine output. Even as they do so, however, they acknowledge that AI has grown out of interest in scientific fields concerned with human cognition and behavior, such as neuroscience, cognitive psychology, and linguistics.[5]

Computer systems using AI are particularly good at recognizing patterns, classifying messy real-world data into categories, estimating and forecasting quantities of interest, solving complex mathematical problems, calculating payoffs in situations requiring strategic decision-making, and identifying clusters of nodes, such as people or computers, interacting in networks. Thus, these systems excel at playing games like Pac-Man, chess, and Go, classifying objects in photos, recognizing human faces and voices, identifying potentially tumorous cells, forecasting outside temperature and stock prices, translating documents, generating sentences and paragraphs, discovering and recommending taste profiles, and much more.

AI's integration into robotic systems, that is, hardware with animal- or human-like motion capabilities, has led to the conflation of *AI* with *robots*. Research in image processing, robotics, and AI indeed have shared roots in the history of science. It is important to disambiguate, however: AI can exist in the absence of robotic components because complex mathematical models and logical formulas contained under the term AI typically do not perform motion-related tasks. To give a simple example: An AI-enabled chatbot that interacts with its users is not a robot. Likewise, not all robots have AI elements that give them automated decision-making capabilities. Therefore, AI-powered robots are at the intersection of the separate fields of AI and robotics.

Alongside AI, the word *data* has moved to the center of technology conversations. It is widely understood that AI is about data collection and analysis. *Data* [sing. datum][6] may refer to any piece of information. A survey response, the color of a photo pixel, a person's heart rate at a given moment, the number of cars crossing an intersection, and the movement of a finger on a screen are all examples of data used by AI algorithms. Sensors with audiovisual data collection capabilities

3 www.oecd.ai/en/ai-principles

4 Russell and Norvig, *Artificial Intelligence: A Modern Approach*: viii.

5 Russell and Norvig.

6 It is worth noting that the use of *data* as a singular noun has become widespread in the recent past.

are everywhere – think smartphone microphones and cameras, touchscreens, voice assistants, and also conventional appliances like street cameras and odometers. Human characteristics – like age, gender, or income – and behavior – like shopping, taking a cab, or going on a vacation – add to the wealth of information to be analyzed. This vast availability of data collection methods, thanks to the ubiquity of internet-connected devices and databases, marks a major difference from the not-so-recent past, not only because of the large quantities of data to be analyzed but also because the data tend to be multifaceted and messy – imagine the kind of data that a web browser collects based on registered users' audiovisual traces, finger movements, shopping behavior, and duration of stay across multiple devices.

Not all AI systems are data-intensive (see the section on Symbolic AI), and not all data require complex AI algorithms to be analyzed. Nonetheless, the use of computer-run algorithms to make sense of vast quantities of data, which do not lend themselves to straightforward human interpretation, has proven so advantageous that nowadays, the terms *data* and *AI* almost always go together. What is more, the need to prepare the datasets for analysis, validate their quality, and store and process them efficiently has led to the growth of adjacent fields of data science, data engineering, data mining, and data analytics, which intersect, but are not synonymous, with AI.

AI experts come from various professional backgrounds. Mathematicians have no doubt laid the theoretical foundations of the field, as have computer scientists. Today, most AI experts work in computer science and software engineering. As AI expertise has become increasingly more specialized, job titles have adapted as well. AI engineers, data scientists, data engineers, and ML specialists all perform different yet complementary tasks. A few businesses have also added a chief AI officer to the C-suite. Not all AI-related job titles have the words *AI* or *data* in them: Many academic researchers and private-sector employees with conventional job descriptions, such as chemists, physicists, or radiologists, have combined their domain knowledge with emerging expertise in AI use cases in their field.

Algorithm has recently become popular as a synonym for AI, but they are not identical, either. The dictionary definition of an algorithm is any procedure that helps to accomplish a task. How I tie my shoes is an algorithm, as is how I navigate a trip to the grocery store. In the AI context, an algorithm refers to a complex mathematical model that helps a computer system to automate tasks and improve performance by making sense of data. In other words, it is an abstract model to achieve the best outcome for a task. The goal of AI research and practice is to find the most accurate, precise, and efficient algorithms to draw insights from data. As the definition suggests, algorithms are designed to focus on achieving substantive tasks. Such tasks include completing a round of Pac-Man with the fewest steps possible; finding the likelihood of a match between two photos; identifying unusual patterns in a photo, video, or audio; completing a sentence with the most plausible arrangement of words; finding the shortest driving time between two addresses; suggesting a person's new friend, favorite movie, or favorite song; and much more. Those tasks are represented abstractly in logic, statistics, calculus, linear algebra, and social network theory in the process of building effective algorithms.

Machine Learning, Neural Networks, and Deep Learning

Talk of AI almost always invokes *ML*, *neural networks*, and *deep learning* these days. ML refers to the ensemble of estimation, prediction, and classification techniques, also known as *algorithms* or *models*, that use statistics, calculus, linear algebra, and social network theory to make sense of data. The mathematical procedures underlying ML algorithms are not novel; basic statistics and calculus have been around for centuries, and research on even sophisticated techniques like neural networks had begun in the early 1960s. However, these techniques are too complex to work through with a pen and paper and do not provide useful insights with small batches of data. The increasing compute-power of processing units since the 1990s and data availability since the late 2000s, thanks in great part to internet-connected devices like smartphones, have revolutionized the usefulness of these algorithms, which take a large quantity of data as input to optimize the parameters of the underlying mathematical model. The real-world concern is to make sense of data as accurately as possible. This translates to statistics as discovering the best fit between the model and the error resulting from the use of that model on data it has not trained itself on.

Machine learning algorithms are categorized by what they do (e.g., classification, estimation, and forecasting), the techniques used (e.g., neural networks, decision trees, K-means clustering, and regression analysis), and the substantive area of use (e.g., natural language processing, computer vision, and voice recognition). The different approaches to *learning*, that is, providing the best fit between the data and the model, include *supervised learning*, *unsupervised learning*, *semi-supervised learning*, and *reinforcement learning*. The difference between supervised and unsupervised learning is about whether humans guide a computer system to determine the expected output or whether algorithms find relevant patterns in the data without human intervention. It is important to note that a task can be tackled with different ML techniques, and each technique may use a variety of approaches to learning. For example, a researcher or product developer who wants to distinguish between photos of dogs and those of cats might use supervised neural networks, whereby the computer program identifies a new photo as a cat or dog based on the data humans have already tagged as cat and dog photos, or unsupervised neural networks, in which the algorithm learns to distinguish between different-looking images with no prior human input. It bears warning that regardless of the approach used, computers do not have an intuitive understanding of what a dog or cat is, or why the distinction matters. Unlike supervised and unsupervised learning, which condition learning on previously collected data, reinforcement learning focuses on a computer system's interaction with the environment to figure out rewards and penalties.

Neural networks are a subcategory of ML, and *deep learning* is a subcategory of neural networks. The word *neural* indicates a conscious effort to imitate the human nervous system, but the success of this line of research is attributed more to what it has inspired than whether it gets the neuroscience right. The basic intuition of neural networks is to minimize error through a process of back-propagation, which ensures the best fit between the data and the algorithmic model. It does so by iterating over the weight of every piece of information that connects the data input to the output. *Weight* is a mathematical abstraction representing the relevance of different elements of a complex web of information. Each iteration brings the algorithm closer to a better solution of the problem at hand thanks to the *hidden layers*, that is, weights assigned to the data input that change to minimize the error. Reassigning these weights can take place over multiple iterations using deeper layers of calculation – hence the term *deep learning*.

The intuition behind neural networks and deep learning appears straightforward, but improving an algorithm's accuracy or performance requires working with datasets with millions, if not billions, of data points. Each data point is quantified into parameters, that is, relevant features that may indicate the color of a single pixel, the pitch in one nanosecond of a sound recording, or the position of a single word in a news article. Today's LLMs are trained with billions of parameters. Simply multiplying the number of data points with the number of parameters and with the number of iterations gives a sense of the complexity and required compute-power to operate neural networks.

Large Language Models (LLMs) and Generative AI

Large language models represent further progress in the application of neural networks. LLM architecture relies on *transformers*, that is, neural networks well-suited to generate output using highly interdependent input elements. Linguistic tasks, such as sentence completion and translation, fit this specification because words in a phrase tend to be interrelated. What is more, the interconnections are not merely sequential: The fifth word in a sentence may be correlated with not only the fourth and sixth words, but also with words farther apart. Think about the sentence: "I am going to the movie theater with a friend because we enjoy movies." The word "enjoy" is conjugated in accordance with "we," which aggregates the "I" and "my friend" – not to mention the semantic connection between "enjoy" and the first part of the sentence through the use of "because."

The critical element of the transformer architecture is *self-attention*, as opposed to the *attention* mechanism found in the standard neural network architecture.[7] While the attention mechanism assigns weights to hidden layers based on a sequence (starting from the input and ending in the output), the self-attention mechanism

7 Vaswani et al., "Attention Is All You Need."

acknowledges dependencies between input elements that are not sequential. In a way, it offers more context to an input element than the standard neural network – though it should be recognized that context refers to the placement of elements in relation to one another, not the kind of spatial and temporal awareness we understand with context in everyday language. What do LLMs know about enjoyment, movies, movie theaters, or cause and effect for that matter? The answer is, they do not have to. Having trained on trillions of letter and word sequences (*tokens* in technical language), they provide statistically plausible options to complete sentences, fill in the blanks, accomplish translation jobs, and generate complex answers to queries.

A related term is *context window*, which refers to the amount of input data that an LLM is capable of storing and processing. The longer the context window, by definition, the larger the amount of data stored and processed, and thus, the more relevant and accurate the results. Long context windows are what enable users to hold conversations with chatbots. A chatbot application with a long context window can structure the current conversation on past ones. In fact, the quality – and consequently, price – of today's chatbot products depends on the length of their context window.

It is worth noting that the word *language* in LLMs does not have to be one of the natural languages humans speak. LLMs tackle scientific and technological challenges as though they were linguistic ones. Uncovering the syntax and grammar of a language through many examples helps to solve linguistic problems; the color of a pixel in a photo or the chord progression in a musical composition can be predicted following a similar logic. Taken to extremes, reimagining complex issues as LLM problems may lead one to claim that massive data and advanced algorithms will obviate the need for area expertise – a claim that has not gone uncontested. In fact, AI pioneer and Nobel Prize laureate Geoffrey Hinton's 2016 recommendation to "stop training radiologists" because deep learning would overtake them in five years has been criticized and ridiculed.[8]

Generative AI has become the catchphrase for AI tools that create novel texts or images. Despite its success in capturing the popular imagination, the term *generative* alludes less to the creativity of AI tools than to the fact that these tools use generative models (i.e., statistical approaches that model the conditional probability of the observed data given a target). The guiding idea is that these models can produce novel data that is statistically plausible given the existing data – to offer an example, an LLM can generate a new recipe in the English language thanks to all the texts (ones unrelated to recipes included) it has trained on. Generative AI and LLMs are technically not synonymous because large quantities of data can be studied using statistical models other than generative ones, and also because generative models

[8] "Geoff Hinton: On Radiology," *Creative Destruction Lab [YouTube]*, November 24, 2016 (www.youtube.com/watch?v=2HMPRXstSvQ).

are used outside the LLM context. Nonetheless, almost all the text and image models that have made the headlines since 2022 use generative AI, so the two concepts are used as if they were synonyms.

Finally, how do we know if an ML-based model is successful? Most users of AI products simply want to get the job done, whatever that job may be. Ensuring reliable success requires standard evaluation metrics, which can be quite challenging to identify and implement in the context of AI.[9] Nonetheless, many metrics exist. The accuracy and usefulness of ML models depend on the fit between a model's expected results and the actual data. Thus, algorithm design aims to minimize *statistical error*, which refers to the gap between expectations and observed reality. In discrete tasks (e.g., tagging photos of dogs), that goal translates to minimizing *false positives* (e.g., tagging a photo with no dog in it as a dog photo) and *false negatives* (e.g., failing to tag a photo with a dog in it as a dog photo) – it is worth noting that ML experts use *accuracy*, *precision*, and *recall*, otherwise-ordinary words with specific technical meanings, to refer to model performance metrics.

In addition, *benchmarks* are used for the performance of algorithmic models vis-à-vis humans and other models. For example, researchers have come up with myriad benchmarks to assess Generative AI models' understanding of language. Typically, these evaluation metrics rely on questions akin to school exams to test a model's performance. The AI Index Report 2025, published by the Stanford Institute for Human-Centered Artificial Intelligence, lists twenty-three benchmarks to assess image classification, reading comprehension, English language understanding, mathematics, science, and multimodal reasoning.[10] Most benchmarks indicate constant progress: The Generative AI models of the mid-2020s are doing much better than their five-years-older predecessors. Nonetheless, not all benchmarks paint a rosy picture of AI advancement: Humanity's Last Exam, which uses 2,700 test questions over 100 subjects to assess leading LLMs' command of human knowledge, reports rather low test-taking skills.[11]

Symbolic AI

Even though they receive less attention currently, fields of AI other than ML deserve mention, in part because they make up the history of AI and in part because the shortcomings of ML have led some voices to call for a reappraisal of these other fields. Before today's neural networks, symbolic AI was the predominant form of making computer systems undertake complex cognitive tasks. The *symbolic* component refers to the ability to build a knowledge base of the world through

[9] Kevin Roose, "A.I. Has a Measurement Problem," *The New York Times*, April 15, 2024 (www.nytimes.com/2024/04/15/technology/ai-models-measurement.html).

[10] Maslej et al., "Artificial Intelligence Index Report 2025."

[11] www.lastexam.ai

representations (i.e., symbols). Humans can identify physical objects and abstract phenomena thanks to their ability to represent them in their minds. Symbolic AI requires an initial set of rules for the computer system to process. Accordingly, explicit rule-making is the basis of successful domain-specific models. A computer system that is good at playing chess thanks to symbolic AI cannot transfer that skill set to language translation.

Symbolic systems were the dominant form of AI from the inception of AI research from the 1950s to the 1990s. The emergence of *expert systems* (a subcategory of symbolic AI that combines a knowledge base that stores rules and facts with an inference engine that processes them) in the 1970s and 1980s made the industry adoption of AI a reality.[12] However, the difficulty of maintaining a knowledge base in domains where decisions require knowledge of an expanding set of rules and facts has always been the greatest shortcoming of these systems. Data availability and increasing computer processing power in the 2000s meant that neural networks, which do not require prior rule-making to obtain insights from data, overtook expert systems.

DEFINITIONAL CONTROVERSIES

Rule-Based, Data-Driven, and Hybrid AI

The tendency to equate AI with data-driven fields like ML, neural networks, and deep learning has been criticized for failing to acknowledge and use other forms of AI – especially the rule-based symbolic AI. The criticism directed at neural networks is that they produce a lot of errors – after all, the complex calculations going into data-driven AI boil down to statistical estimation and prediction techniques susceptible to statistical error. While it is true that some error is tolerable, especially in domains in which human decision-makers are prone to error, too, statistical error may be a matter of life and death in domains in which accuracy matters (think medical diagnostics, psychotherapy, journalism, or driving). Furthermore, neural networks require a lot of data for training, which is expensive, resource-intensive, and, in the case of human data subjects, susceptible to privacy violations. Furthermore, if AI research has set as its goal outperforming humans, then the task of learning from small amounts of data, which is what humans – especially children – are exceptionally good at, remains an outstanding challenge for data-driven AI.

Critics of neural networks typically advocate a hybrid approach rather than a full-fledged return to symbolic AI, whose Achilles' heel is its reliance on domain-specific rules given by humans. Proponents of *hybrid AI* – or what is sometimes called *neurosymbolic AI* – want to combine the strengths of rule-based and data-driven AI to maximize the benefits of both, namely the accuracy and robustness of the former

[12] Cercone and Murchison, "Integrating Artificial Intelligence into Literary Research"; Bundy, "Artificial Intelligence: Art or Science?"

and the scalability and creative potential of the latter.[13] Whether this is desirable or feasible has proven to be one of the major controversies in contemporary AI research and practice. As of this writing, major AI companies have been continuing to invest in data-driven AI, with little or no acknowledgment of the need for a hybrid component.

AI and Human-Like Qualities

AI terminology has fueled deep disagreements about what it means to be an intelligent agent and, consequently, a human. The entire field is built around concepts typically associated with human cognitive capabilities, like *intelligence* itself, *learning, reasoning*, and *perception*. To add to that, AI-powered products are said to converse, decide, read someone's mind, maintain a friendship or romantic relationship, invest, defeat an opponent, and more. The human-centric language around machine intelligence raises philosophical questions. Do computer systems learn, think, or act in ways identical or similar to humans? Does the manipulation of binary electric signals going in and out of computers, no matter how complex, count as intelligence? Or is the whole terminology around intelligence a marketing and sales pitch rather than an accurate description of how computers work? Alternatively, does the human brain work all that differently from a computer's processing unit? Are humans relatively complex yet imperfect input–output machines made of organic matter or is there more to being human?

For some, the qualitative difference between machines and humans is nonexistent or irrelevant. Accordingly, machines, just like humans, process sensory data to estimate, categorize, and predict outcomes of interest, which they use to decide on the best course of future action. AI agents are cognitively more capable than humans in some areas and less capable but catching up quickly in others. What is more, the hope that future AI agents will be intelligent in multiple tasks (imagine a single computer program that plays chess, detects cancer cells, and manages an investment portfolio) has heightened the prospect of versatile machine intelligence. The epitome of such thinking is *artificial general intelligence* (AGI) – a computer system capable of reaching or surpassing human intelligence in many, most, or all tasks. "We started DeepMind in 2010 as an industrial research lab with a mission to build Artificial General Intelligence" is how DeepMind CEO Demis Hassabis introduced his company at the Nobel Prize in Chemistry 2024 lecture.[14] Spokespersons for well-resourced technology companies often describe the nature of the competition in their industry as a race to build AGI. A few industry leaders

[13] Steels and Lopez de Mantaras, "The Barcelona Declaration for the Proper Development and Usage of Artificial Intelligence in Europe"; Marcus, "The Next Decade in AI: Four Steps Towards Robust Artificial Intelligence"; Garcez and Lamb, "Neurosymbolic AI"; DeLong, Mir, and Fleuriot, "Neurosymbolic AI for Reasoning over Knowledge Graphs."

[14] www.youtube.com/watch?v=YtPaZsasmNA

who have turned away from the hype associated with AGI use alternative wording to arrive at the same aspirations – Anthropic CEO Dario Amodei, for example, prefers "powerful AI."[15]

A more nuanced position among those who are sympathetic to machine *intelligence* is to acknowledge the differences between machines and humans, at least for now. Law professor Flynn Coleman, for example, argues that machine intelligence is still not endowed with "common sense," and cannot think or act on the fly.[16] In science writer Philip Ball's words, "Computers today, for all their staggering capabilities, remain closer to complicated arrays of light switches than even to rudimentary insect brains."[17]

Skeptics believe that computer systems will never develop human-like intelligence. AI pioneer Joseph Weizenbaum once called the notion that a machine could learn like a human a "perverse grand fantasy."[18] Critics point out that the supposed intelligence of computer systems is not much more than hyperbolic marketing. Emily Bender, Timnit Gebru, Angelina McMillan-Major, and Margaret Mitchell have coined the term "stochastic parrots" to refer to today's complex language models that produce statistically plausible text with no understanding of its meaning.[19] Critics in general argue that the use of anthropomorphic words to refer to tasks completed by computers, starting with the word *intelligence*, may be effective in exciting investors, technology journalists, and the lay public by evoking a mixture of futuristic optimism and dread but lacks scientific or philosophical foundations. Intuitive knowledge of others' thoughts and emotions, awareness of spatial-temporal context, cultural nuance, and meaning-making are human capabilities that machines will forever lack, it is argued. From this perspective, saying that a machine is intelligent is not much different from saying that an Excel sheet is intelligent.

AI as Hype

In 2019, London-based venture capital firm MMC released a survey of AI startups in thirteen European countries, finding that "[i]n approximately 60% of the cases … there was evidence of AI material to a company's value proposition,"[20] or in other words, about 40 percent did not have much use for AI. Two years earlier, Hanson Robotics presented the world with Sophia, which, according to the company's

[15] Dario Amodei, "Machines of Loving Grace: How AI Could Transform the World for the Better," October 2024 (www.darioamodei.com/essay/machines-of-loving-grace).

[16] Coleman, *A Human Algorithm: How Artificial Intelligence Is Redefining Who We Are*: 36–39.

[17] Ball, *The Book of Minds: How to Understand Ourselves and Other Beings, from Animals to AI to Aliens*: 270.

[18] Weizenbaum, *Computer Power and Human Reason: From Judgment to Calculation*: 203.

[19] Bender et al., "On the Dangers of Stochastic Parrots."

[20] MMC Ventures, "The State of AI 2019: Divergence," 99 (www.mmc.vc/resources/fund-brochures/The-MMC-State-of-AI-2019-Report.pdf).

website, is the "world's first robot citizen and the first robot Innovation Ambassador for the United Nations Development Programme."[21] It was given Saudi citizenship in November 2017, and a month later, company CEO David Hanson announced that she was "reaching out about women's rights in Saudi Arabia" and human rights elsewhere.[22] The company's efforts to anthropomorphize Sophia and some technology journalists' tendency to cheerlead them generated immense anger among AI researchers and developers, who published thoughtful warnings against this misrepresentation of AI progress.[23] Sophia did not even have autonomous text-generation capabilities, much less an ability to understand, reason, or defend rights.

AI has been thrown around as a marketing and sales pitch. The two magic letters are made to stand for everything that is data-intensive, computational, mathematically complex, useful, creative, and dangerous. Some supposed AI applications have no AI component at all. A more common situation is one in which businesses throw in AI to endow their goods and services with an aura of modernity, slickness, and prestige even if it adds little of substance. That deep learning is in most cases just a more expensive way to arrive at the same results as simple statistics is a common joke in the data science and ML communities. The joke gets the technology right but ignores the marketing and sales side of running a business. On the day Microsoft announced that it would charge business customers $30 extra per month for its AI-powered Office software called Microsoft 365 Copilot, its shares went up as much as 3.8 percent.[24] Share price as an indicator of expectations may contain informed valuation of business decisions as well as incorrect assumptions, and as such, it is difficult to argue that a thorough analysis rather than hype informs such immediate market reactions.

CONCLUSION

AI refers to computer programs that automate tasks. Automation is generally associated with increased efficiency, accuracy, or performance. Historically, *symbolic AI*, which consists of incorporating human-given rules, facts, and logical statements into computer systems, was the dominant type of AI, but data-intensive techniques subsumed under the term *ML* have led the advances in AI since the 2010s. AI and related terminology around it expose the moral and political disagreements societies

[21] www.hansonrobotics.com/sophia/

[22] Ryan Browne, "World's first robot 'citizen' Sophia is calling for women's rights in Saudi Arabia," *CNBC*, December 5, 2017 (www.cnbc.com/2017/12/05/hanson-robotics-ceo-sophia-the-robot-an-advocate-for-womens-rights.html).

[23] James Vincent, "Facebook's head of AI really hates Sophia the robot (and with good reason)," *The Verge*, January 18, 2018 (www.theverge.com/2018/1/18/16904742/sophia-the-robot-ai-real-fake-yann-lecun-criticism).

[24] Dina Bass and Bloomberg, "Microsoft will charge you $30 per month to use A.I. tools with Office – on top of what you already pay," *Fortune*, July 17, 2023 (fortune.com/2023/07/18/microsoft-office-365-copilot-openai-30-dollars-per-month/).

have developed over AI. Terms like *AI*, *ML*, *LLMs*, *robots*, and *algorithms* have their roots in technical fields, but their connotations go above and beyond the technical to capture what we desire and dread about technology.

I believe that the skeptical position that cautions against attributing human-like faculties to AI is much closer to the truth of AI today than futuristic narratives of human-like AI. The mixture of statistics, calculus, linear algebra, and social network theory that underpins today's AI is an unlikely candidate for producing a generally intelligent artificial agent with complex mental mapping, contextual awareness, cultural nuance, and meaning-making. It is true that LLM output can be astonishingly human-like, but researchers' inability to explain how a computer system generates an outcome is not necessarily proof of its superior intelligence. For all the hype around the cognitive abilities of LLMs, no one has yet published a peer-reviewed scientific article to corroborate a theory of the mind. Therefore, I am led to conclude that words like *learning* and *intelligence* should be used with caution because the processes through which computer programs arrive at human-like outcomes are not human-like.

What happened to Sophia, the robot? If anyone thinks technology journalists and politicians may have reflected on the silliness and irresponsibility of attributing human capabilities to a machine that obviously lacks them, that is sadly not what happened. The United Nations brought in Sophia and several other humanoid robots to its 2023 AI for Good Global Summit![25] This anecdote uncovers just so much of what needs to change about modern technology discourse: A machine with little or no AI capability should not be the face of AI; technology journalists should scrutinize developers' narratives about AI rather than publish them uncritically; nation-states and companies should not be allowed to hijack technology discourse with gimmicks; public education should be aimed at explaining the gap between human cognitive capabilities and machine capabilities; and the hard work of understanding and addressing the risks and harms of AI should receive the attention it deserves.

Questioning narratives of machine superintelligence and sentience is not technophobia. Being honest about what technology can and cannot do would make the public appreciate the achievements and temper expectations. In fact, skeptics of the AI hype tend to be specialists who have themselves contributed to the advancement of science and technology. AI-powered technologies have been making the world a better place by transforming medical diagnostics, drug discovery, urban planning, translation, and many other walks of life. Wild speculation about their future capabilities makes for fun conversation and attracts investors but also detracts from a realistic assessment of their uses and risks. Conversely, an honest reckoning with AI producers about their ability to deliver on promises can alleviate the public's fear and mistrust around AI.

[25] www.news.un.org/en/story/2023/07/1138412

2

The Quest for Good AI

AI ethics is a rising academic and business field, some days outshining the very technology it is expected to keep in check. The arXiv repository of scientific preprints lists over 568,000 computer science entries, about 85 percent of which are from 2016 or later (Figure 2.1). Table 2.1 shows that the share of articles including the term *artificial intelligence* has declined slowly but steadily from 31.7 percent to 24.1 percent between 2016 and 2024,[1] while at the same time, the share of articles that mention *artificial intelligence ethics* has risen from 0.6 percent to 3.2 percent.

The sheer number and variety of adjectives attached to AI development are breathtaking: We want AI to be ethical, responsible, safe, trustworthy, explainable, accurate, just, transparent, accountable, sustainable, fair, robust, accessible, and much more, all at once.[2] We want it to be good (*beneficent*) or at least not bad (*non-maleficent*).[3] These expectations do not just form a wish list; they speak to our anxieties about the harm AI can do, and, worse yet, has already done when not tethered to a value system.

But what do these words mean? The academic and journalistic literature on AI reveals a complex picture: There is some overlap across authors, but divergence in the definitions of these adjectives is frequent, too.[4] What is more, definitions tend to

1 The query terms used are "artificial intelligence" and "algorithm" for the category *AI*, and "responsible AI," "ethical AI," "trustworthy AI," "algorithmic fairness," and "fairness in algorithm" for the category *AI ethics*.

2 The adjectives are the most commonly used ones in relation to AI. A simple Google search yields the following ranking in the number of query results: ethical AI, ethics in AI or AI ethics (4.46M); responsible AI or responsibility in AI (2.95M); safe AI, AI safety or safety in AI (1.66M); trustworthy AI or trust in AI (1.4M); explainable AI, explainability in AI or AI explainability; accurate AI, accuracy in AI or AI accuracy (404K); just AI, justice in AI or AI justice (360K); transparent AI, transparency in AI or AI transparency (253K); accountable AI, accountability in AI, AI accountability; sustainable AI, sustainability in AI or AI sustainability (218K); fair AI, fairness in AI or AI fairness (188K); robust AI, robustness in AI or AI robustness (164K); and accessible AI, accessibility in AI or AI accessibility (79K). Other nouns and adjectives yield fewer than 10K results.

3 Floridi et al., "How to Design AI for Social Good."

4 De Laat, "Companies Committed to Responsible AI."

TABLE 2.1 *Count of computer science, AI, and AI ethics terms in arXiv articles over time*

Subject	2016	2017	2018	2019	2020	2021	2022	2023	2024
All computer science	21,411	27,681	37,370	47,876	61,834	70,607	75,302	90,720	128,425
AI	2,774	3,739	5,525	6,670	9,273	14,444	17,065	23,773	39,268
AI ethics	86	152	251	379	612	832	952	1,553	2,849

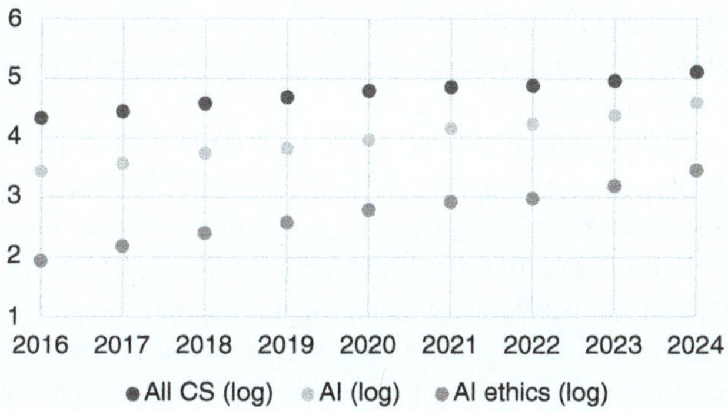

FIGURE 2.1 Count of computer science, AI, and AI ethics terms in arXiv articles over time

be circular: It is not uncommon to read, for example, that safe AI should be ethical, and ethical AI should be safe or that accountability is a component of explainability, and vice versa. Microsoft's Responsible AI Standard lists accountability, transparency, fairness, safety & reliability, privacy & security, and inclusiveness as its goals.[5] The tendency to use concepts together should be noted, too: For example, one of the largest conferences on algorithms, organized annually by the Association for Computing Machinery, is called Fairness, Accountability and Transparency; likewise, Microsoft has a Fairness, Accountability, Transparency, and Ethics in AI team.[6]

As it will become clear, when used in the context of AI, the words *ethical*, *responsible*, *safe*, and *trustworthy* do not always have distinctive meanings; rather, they are used as umbrella categories under which other nouns and adjectives are huddled together. To complicate matters, similar ideas, goals, and practices tend to be under different names. For example, IBM has trust and transparency principles as part of its AI ethics initiative,[7] and Deloitte has developed a trustworthy AI framework,[8]

5 Microsoft, Responsible AI Standard, v2 (www.blogs.microsoft.com/wp-content/uploads/prod/sites/5/2022/06/Microsoft-Responsible-AI-Standard-v2-General-Requirements-3.pdf).

6 www.microsoft.com/en-us/research/theme/fate/

7 www.ibm.com/policy/trust-principles/; also see: www.research.ibm.com/topics/trustworthy-ai

8 www2.deloitte.com/us/en/pages/deloitte-analytics/solutions/ethics-of-ai-framework.html

while Google and Microsoft have developed responsible AI practices and principles, and it is not clear what is different about each one of these initiatives.[9] OpenAI's safety research is exclusively about existential AI risks, to the exclusion of present-day risks that others in the AI safety field are preoccupied with.

This chapter presents concepts with a connotation of good, socially beneficial uses of AI. The goal is to provide as clear definitions as possible while keeping in mind that academics, journalists, and industry professionals disagree on those very definitions.[10] In order to overcome confusions arising from the fact that the same term tends to have multiple uses or multiple terms have roughly similar meanings, this chapter will disambiguate across concepts and interpretations. Furthermore, if specific individuals or organizations use a term more frequently than others, such special use is acknowledged.

Terms like *AI ethics* appear to have galvanized research and practice since the mid-2010s, but they are not entirely novel. Criticism of AI systems can be traced back to the 1960s, when pioneers like Joseph Weizenbaum began to caution against early chatbots.[11] Even before that time, the concern that machines in general, and computerized systems in particular, would pose unforeseen dangers to their creators and the rest of humanity was a theme in fiction and social thought. A second reason to argue that AI ethics is not all that new is that terms like *computer ethics*, *machine ethics*, *robot ethics*, *business ethics* and *data ethics* already cover some, but not all, of the concerns around AI today[12] – not to mention the many guidelines, standards, and practices that have long aimed to make professional fields as varied as medicine, military, car manufacturing, biological sciences, and construction safe, ethical, and responsible.[13] The need to develop AI ethics within existing ethical frameworks was not lost on pioneering efforts: One of the most famous texts on AI ethics, called the Asilomar AI Principles, gets its name from the Asilomar Conference of 1975 that aimed to develop biotechnology responsibly.[14] Thus, it is worth acknowledging both the continuity and discontinuity of today's academic and industry discourse around AI with earlier technology ethics efforts.

This chapter introduces *ethical*, *responsible*, *safe*, *trustworthy*, *transparent* (and *explainable*), *accurate*, *just* (and *fair*), *accountable*, *sustainable*, *robust*, *accessible* and *inclusive* as adjectives with a positive association. The rank order reflects the frequency

9 www.ai.google/responsibility/responsible-ai-practices/; www.microsoft.com/en-us/ai/responsible-ai

10 Jobin, Ienca, and Vayena, "Artificial Intelligence: The Global Landscape of Ethics Guidelines"; Gabriel, "Artificial Intelligence, Values, and Alignment."

11 Tavani, "Expanding the Standard ICT-Ethics Framework in an Era of AI."

12 Baird and Schuller, "Considerations for a More Ethical Approach to Data in AI"; Schultz and Seele, "Towards AI Ethics' Institutionalization."

13 Martin and Villegas-Galaviz, "AI and Corporate Responsibility"; Gundersen and Bærøe, "The Future Ethics of Artificial Intelligence in Medicine."

14 Ball, *The Book of Minds: How to Understand Ourselves and Other Beings, from Animals to AI to Aliens*: 269.

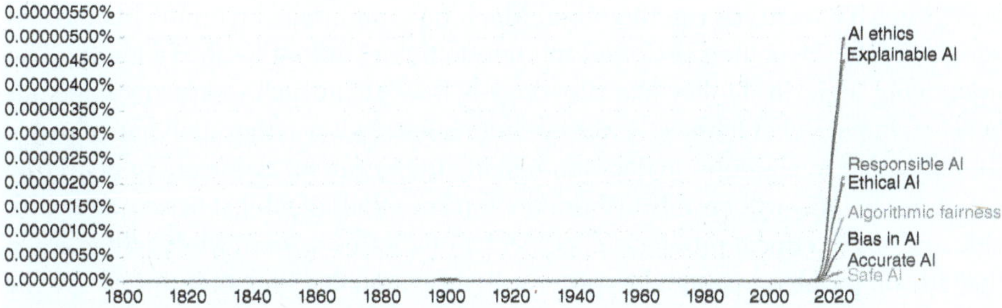

FIGURE 2.2 Count of AI-related terms in Google Books Ngrams, 1980–2022 (other terms not found)

of use in popular media and academia. This chapter then discusses briefly the synergies and potential discrepancies among these values. Ultimately, this chapter's goal is to lay out the complex conceptual and empirical debates on AI governance.

POSITIVE ADJECTIVES ASSOCIATED WITH AI

Ethical

AI ethics is arguably the concept that unites an entire epistemic and practitioner community. In comparison to other AI-related concepts, it yields by far the largest number of query results on Google, Google Scholar, and Google Book Ngrams (Figure 2.2). Ethics generally denotes morally upright professional conduct; AI ethics, therefore, refers to developing, designing, deploying, and using AI tools in accordance with some notion of professional morality.

Beyond this commitment to doing the right thing, however, definitions diverge significantly. One study divides AI ethics topics into three streams: Specific issues related to the application of machine learning; social and political questions arising from digital society; and metaphysical questions about the nature of reality and humanity.[15] Clearly, the first conception converges with professional ethics, the second one invites a much more profound analysis of the economic, political, and cultural context in which AI is embedded, and the third scrutinizes the existential dimensions of the human–machine interaction. Most of this chapter focuses on the first and second conceptions.

For some commentators, AI ethics explores Trolley Problem-like dilemmas that prompt hard decisions.[16] Should a driverless car prioritize the safety of its passengers or that of pedestrians in the event of an unavoidable crash? Does the answer change if the passerby is identified as a child, elderly person, criminal, man, woman, cat, or

[15] Stahl et al., "Artificial Intelligence for Human Flourishing – Beyond Principles for Machine Learning."

[16] Belenguer, "AI Bias."

dog?[17] An MIT team has run the Moral Machine experiment, an online platform in which people select their preferred solution to these kinds of hard problems.[18] The underlying logic in Trolley-like situations is that AI inevitably presents trade-offs between imperfect outcomes. A second-order question is whether such hard choices should be left to algorithmic decision-making in the future. Some are hopeful that computer systems will be able to learn the fundamentals of ethical reasoning to provide answers to ethical problems consistent with a value system, while others argue that ethical problems cannot be solved with an automated rank-ordering of options if those options carry equal moral value.[19]

Associating ethics with choice in the face of unappealing alternatives has drawn criticism for ethical reductionism.[20] Another conception of ethics concerns a set of principles and actionable rules with broad applicability based on three major families of ethical thought, namely deontology, utilitarianism, and virtue ethics, as potential guiding philosophies of AI ethics.[21] The deontological approach, associated with the writings of Immanuel Kant, and his followers, advocates for general principles that apply across all contexts. The utilitarian perspective, associated with the works of Jeremy Bentham, John Stuart Mill, and their followers, measures the value of an action by the amount of happiness, income, or some other positive outcome it brings to the broadest number of people. Virtue ethics calls for a contextual analysis of situations requiring ethical decision-making to cultivate virtue.[22] The virtue ethics tradition in the global West is often associated with the revival of Aristotle, but multiple philosophical and spiritual traditions have developed virtue-centered moral doctrines.

Defining AI ethics as the implementation of these philosophical paradigms to real-world situations is a common tendency, in great part because deontology, utilitarianism, and virtue ethics are often taught as the exhaustive list of ethics paradigms in professional ethics education. Beyond these three broad families of thought, contemporary philosophers demand that AI be aligned with the ethics of non-domination,[23] ethics of care,[24] relational ethics,[25] intersectionality,[26] human rights,[27] and human emancipation and empowerment.[28] These alternative conceptions

17 Awad et al., "The Moral Machine Experiment."
18 moralmachine.net
19 Atay Kozlovski, "Should We Leave It to AI to Make Our Hard Choices?" *Tech Policy Press Blog*, August 3, 2023 (www.techpolicy.press/should-we-leave-it-to-ai-to-make-our-hard-choices/).
20 Etienne, "The Dark Side of the 'Moral Machine' and the Fallacy of Computational Ethical Decision-Making for Autonomous Vehicles."
21 Stahl, Schroeder, and Rodrigues, *Ethics of Artificial Intelligence*.
22 Quinn, *Ethics for the Information Age*.
23 Rochel and Evéquoz, "Getting into the Engine Room: A Blueprint to Investigate the Shadowy Steps of AI Ethics."
24 Asaro, "AI Ethics in Predictive Policing: From Models of Threat to an Ethics of Care."
25 Colonna, "Artificial Intelligence in Higher Education: Towards a More Relational Approach."
26 Bauer and Lizotte, "Artificial Intelligence, Intersectionality, and the Future of Public Health."
27 Mantelero, *Beyond Data*.
28 Waelen, "Why AI Ethics Is a Critical Theory."

promise to ground AI ethics in social and political thought; that is to say, they derive principles of ethics from concrete social, economic, and cultural contexts in which AI produces potential risks and actual harms. For example, an alternative conception that goes beyond Trolley-like situations includes meaningful human oversight and control of AI, algorithmic opacity and hidden machine bias, widespread technological unemployment, psychological and emotional manipulation of humans by AI, and automation bias as components of AI ethics.[29]

Who decides what the relevant ethical philosophies and decisions should be? As is obvious from above, there is no unifying ethical principle in AI ethics.[30] A cross-national survey of citizens' attitudes towards AI concerns reveals individual-level variation on the basis of economic and normative attributes, as well as country-level variation.[31] Thus, the naming and operationalization of AI ethics principles, and the accompanying proposed solutions to risks and harms, remain a field of struggles over interests, values, and meanings.

Responsible

The word *responsible* connotes a sense of agency that is missing in most other good AI concepts. Someone has to do the right thing for AI to be responsible. As a result of this conceptual complexity, responsible AI remains an umbrella term with diverse and vague definitions.[32] It invokes other concepts, such as explainability, fairness, transparency, and privacy (see below).[33] Some scholars interpret responsibility as the translation of AI ethics principles into practice through human choices.[34] One way to accomplish that is by building responsibility into AI systems by design,[35] but responsibility can also be understood as a legal and governance challenge in addition to a design and development one.[36] What is less clear is who should assume that responsibility. Researchers, computer scientists, and other workers in design and development come to mind, of course. However, AI risks and harms tend to go above and beyond individual workers or teams, as business models and decisions may be at their root.[37] Thus, businesses and even entire industries can be tasked to bear responsibility.

29 Vallor and Bekey, "Artificial Intelligence and the Ethics of Self-Learning Robots."

30 Baum, "Social Choice Ethics in Artificial Intelligence."

31 Ehret, "Public Preferences for Governing AI Technology."

32 Tigard, "Responsible AI and Moral Responsibility."

33 Barredo Arrieta et al., "Explainable Artificial Intelligence (XAI)."

34 Peters et al., "Responsible AI – Two Frameworks for Ethical Design Practice"; Shneiderman, "Responsible AI."

35 Benjamins, Barbado, and Sierra, "Responsible AI by Design in Practice."

36 Mikalef et al., "Thinking Responsibly about Responsible AI and 'the Dark Side' of AI"; Cheng, Varshney, and Liu, "Socially Responsible AI Algorithms."

37 Schiff et al., "Principles to Practices for Responsible AI."

Attributing responsibility to organizational actors generates more questions than it answers, though. First and foremost, it is ambiguous whether any consequence follows from irresponsible behavior in the absence of binding rules. Furthermore, AI systems tend to produce unintentional, even unforeseen risks and harms, which means that the standard of responsibility should be more rigorous than avoiding malicious harm. Just like ethical AI, therefore, responsible AI connotes the possibility of doing the right thing above and beyond strict statutory requirements, but the flexible interpretations of the term leave the designers, developers, and users of AI tools with too much discretion.

Safe

The demand for safety comes from the realization that applications of AI may harm individuals and communities. The unpredictable and unreliable character of some AI systems accentuates these fears. Self-driving vehicles may crash into pedestrians or other vehicles; people may be denied opportunities or framed as criminals by algorithmic decisions; and chatbots may give harmful advice to users who turn to them for guidance. Thus, safety in AI goes hand in hand with harm avoidance, fairness, and accuracy, among others.

The safety framework comes from engineering practice, where safe design, development, deployment, and use have a long history. It is perhaps not surprising that advocates for AI safety often bring up examples like civilian airplanes and automobiles to argue that safety standards are possible and necessary. Likewise, professional ethics standards in science, which began with a horrifying record of ethics violations until scientific fields began to address conduct, can show the way.

Making AI products generally more accurate is likely to improve their safety. More specific interventions deserve mention, too. One research paper advocates the validation of AI data and models not only for statistical metrics but also for usability, real-world functionality, and social and environmental fit.[38] If one part of safety is avoiding wrongs, another component is the possibility of rectification in case something goes wrong. This second formulation means that efforts to ensure safety are deeply intertwined with accountability in AI.[39]

For whom is AI supposed to be safe? The users or customers of AI systems come to mind in most cases. However, as the dilemma of setting safety standards for a self-driving car suggests, what is safe for a customer may not be safe for a pedestrian affected by an automated decision. To give another example, those adversely affected by facial recognition software, say, individuals wrongly identified as criminal offenders, are not its customers. Furthermore, modern machine learning applications almost always come with statistical error, which, depending on the specific

[38] Morales-Forero, Bassetto, and Coatanea, "Toward Safe AI."

[39] www.digital-strategy.ec.europa.eu/en/library/ethics-guidelines-trustworthy-ai

field of application, can generate unsafe outcomes for some target populations. Therefore, the question of safety is not only technical but also deeply political: It is about how the risks and harms are distributed across social groups as a result of technological developments.

Trustworthy

Trustworthy AI is often understood as a meta-category, to which different businesses, non-profits, and academic researchers attribute desirable goals such as safety, robustness, accuracy, fairness, privacy, beneficence, and autonomy.[40] More specifically, trust implies the belief that the output of an AI system is accurate, useful, and safe enough for people to trust it. As such, the concept evokes an external measure of accuracy, robustness, and reliability. It has also been suggested that the explainability of AI, and particularly the extent to which the users of AI can achieve some level of causal understanding, improves trustworthiness.[41] Alternatively, earning trust is said to require building robust systems whose output can be verified.[42] Likewise, accusations targeting AI companies for not doing enough to ensure the safety of their products erode trust.[43]

Businesses like IBM and Deloitte have taken the lead in developing what they call trustworthy AI. The term has also attracted lawmakers' attention: The European Commission's High-Level Expert Group, which was instrumental in drafting the first version of the EU's AI Act, called for a foundation of excellence and trust in AI. The Group defined trustworthy AI as lawful, ethical, and robust.[44] Trust in AI was a key policy objective under the Biden administration in the US.[45]

Surveys conducted by academics and businesses suggest that considerable pluralities, and in some cases majorities, do not trust AI. A survey of over 17,000 participants from 17 countries reveals that people are evenly divided over the question of trusting AI in the workplace.[46] Such mistrust may result from the reported shortcomings of contemporary AI tools, worries about AI's long-term effects on lives and

40 Thiebes, Lins, and Sunyaev, "Trustworthy Artificial Intelligence."

41 Shin, "The Effects of Explainability and Causability on Perception, Trust, and Acceptance."

42 K.N.C., "Don't trust AI until we build systems that earn trust," *The Economist*, December 28, 2019 (www.economist.com/open-future/2019/12/18/dont-trust-ai-until-we-build-systems-that-earn-trust).

43 Editorial Board, "Building trust in AI systems is essential," *Financial Times*, March 2, 2021 (www.ft.com/content/85b0882e-3e93-42e7-8411-54f4e24c7f87).

44 www.digital-strategy.ec.europa.eu/en/library/ethics-guidelines-trustworthy-ai. Also see: Smuha, "From a 'Race to AI' to a 'Race to AI Regulation.'"

45 Gopal Ratnam, "Congress, White House race to get arms around AI systems," *Roll Call*, June 21, 2023 (www.rollcall.com/2023/06/21/congress-white-house-race-to-get-arms-around-ai-systems/).

46 Gillespie et al., "Trust in Artificial Intelligence: A Global Study"; Vivian Lam, "A survey of over 17,000 people indicates only half of us are willing to trust AI at work," *The Conversation*, February 22, 2023 (www.theconversation.com/a-survey-of-over-17-000-people-indicates-only-half-of-us-are-willing-to-trust-ai-at-work-200256).

livelihoods, or people's affective distance from a non-human decision authority – although, paradoxically, the perception of AI as a form of superintelligence free from human bias sometimes leads people to place undue trust, too.[47]

Conceptual work on trustworthy AI does not always specify whose trust AI should earn. In some definitions there is mention of customers, but earning the trust of AI experts, communities affected by AI decisions, or the public in general can be considered viable alternatives to focusing on customers only.[48] All in all, the *trust* in trustworthy AI does not receive much attention, with notable exceptions: An analysis of the term cautions against anthropomorphizing AI by expecting it to conform to our affective and normative notions of trust, arguing that AI can at best be reliable, that is, performing as expected even while lacking a motivation to be trustworthy.[49] In her blog post titled "AI & Global Governance: No One Should Trust AI," AI ethics and technology policy scholar Joanna Bryson argues that instead of using the language of *trust* to describe our relationship to software development techniques, we should hold the humans behind them *accountable* and thereby enhance the trustworthiness of our institutions.[50]

Transparent and Explainable

One of the defining features of the mathematical models characterizing today's AI is that they rely on numbers and calculations that defy straightforward interpretation. Modern machine learning models take in text, image, sound, video, and other data types as input, turn some of their features into numbers, and then iterate over a mathematical function to minimize the mismatch between an expected output and the resulting output. The numbers in those iterations do not make intuitive sense (see the section on deep learning in Chapter 1). In practice, this means that the reasoning behind decision-making models that grant or deny a mortgage, job, school admission, and even release from prison cannot be understood, explained, or objected to. Algorithmic opaqueness has yet another meaning: Businesses typically do not publicize their data sources, data, or algorithms. Trade secrets are valued for incentivizing innovation, but decisions based on proprietary data and algorithms affect people who are not allowed to raise informed objections to them.

Whether the cause is technical complexity or business secretiveness, the phenomenon of black-box algorithms accounts for many of the risks and harms associated with

47 Baria and Cross, "The Brain Is a Computer Is a Brain: Neuroscience's Internal Debate and the Social Significance of the Computational Metaphor."

48 Floridi et al., "AI4People – An Ethical Framework for a Good AI Society."

49 Ryan, "In AI We Trust."

50 Joanna Bryson, "AI & Global Governance: No One Should Trust AI," *United Nations Centre for Policy Research*. November 13, 2018 (www.cpr.unu.edu/publications/articles/ai-global-governance-no-one-should-trust-ai.html).

AI today. A 2018 survey of about 5,000 executives finds that 60 percent are concerned about explaining how AI makes decisions.[51] Lael Brainard, former member of the US Federal Reserve Board of Governors, gave a speech in which she questioned the suitability of opaque AI systems in financial institutions that are required by law to incorporate transparency and explainability into their decisions to ensure fair lending.[52]

AI systems can be made more transparent than they typically are, even if full transparency in technical matters may be intractable. The commitment to transparency may mean a commitment to interpretability, explainability, justified opacity, or auditability.[53] In other words, transparency may mean sharing as much information about data and methods as possible, or more minimally, justifying why some information may not be shared, or at a bare minimum, shielding the population from the harms of an opaque system.

In operational terms, it has been suggested that human users should at least be made aware that they are interacting with an AI system, and "must be informed of the system's capabilities and limitations."[54] As AI-generated text, image, sound, and video content is likely to increase dramatically in the future, information about the origin of such content will prove crucial in fighting disinformation. Above and beyond this bare-minimum consideration, explainable AI has garnered considerable practitioner interest. In part, the term refers to technical solutions to explain the internal working of ML algorithms. Some of the proposed technical solutions in Chapter 4 aim to reverse-engineer algorithmic processes to make the intermediary steps connecting the input to the output more explainable.

Explainability is not limited to what goes on inside the algorithm. Researchers at the US National Institute for Standards & Technology present a fourfold scheme for explainable AI: An AI system should contain an explanation, which amounts to "accompanying evidence and reason(s)" for outputs and/or processes; the explanation should be understandable to consumers; the explanation should be accurate; and the system should always operate under conditions for which it was designed.[55] Likewise, the EU's General Data Protection Regulation, in effect since 2018, acknowledges the "right to explanation," interpreted as a simple overview of system functionality.[56] In other words, providing those affected by AI with an explanation of the data collection and analysis methods can work towards explainability in the absence of technical elaboration.

51 Sara Castellanos, "Corporations Confront Need for Transparency in AI-Driven Decisions," *The Wall Street Journal*, December 4, 2018 (www.wsj.com/articles/corporations-confront-need-for-transparency-in-ai-driven-decisions-1543977978).

52 Lael Brainard, "What Are We Learning about Artificial Intelligence in Financial Services?" Speech at the New Financial Landscape, Philadelphia, PA, November 13, 2018 (www.federalreserve.gov/newsevents/speech/brainard20181113a.htm).

53 Basl, Sandler, and Tiell, "Getting from Commitment to Content in AI and Data Ethics."

54 www.digital-strategy.ec.europa.eu/en/library/ethics-guidelines-trustworthy-ai

55 Phillips et al., "Four Principles of Explainable Artificial Intelligence."

56 Wachter, Mittelstadt, and Floridi, "Transparent, Explainable, and Accountable AI for Robotics."

Accurate

In everyday language, *accuracy* is about getting correct results.[57] *Reliability* is about getting the same – hopefully accurate – result consistently. Minimizing statistical error is essential to scientific, technological and business success, of course, but it is also a cornerstone of moral conduct, as correct output is a necessary (though not sufficient) condition for reaping the societal benefits of AI. Diagnostic medical AI should be as error-free as possible, as should facial recognition software and large language models. In that sense, accuracy and reliability connote the alignment of strategic incentives and moral considerations: It is safe to argue that businesses would rather get the output correct than not.

Incorrect or inconsistent output is one among many reasons why AI can produce risks and harms (see Chapter 3). Even accuracy-enhancing data collection and analysis practices do not necessarily enhance the morality of decision-making. To give an obvious example: If facial recognition correctly identifies an unarmed civilian in order to not target them, that would improve safety, but in an alternative scenario in which a decision-making system encourages the lethal targeting of civilians, accurate AI would simply enable immoral and illegal conduct. Therefore, accuracy is necessary but not sufficient for fair, substantively unbiased and morally defensible uses of AI.

Just and Fair

Fairness in AI accompanies acknowledgment of bias and discrimination against vulnerable social groups.[58] A recent survey defines fairness in AI as the absence of "any prejudice or favoritism toward an individual or a group based on their inherent or acquired characteristics."[59] AI tools are said to reproduce and at times amplify bias, discrimination, hate speech, incitement to violence, disinformation, and privacy violations. These potential risks and actual harms are not uniformly distributed across society: They target the poor, persons with disabilities, ethnic and racialized minorities, women, persons of diverse sex, sexual orientation and gender identity, children, the elderly, migrants, and people at the intersection of these identities disproportionately.[60]

57 By way of disambiguation, accuracy in classification algorithms refers to the ratio of true predictions to the total number of predictions. For example, if an image dataset has fifty photos of dogs and fifty photos of other animals, and if the classification methodology correctly identifies forty of the fifty dog photos, and incorrectly identifies fifteen non-dog photos as dog photos, a total of seventy-five out of a hundred will have been accurately identified.

58 Lauren Kirchner, "When Discrimination Is Baked into Algorithms," *The Atlantic*, September 6, 2015 (www.theatlantic.com/business/archive/2015/09/discrimination-algorithms-disparate-impact/403969/).

59 Mehrabi et al., "A Survey on Bias and Fairness in Machine Learning."

60 Molnar, "Technology on the Margins"; Noble, *Algorithms of Oppression: How Search Engines Reinforce Racism*; O'Neil, *Weapons of Math Destruction: How Big Data Increases Inequality and*

The inaccuracy and unreliability of AI output are partly responsible for the listed risks and harms. Unfair outcomes do not result only from technological failures, however. Researchers at the US National Institute for Standards & Technology distinguish between statistical, human, and systemic bias.[61] Today's probabilistic machine learning algorithms will carry some degree of error in their classifications, estimations, and predictions. When those errors target certain groups in the population more than others, questions of fairness arise (see the section on bias and discrimination in Chapter 3). Unintentional algorithmic discrimination as a product of systemic bias and discrimination is not the end of the story, either: Today's increasingly sophisticated surveillance technologies make the intentional targeting of disadvantaged social groups or dissidents more likely. Thus, the fight for justice in today's world should take many different shapes and forms.

From a technical standpoint, measuring fairness in AI requires assessing it for unbiased outcomes and processes.[62] Another definition emphasizes fairness not only in the process and outcome of data collection and analysis but also in how individuals are treated by algorithmic systems. Accordingly, explainability constitutes an important component of fairness if algorithms have a tendency to introduce bias and discrimination implicitly, that is, when sensitive population characteristics are picked up even when they are not attributes of the training dataset.[63]

A survey of computer scientists' conceptions of fairness groups more than twenty notions under three categories: Individual fairness (achieving equality of opportunity across individuals), group fairness (achieving equality across groups or rectifying inequality through affirmative action), and causal reasoning (using counterfactuals to achieve some notion of due process).[64] Incorporating equality concerns into research and product design has been both praised for its potential for improving the fairness of decision-making, and criticized for failing to take into account the socio-technical context in which inequalities manifest themselves.[65]

Value diversity in terms of what people acknowledge as fair or just creates another challenge for fairness and justice work in AI. Interviews with AI practitioners working to reduce disparities across demographic groups reveal that they face challenges in choosing performance metrics, identifying the relevant stakeholders and

Threatens Democracy; Eubanks, *Automating Inequality: How High-Tech Tools Profile, Police, and Punish the Poor*; Zuiderveen Borgesius, "Strengthening Legal Protection against Discrimination by Algorithms and Artificial Intelligence"; Buolamwini and Gebru, "Gender Shades: Intersectional Accuracy Disparities in Commercial Gender Classification"; Turner Lee, *Digitally Invisible: How the Internet Is Creating the New Underclass*.

61 Schwartz et al., "Towards a Standard for Identifying and Managing Bias in Artificial Intelligence."

62 Benjamins, Barbado, and Sierra, "Responsible AI by Design in Practice."

63 Barredo Arrieta et al., "Explainable Artificial Intelligence (XAI)."

64 Abu-Elyounes, "Contextual Fairness."

65 John-Mathews, Cardon, and Balagué, "From Reality to World. A Critical Perspective on AI Fairness"; Selbst et al., "Fairness and Abstraction in Sociotechnical Systems."

demographic groups, and collecting relevant data.[66] What is more, the justice and fairness perspective involves much more than picking metrics for an algorithm; it invites a more profound conversation about the broader sociocultural systems within which AI is embedded.[67] Put simply, justice and fairness are as much about AI as what kind of society we all want to live in.

Accountable

Over time, the term *accountability* has come to mean good business practices that avoid risks and harms in AI. In a way, accountable behavior is about ensuring ethical, responsible, safe, or explainable uses of AI, monitoring risks and harms, and attributing responsibility in cases of harm. Monitoring and responsibility attribution have received increasing attention because AI risks and harms are not always visible, the observed problems result from highly technical applications, and the potential victims are diffuse groups of people. Accountability in AI, therefore, refers in part to monitoring AI systems for potential or real harms, either as part of business practice or through interventions from outside. An example of internal monitoring is what the European Commission's High-Level Expert Group calls *auditability*,[68] which includes the assessment of data, algorithms and design, and adequate and accessible redress.[69] Businesses may self-monitor or journalists, academic researchers, and administrative bodies may be expected to monitor externally. This task has fallen disproportionately on journalists, researchers, and non-governmental organizations in the absence of laws and policies requiring government agencies to do so. Regardless of who does the monitoring, publicizing the findings of AI-related risks and harms is an essential component of explainability as well as accountability.

The assignment of moral and legal responsibility when autonomous decisions made by AI systems pose risks and harms is a closely related conception of accountability. Legal personhood is not an attribute of AI systems, so human individuals and organizations should bear responsibility. It is not always clear, however, who must be held accountable in the long value chain in which academic researchers, coders, designers, managers, shareholders, intermediaries, and end users participate.[70] In other words, the difficulties of establishing responsibility also complicate this notion of accountability.

66 Madaio et al., "Assessing the Fairness of AI Systems."

67 Dancy and Saucier, "AI and Blackness."

68 Thiebes, Lins, and Sunyaev, "Trustworthy Artificial Intelligence."

69 www.digital-strategy.ec.europa.eu/en/library/ethics-guidelines-trustworthy-ai

70 Mary K. Pratt, "AI accountability: Who's responsible when AI goes wrong?" *TechTarget*, August 19, 2021 (www.techtarget.com/searchenterpriseai/feature/AI-accountability-Whos-responsible-when-AI-goes-wrong).

Sustainable

The advent of contemporary AI has coincided with worldwide concern about environmental degradation, and along with it, calls for businesses and lawmakers to place economic sustainability at the center of economic development and legislation. Over time, the term sustainability underwent conceptual stretching to include not only environmental but also socioeconomic and governance concerns – as evidenced by the adoption of Sustainable Development Goals (SDGs) by the United Nations General Assembly in 2015. Sustainable AI, likewise, starts from the scrutiny of AI's environmental impact, but has far-reaching implications.

Part of the sustainable AI agenda is a nudge to businesses toward relatively energy-efficient AI development. The energy and water usage of large language models has led to calls to curb AI's negative environmental impact. Conversely, AI systems that identify sources of environmental waste and inefficiency, say, by monitoring deforestation and illegal fishing or improving heating, ventilation, and air conditioning systems, can be part of sustainable solutions.[71] Some businesses and consultancies claim to offer sustainability services, including in areas like AI and data science, to clients.[72]

Mirroring the central premise of SDGs that environmental goals cannot be separated from broader social justice agendas, sustainable AI advocates look not only for ways to reduce the negative environmental impact of AI systems but also call for embedding environmental concerns in broader social, political, and cultural ones. Thus, the term *sustainability* in AI converges, to a great extent, with the comprehensive outlook on sustainability.[73] Sustainable AI advocates recommend building a social justice perspective into the entire AI lifecycle, which includes collecting, exploring, validating, and cleaning data, then training and testing the data using model engineering and model evaluation, followed by model packaging, coding to build and test the model, and ultimately deploying and monitoring.[74]

The demand for sustainable AI is a call for radical change: The aspiration of environmental, social, and political transformation requires systemic and global progress, including but not limited to the AI industry. In a way, the call for sustainable AI reflects the frustrations of the environmental movement: Significant changes should take place urgently, but existing political and economic realities create enormous obstacles for all but relatively minor adjustments to systems at the root of the problems.

71 van Rijmenam, "Building a Greener Future: The Importance of Sustainable Ai."

72 Lawmakers around the world are catching up, too: for example, the Swedish presidency of the Council of the EU and Sweden's ministry of finance co-hosted a sustainable AI conference on May 2–3, 2023. www.swedish-presidency.consilium.europa.eu/en/news/sustainable-ai-and-ai-for-sustainability/

73 van Wynsberghe, "Sustainable AI"; Renda, *Artificial Intelligence*.

74 Gupta, "The Imperative for Sustainable AI Systems."

Robust

In science terminology, robustness refers to the validity of results in the face of adjustments to data and methods. If a hypothesis is robust, it should hold with new data generated with the same underlying method subject to the same evaluation metrics. AI would be considered robust if it generated reliably correct output when data, methods or contexts change.[75] Robustness is a necessary condition for accuracy; the difference is that while accuracy is more concerned with the outcome, robustness is concerned with the methods to arrive at the outcome. To give a high-profile example: Google's Flu Trends appeared to have produced surprisingly accurate estimates of influenza activity using disease-related Google queries in many countries between 2008 and 2010, but its failure starting in 2011 indicates that the underlying model was not robust to changes in the query data.[76]

Critics of deep learning have long argued that relying on an analysis of statistically plausible outcomes does not ensure robustness in AI.[77] Gary Marcus, a critic of the inaccuracy and unreliability of contemporary machine learning applications, argues that contemporary AI should incorporate components of symbolic AI in order to overcome the shortcomings of machine learning methods.

Since it is closely related to accurate outcomes, robustness tends to attract the interest of AI business and research communities. For example, the term has risen to prominence in official circles in the European Union (EU): It is one of the three pillars of trustworthy AI, and technical robustness is one of the seven requirements of trustworthy AI, according to the European Commission's High-Level Expert Group.[78] As Chapter 6 shows, reliability is an important component of the EU's AI Act.

Accessible

The term accessible AI refers to access regardless of disability status.[79] Accessibility in the context of AI has been used both as enabling – or at least as not blocking – access to persons with disabilities. In terms of enabling access, the development of assistive technologies through the use of AI is the most promising avenue. For example, chatbots can help persons with communication disabilities to convey their message more efficiently and effectively.[80] Unblocking access to persons with disabilities

75 Obafemi-Ajayi et al., "No-Boundary Thinking."

76 David Lazer and Ryan Kennedy, "What We Can Learn from the Epic Failure of Google Flu Trends," *Wired*, October 1, 2015 (www.wired.com/2015/10/can-learn-epic-failure-google-flu-trends/).

77 Marcus, "The Next Decade in AI: Four Steps Towards Robust Artificial Intelligence."

78 The High-Level Expert Group on AI, "Ethics Guidelines for Trustworthy AI."

79 www.digital-strategy.ec.europa.eu/en/library/ethics-guidelines-trustworthy-ai

80 Bronwyn Hemsley, Emma Power, and Fiona Given, "Will AI tech like ChatGPT improve inclusion for people with communication disability?" *The Conversation*, January 18, 2023 (www.theconversation.com/will-ai-tech-like-chatgpt-improve-inclusion-for-people-with-communication-disability-196481).

includes avoiding bias and discrimination – a key element of fairness in AI.[81] Design choices that do not restrict access, intentionally or otherwise, constitute another crucial element.[82] The European Commission's High-Level Expert Group report states: "Fostering diversity, AI systems should be accessible to all, regardless of any disability, and involve relevant stakeholders throughout their entire life circle."[83]

Accessibility for persons with disabilities is closely aligned with ethical, safe, and fair AI. Accessible AI requires intentional and thoughtful choices as early as the research and design stages and beyond them – in that sense, it departs from the "move fast and break things" mentality voiced by Mark Zuckerberg and endorsed by much of the AI industry. What is more, the inclusion of affected communities at every stage of AI development, something that technology companies typically assume to be unnecessary, is built into the goal of accessibility. All in all, accessibility for persons with disabilities would ideally push AI companies to make choices for inclusionary processes and outcomes.

Inclusive

Inclusive AI refers to the process of making available the end products, the data and code going into those products, or an explanation of AI procedures to the relevant stakeholders, which may include the entire population, affected persons, or communities of experts.[84] Media coverage sometimes refers to ChatGPT as inclusive because a simple version of the end product is available to the masses. Similarly, open-sourcing the data, algorithms, model weights and code, making the wider internet and AI infrastructure available within and across countries, and improving the transparency and explainability of AI products are seen as elements of inclusive AI.[85]

The demand for inclusive AI deserves further scrutiny. Overcoming inequalities in access to AI infrastructure requires socioeconomic transformations that go above and beyond what the AI industry can or wants to achieve. AI companies can do more to make their products, data and algorithms publicly available. However, this demand carries with it promises as well as risks: Availability can drive further innovation and crowd-source necessary auditing and testing tasks, but also increases the likelihood of misuse and makes regulation more difficult.

Inclusion may mean more than public availability of products or open-sourcing. Overcoming economic barriers to access is key. Empowering affected persons and communities to make technology governance decisions that shape their lives is the

81 Barredo Arrieta et al., "Explainable Artificial Intelligence (XAI)"; Schwartz et al., "Towards a Standard for Identifying and Managing Bias in Artificial Intelligence."

82 Tanweer, "Tradeoffs All the Way Down."

83 The High-Level Expert Group on AI, "Ethics Guidelines for Trustworthy AI."

84 Barredo Arrieta et al., "Explainable Artificial Intelligence (XAI)."

85 Cowls et al., "The AI Gambit."

ultimate test of inclusivity that requires changes not only within companies but also at the industry level. An informed citizenry with a high level of AI and information literacy is needed to achieve genuine inclusion in shaping the future of AI.

"GOOD" AI GOALS: MUTUALLY REINFORCING OR MUTUALLY EXCLUSIVE?

The synergy between different conceptions of "good" AI cannot be overstated. A clearly defined chain of responsibility is likely to make products safe and company decisions accountable. Data and algorithmic transparency keep the process and outcome accountable. Nondiscriminatory datasets are likely to improve accuracy. However, rarely do all good things go together in life, and AI is no exception. The trade-offs between the goals of good AI should not be ignored. For example, given the dataset and model choice, there exists a trade-off between minimizing false positives and minimizing false negatives. Making a dataset fully available to the public runs the risk of violating the privacy of individuals whose data are stored in that dataset. To give another example: Fair classification, estimation, and forecasting may require the inclusion of more features in datasets, which may interfere with the data subjects' privacy. Transparency is a major check against errors and misuse in the design, development, and deployment of AI tools, but failing to set principled limits on who should have access to data and algorithms for review can produce novel risks to public safety. Maximizing overall prediction accuracy may violate fairness for subpopulations, and vice versa. A research team offers users a visualization tool that illustrates these technical trade-offs in the analysis of recidivism prediction data.[86]

These trade-offs are sometimes portrayed as Trolley Problem situations requiring hard decisions. Those who design, develop, and deploy AI tools indeed face difficult dilemmas at times, and are right to claim that no universally agreed-upon value system exists to orient their decisions. However, it would be disingenuous to let the AI industry off the hook: Moral complexity is not an excuse for cynicism. As with any other walk of life in which moral decision-making involves hard choices, getting AI right is about the priorities of those making the decisions and the processes through which the decisions are made. Decisions about calibrating the values embodied in AI systems are more political than technical. For example, take the impossibility of minimizing both false positives and false negatives: For crime prediction software, this means making a choice between letting some crime go undetected or accusing some innocent people of crime. For an industry whose chief customers are law-enforcement agencies, the latter seems to be the obvious choice, even if that puts the life and liberty of innocent people at risk. Thus, value pluralism in AI ethics should motivate informed democratic decision-making, not inaction.

[86] Yu et al., "Keeping Designers in the Loop."

CONCLUSION

The social and political implications of AI can also be studied under terms like human rights and corporate social responsibility,[87] but the adjectives attached to AI appear to have captured the zeitgeist of the mid-2010s and early 2020s. Regardless of how one conceptualizes a term like *AI ethics*, it should be acknowledged that its popularity owes in great part to what it is not: legal compliance. Producing and using AI tools ethically has become a general expectation because existing laws around the world, and in particular in the US, where most early AI development has taken place, do not regulate the potential risks and harms adequately. Doing the right thing, therefore, has depended on companies' voluntary compliance with guidelines, standards, and principles published by academics, non-profits, industry organizations and companies themselves. Thus, bridging the gap between AI ethics principles and implementation has been the defining challenge of the 2010s and early 2020s, when government regulation was slow to catch up with technological change.[88]

It is perhaps safe to argue that most scholarship on AI does not clarify what ethics means, much less subscribe to an ethical philosophy; rather, ethics is understood as avoiding harmful or risky conduct. A survey of AI-related journal articles in law, business, medical, science, and engineering journals finds that only very few of them even mention professional ethics paradigms, such as deontology, utilitarianism, or virtue ethics.[89] The inattention to concepts and their philosophical foundations runs the risk of reducing important and difficult conversations about AI to simplistic formulae like "do no harm."

The desirable qualities discussed in this chapter are often mutually supportive, but tensions between them deserve to be acknowledged, too. However, the implication should not be that trade-offs like the one between privacy and transparency always require zero-sum thinking. For example, collecting identifiable personal data is not always necessary, and even if such data are collected, techniques for anonymizing or pseudonymizing sensitive information can alleviate the violation of privacy. Thus, possibilities of mitigation and balancing do exist between contending values and priorities.

As Chapter 4 makes clear, technical solutions that ground AI systems in human values are necessary and at times useful, but doing the right thing cannot be reduced to such technical fixes. For example, improving the accuracy of an AI system may or may not improve its safety, depending on the intention with which an AI tool is used. There exists no perfect definition of AI ethics, fairness, or transparency to accommodate everyone's values and interests. Aligning AI with human values

87 Ebert, Wildhaber, and Adams-Prassl, "Big Data in the Workplace."

88 Baxter et al., "Bridging the Gap from AI Ethics Research to Practice"; Morley et al., "From What to How."

89 Bakiner, "What Do Academics Say about Artificial Intelligence Ethics?"

depends on what kind of society we want to live in, and that is ultimately a political question about how we make collective decisions and distribute society's resources. What some people experience as freedom of speech is experienced by others as a life-ruining disinformation campaign. The kind of data-driven policing some people desire for their safety ends up getting innocent citizens arrested or worse. An AI-assisted productivity tool may deliver shorter, more enjoyable workdays or massive unemployment depending on who uses it and to what end. The opportunities and risks associated with AI are not randomly assigned: Those at the losing end of technology are likely to be members of historically disadvantaged and marginalized social groups.

What kind of ethics should foreground AI governance? This is obviously an open-ended question, but value diversity is not an excuse for not doing the right thing. Anyone who wants technology to be an ally for social justice – or at least not its enemy – should think and act from the perspective of individuals and communities most likely to be systematically disadvantaged for the ethical, fair, responsible and safe development and use of technology. Of course, there are no perfect solutions in ethics. That is precisely why we have democracies in which differences about what is good and right are expressed, debated, negotiated, voted on, and rethought. The problem with AI governance so far has been the exclusion of those affected by AI from any sense of meaningful agency. The leadership in businesses developing and using AI has closed off the rest of society from ethical decision-making. Exceptions notwithstanding, lawmakers have been too deferential to business-led conceptions of ethical conduct. Critical researchers, journalists, and social movement activists do their best to give voice to affected persons and communities, but their power remains limited. The future of AI ethics depends on whether venues to debate and decide on ethical issues are democratized – a topic I will pick up in further detail in Chapter 7.

3

When Things Go Wrong

Understanding AI Risks and Harms

AI has earned the dubious distinction of attracting immediate and vocal negative attention while being developed. Unlike cigarettes or pre-seatbelt automobiles, the negative impact of AI on individuals and communities did not have to wait decades to become commonsense knowledge. If celebration of the mind-bending things AI could do inundated TED Talks and airport bookstores around the time deep-learning models began to deliver results in 2013, question marks around bias, discrimination, inaccuracy, and privacy violations were already on their way to haunt AI optimism by 2015. Since then, critical voices, which at times include the very producers and marketers of AI tools, have only grown louder.

This chapter introduces the potential risks and actual harms associated with AI systems. *Harm* itself is an essentially contested concept; for the purposes of this chapter, actual harm is defined as negative impact on the life, livelihood and well-being of individuals, communities and society as a whole. *Potential risk* is about harms that have not occurred yet but may result from the unregulated development and use of AI. Building on the critical academic and journalistic literature on AI, this chapter identifies the following as the risks and harms arising from the use of AI tools by individuals, businesses, and public agencies:

- bias and discrimination
- surveillance
- inaccurate, incorrect, and unreliable output
- disinformation, misinformation, or manipulation
- harm to life, livelihood, and well-being
- privacy violations
- decline in product and service quality
- political polarization, online radicalization, and algorithmic censorship
- job replacement.

Academics and journalists report ample evidence for bias and discrimination, surveillance, inaccurate, incorrect and unreliable output, disinformation and privacy violations. There are comparatively fewer episodes of harm to life, livelihood and well-being, but those cases understandably raise alarm for the algorithmic amplification of physical harm. The extent to which AI amplifies polarization and radicalization has proven divisive in academic scholarship. There is no doubt that AI use has improved product and service quality in multiple sectors, which is the reason why so many people want to use AI tools in the first place, but it is also true that uncritical AI adoption has made things worse – for example, in journalism and education. Job replacement has already become a real concern in a few industries, but massive disruptions to the global economy have not happened yet. It is possible that many tasks that are performed entirely by human workers will be handled primarily or exclusively by AI systems in the near future. Finally, accusations of algorithmic censorship and shadow banning on social media platforms are common across the political spectrum, but evidence is scant.

Needless to say, not all AI tools come with all these problems. Some back-end AI applications have little or no impact on individuals and communities. Automated decision-making systems are more likely to be accused of bias and discrimination than other AI systems; recommender systems on digital platforms are often criticized for amplifying violent and hateful speech; and chatbots come to mind when we think about AI systems sharing wildly inaccurate information and producing deepfakes. These nuances will be noted throughout this chapter.

Understanding the extent and causes of these problems warrants nuance for another reason. Commercial AI tools have already caused real harm, but some have done so more than others. To give an example, disinformation campaigns amplified by algorithms have rightly worried people around the world, while job losses due to AI have so far remained confined to certain industries in a few countries. Furthermore, the negative impact is rarely experienced uniformly: Bias and discrimination have hit historically disadvantaged and marginalized groups disproportionately, for example. In fact, the central message of this chapter is that AI risks and harms are inherently political, in that their consequences are borne by some social groups more than others.

In addition to risks and harms that emerge from the use and development of specific AI tools, AI threatens to aggravate systemic problems. The effect of using any one AI tool may be miniscule at the system level, but the investments in AI and its societywide adoption in the past decade have generated a massive cumulative impact. Such system-level issues are as follows:

- environmental degradation
- exploitation of labor
- market concentration.

Not all the social and political ills associated with AI are inherent to it. Rather, AI systems interact with social, political, economic, cultural, and military realities to aggravate existing problems. For example, disinformation has existed with or without AI, but the availability of recommender systems and proliferation of AI-powered chatbots have exacerbated disinformation. Likewise, digital platforms violate data subjects' privacy in the absence of AI, too, but the need for vast quantities of data to train and test AI algorithms reinforces the reckless data collection methods that result in privacy violations.

This chapter also discusses some of the underlying reasons for AI risks and harms. On-the-ground analyses find fault with biased, non-representative and low-quality data and problematic algorithms. A deep dive into the production and use of AI systems suggests that human decisions in the design, development, and use of AI systems and demographic uniformity in the technology sector may well be at the root of AI risks and harms. In other words, above and beyond data and algorithms, one should look into business organization and culture to understand what has gone wrong with AI.

THE POTENTIAL RISKS AND ACTUAL HARMS ARISING FROM THE USE OF AI TOOLS

Bias and Discrimination

Robert Williams, Michael Oliver, and Nijeer Parks were arrested for crimes they did not commit between 2019 and 2020. The charges were dropped in all three cases, but Parks spent ten days in jail for a theft that happened thirty miles away from where he was at the time. The cases shared commonalities: All three men are fathers, Oliver and Parks had prior criminal records, Oliver and Williams were investigated by the same Detroit detective, all three arrests took place as a result of misidentification by a facial recognition software, and … all three men are Black.[1] At the time of the arrests, researchers had already published findings of a high degree of misidentification or non-identification of Black people's faces, and especially those of Black women, by facial recognition software.[2] In fact, Detroit police chief James Craig admitted that the software's misidentification rate was at around 96 percent![3] Yet, knowledge of misidentification did not stop police departments from using the software. By early 2025, a total of eight men, seven of them Black, were wrongfully arrested as a result of facial recognition technology.[4]

Recent algorithmically driven wrongful arrests may not sound too significant in the long history of human-led miscarriages of justice in the United States, but

1 Khari Johnson, "How Wrongful Arrests Based on AI Derailed 3 Men's Lives," *Wired*, March 7, 2022 (www.wired.com/story/wrongful-arrests-ai-derailed-3-mens-lives/).

2 Buolamwini and Gebru, "Gender Shades: Intersectional Accuracy Disparities in Commercial Gender Classification."

3 Jason Koebler, "Detroit Police Chief: Facial Recognition Software Misidentifies 96% of the Time," *Vice*, June 29, 2020 (www.vice.com/en/article/dyzykz/detroit-police-chief-facial-recognition-software-misidentifies-96-of-the-time).

4 Douglas MacMillan, David Ovalle, and Aaron Schaffer, "Arrested by AI: Police ignore standards after facial recognition matches," *The Washington Post*, January 13, 2025 (www.washingtonpost.com/business/interactive/2025/police-artificial-intelligence-facial-recognition).

considering that wrong decisions, algorithmic or otherwise, do not always get rectified, the actual number of people affected by facial recognition inaccuracies may be higher. The pressure to get criminal defendants, even innocent ones, to agree to a plea deal aggravates the problem: "Defense attorneys and legal experts say some people wrongly accused by facial recognition agree to plea deals, suggesting wrongful arrests are more common than generally realized."[5] One silver lining from Robert Williams's arrest was that two years later Prosecutor Kym Worthy of Wayne County, MI, decided not to adopt a directive allowing Detroit's Police Department to use facial recognition software.[6]

Accusations of racial bias in algorithmically enhanced law enforcement deserve special mention.[7] The Correctional Offender Management Profiling for Alternative Sanctions (COMPAS) is a recidivism prediction software developed by Equivant (formerly Northpointe). The algorithm underlying COMPAS has been marketed as accurate and free of human judgment error. However, *ProPublica* researchers found that the COMPAS algorithm generated racially biased predictions.[8] The report sparked a series of rejoinders between *ProPublica* and COMPAS. Later, a *Washington Post* article replicated the *ProPublica* study, finding that the COMPAS algorithm had a built-in racial bias in predicting false positives, even if it predicted fairly for true positives. In substantive terms, it means that while COMPAS predicted the likelihood of re-offense with high levels of accuracy regardless of race, it failed to predict accurately whether a former convict would not reoffend in the future. Black non-reoffenders were twice as likely to be misclassified as potential reoffenders than white ones.[9]

Accusations of racism are not confined to law enforcement. SafeRent, an AI-powered tenant screening tool, was sued for racial discrimination after two tenants claimed that the algorithm's tenancy eligibility score discriminated against Black and Hispanic applicants.[10] In other cases, algorithms face criticism not for producing discriminatory output, but for failing to stop humans who discriminate. A 2017 study of Airbnb guests and hosts finds that guests with distinctively

5 Khari Johnson, "How Wrongful Arrests Based on AI Derailed 3 Men's Lives."

6 Ibid.

7 Vyacheslav Polonski. "AI is convicting criminals and determining jail time, but is it fair," *World Economic Forum*, November 2018 (www.weforum.org/agenda/2018/11/algorithms-court-criminals-jail-time-fair/).

8 Julia Angwin, Jeff Larson, Surya Mattu, and Lauren Kirchner, "Machine Bias: There's Software Used Across the Country to Predict Future Criminals. And it's Biased Against Blacks," *ProPublica*, May 23, 2016 (www.propublica.org/article/machine-bias-risk-assessments-in-criminal-sentencing).

9 Sam Corbett-Davies, Emma Pierson, Feller, Avi, and Goel, Sharad, "A computer program used for bail and sentencing decisions was labeled biased against blacks. It's actually not that clear," *The Washington Post*, October 17, 2016 (www.washingtonpost.com/news/monkey-cage/wp/2016/10/17/can-an-algorithm-be-racist-our-analysis-is-more-cautious-than-propublicas/).

10 www.justice.gov/crt/case/louis-et-al-v-saferent-et-al-d-mass. Also see: Johana Bhuiyan, "She didn't get an apartment because of an AI-generated score – and sued to help others avoid the same fate," *The Guardian*, December 14, 2024 (www.theguardian.com/technology/2024/dec/14/saferent-ai-tenant-screening-lawsuit).

African–American-sounding names are 16 percent less likely to be accepted relative to identical guests with distinctively white-sounding names.[11] Airbnb established the Work to Fight Discrimination and Build Inclusion initiative in 2016 and launched Project Lighthouse in 2020 to rectify the problem of discrimination. However, according to a report released by the company, "guests perceived to be Black were able to successfully book the stay of their choice 91.4 percent of the time, versus 94.1 percent for guests perceived to be white" in 2021.[12]

Explicitly racist and racially discriminatory content is known to plague social media platforms, chatbots, and search engines. Search engines, arguably the main tools with which billions of people seek useful, correct, truthful, and accurate information, are not free from racist and sexist bias and discrimination. After her initial shock while reading the query results for "Black girls" on Google, Safiya Noble asked colleagues to run the same query on their computers. Confirming that the hyper-sexualized and degrading representations of girls and women of color are a systematic problem, she has taken to investigating the sources of bias.[13] Tay, a chatbot developed by Microsoft's Technology and Research and Bing teams, had to be taken off Twitter shortly after its launch because it began to spit out racist and sexist content. This early experiment in March 2016 pushed companies to pay more attention to content moderation in later iterations of chatbots. For example, the version of OpenAI's ChatGPT that is available to users already filters out content classified as hateful, threatening, self-harm-promoting, sexually explicit, or violent.[14]

An interesting experiment exposing bias and discrimination is ImageNet Roulette, which, according to co-creator Trevor Paglen, is meant as a "provocation" directed at large image datasets.[15] The idea is simple: The user uploads a photo, and the algorithm returns its description using adjectives and generic nouns. While most photos were matched with uncontroversial descriptions, at times the system ended up producing ethnic slurs,[16] sexist and racist stereotypes, demeaning words, and outright silly or absurd descriptions. Co-creators Kate Crawford and Trevor Paglen argue that ImageNet, the gigantic training dataset for images that was developed by a Stanford University team in 2009, reflects many of the unquestioned assumptions of its developers and contributors. The ambition to represent and organize the entire world of objects in 14 billion images and over 20,000 tags leads inevitably to

[11] Edelman, Luca, and Svirsky, "Racial Discrimination in the Sharing Economy."

[12] Airbnb, "A Six-Year Update on Airbnb's Work to Fight Discrimination and Build Inclusion," December 13, 2022 (www.news.airbnb.com/wp-content/uploads/sites/4/2022/12/A-Six-Year-Update-on-Airbnbs-Work-to-Fight-Discrimination-and-Build-Inclusion-12122022.pdf).

[13] Noble, *Algorithms of Oppression: How Search Engines Reinforce Racism*.

[14] www.platform.openai.com/docs/guides/moderation/overview

[15] www.paglen.studio/2020/04/29/imagenet-roulette/

[16] Julia Carrie Wong, "The viral selfie app ImageNet Roulette seemed fun – until it called me a racist slur," *The Guardian*, September 18, 2019 (www.theguardian.com/technology/2019/sep/17/imagenet-roulette-asian-racist-slur-selfie).

the exclusion of some identities and experiences, and the use of biased or offensive categories to describe some images.[17]

The aggravation of sexist bias and discrimination in the age of algorithms has caught global attention. A frequently cited analysis of models that predict the (binary) gender of people visualized while doing things shows massive gender bias: Tasks such as shopping, microwaving, and washing are assigned to a female agent, while driving, shooting, and coaching are biased toward a male one. This is in part a function of the training dataset, but the predictive model further amplifies the bias.[18] Studies of word-embedding associations – co-occurrence of some words with others – find that algorithms replicate human stereotypes about age and gender categories.[19] Voice assistants tend to have female-sounding names, such as Alexa, Cortana, and Siri, and female-sounding default voice settings. It is difficult not to conclude that their designers associated secretarial tasks with women. The gender bias in everyday human–computer interaction does not end there, however: The AI systems underlying them tend to replicate stereotypical gender expectations and language. For example, they may offer flirtatious responses in the face of inappropriate human prompts or set no boundaries when those prompts include demeaning or harassing language.[20] Abusive human responses became so widespread that eventually, Amazon added a "disengage mode" when users made inappropriate comments or requests. It is perhaps no wonder that multiple surveys report women being more worried than men about AI-generated sexual abuse content and AI-induced structural changes in the economy and society, especially around socioeconomic inequality and job security.[21]

AI or no AI, data collection and processing by governments and technology platforms have often reproduced the gender binary at the expense of gender-nonconforming people. Forcing survey respondents to check the 'M' or 'F' box denies lives and experiences on the gender spectrum. Even tech companies that claim to be gender-inclusive do not always help: Facebook users can customize their gender, but the collected data are sold to advertisers as either male or female.[22]

Contemporary AI developments raise the prospects of assisting persons with disabilities and eliminating procedures that discriminate against them. However, failure to

17 Kate Crawford and Trevor Paglen, "Excavating AI: The Politics of Images in Machine Learning Training Sets" (www.excavating.ai).

18 Zhao et al., "Men Also Like Shopping."

19 Matthew Hutson, "Even artificial intelligence can acquire biases against race and gender," *Science*, April 13, 2017 (www.science.org/content/article/even-artificial-intelligence-can-acquire-biases-against-race-and-gender).

20 Jacqueline Feldman, "A Human Wrote This," *Statorec* (blog), 2023 (www.statorec.com/a-human-wrote-this-by-jacqueline-feldman/).

21 Darrell M. West, "AI poses disproportionate risks to women," *Brookings Institute* (blog), November 20, 2023 (www.brookings.edu/articles/ai-poses-disproportionate-risks-to-women/).

22 Meredith Broussard, "Coding Needs to Get Beyond the Gender Binary," *Time*, June 15, 2023 (www.time.com/6287271/coding-beyond-gender-binary/).

account for the needs of persons with disabilities in design and deployment remains a major accessibility issue. One commentator refers to the inattention of the vendors and buyers of human resources technology to the needs of persons with disabilities as a market failure.[23] To give some examples: The speech and gesture analysis algorithms used by the hiring platform HireVue were found to discriminate against candidates "who have speech impediments, are deaf, blind, or have had a stroke."[24] AI video generators reportedly perpetuate stereotypes about people with disabilities.[25] Penn State researchers find that sentiment and toxicity analysis models exhibit bias against persons with disabilities, as they tend to classify disability-related terms as negative or toxic without proper understanding of context.[26] The use of algorithms in human resource management may discriminate against persons with disabilities, whose capabilities and needs are not reflected as the norm in algorithmic data analysis methods.[27]

All in all, algorithmic systems have made bias and discrimination worse. While it is true that much of that bias is a reflection of the structures of inequality in contemporary societies, algorithms *aggravate* and *normalize* unequal and oppressive structures.[28] Aggravation happens when an existing injustice or stereotype is amplified – say, when facial recognition software adds another layer to racial discrimination in law enforcement, or when an AI photo generation tool reproduces traditional gender roles across dozens of examples. Normalization refers to the misconception that computer-generated results must be impartial and robust because mathematics and computers do not hold discriminatory attitudes. Awareness of how today's AI intersects with existing social, political, economic, and cultural issues is therefore necessary for developing governance responses.

Surveillance

Advances in data collection, storage, and analysis tools have made mass surveillance easier and cheaper. Video camera networks, armed with AI-powered facial recognition software and installed in virtually every corner of cities like London, can track people's physical features and movements. The marketing and use of these tools are justified on the grounds of public safety and convenience – for example, in the

[23] Susan Scott-Parker, "AI-powered HR technology has a disability problem," *OECD Forum Network*, July 18, 2023 (www.oecd-forum.org/posts/ai-powered-hr-technology-has-a-disability-problem).

[24] Alyssa Lung, "Disabled and Rejected from a Job? Maybe AI-Discrimination is to Blame!" UCLA Advanced Research Computing, Disabilities & Computing Program, August 4, 2023 (www.dcp.ucla.edu/job-ai-discrimination).

[25] Reece Rogers and Victoria Turk, "OpenAI's Sora Is Plagued by Sexist, Racist, and Ableist Biases," Wired, March 23, 2025 (www.wired.com/story/openai-sora-video-generator-bias/).

[26] Narayanan Venkit, Srinath, and Wilson, "Automated Ableism."

[27] Nancy Doyle, "Artificial Intelligence is Dangerous for Disabled People at Work: 4 Takeaways for Developers and Buyers," *Forbes*, October 11, 2022 (www.forbes.com/sites/drnancydoyle/2022/10/11/artificial-intelligence-is-dangerous-for-disabled-people-at-work-4-takeaways-for-developers-and-buyers).

[28] Hoffmann, "Terms of Inclusion"; Deranty and Corbin, "Artificial Intelligence and Work."

case of airport facial recognition that expedites screening and security procedures. However, AI-led surveillance may also result in excessive policing, loss of privacy, and, in the hands of authoritarian and repressive governments, massive human rights violations. The businesses that collect or purchase personal data often use such data for advertising and marketing without the data subjects' informed consent.

When surveillance intersects with bias, it deepens existing societal inequalities. The negative impact of surveillance on individuals and communities does not always manifest itself in the form of algorithmic bias, however. Expanding on Michael P. Jefferson's description of the debasement, indifference, and denial characterizing responses to Black experiences as *anti-Blackness*, Mutale Nkonde coins the term *automated anti-Blackness*.[29] Her specific example is the deployment of facial recognition technology for surveillance of residents at the Atlantic Towers in the Brownsville section of Brooklyn. She connects the use of novel technologies to fine tenants for minor infractions to the much longer history of surveilling Black people to argue that facial recognition "sees" through the eyes of its creators, almost entirely non-Black, and consequently, these technologies are weaponized against Black people. Unlike earlier examples, what is happening at the Atlantic Towers is not technological error; rather, powerful humans choose to reproduce racially motivated inequality through algorithmic tools.

Surveillance at the borders has taken on a new meaning in the age of powerful facial recognition and biometric identification techniques. Legal anthropologist Petra Molnar argues that states hold off on the legal regulation of AI as they consider migrants, historically vulnerable populations whose rights are not recognized by host states, a "testing ground" for new technologies. The development of migrant management technologies blurs the distinction between public and private accountability in cases where migrants' rights to non-discrimination, privacy, and due-process rights are threatened.[30]

Incorrect, Inaccurate, and Unreliable Output

Chatbots and image generators using the latest large language models (LLMs) can be useful and entertaining – some people find them even creative. Can they tell us the truth, though? There have been too many examples of chatbot failures to provide users with correct, accurate, and reliable answers in response to mathematical, logical, scientific, historical, and political questions. These errors are collectively known as chatbot *hallucinations*. *Correct* here is defined as the factually right ("Botswana is in Africa") or logically true (there are three r's in the word strawberry) answer, or set of answers, to a question. *Accurate* answers refer to the closest approximation to correct answers given present or future uncertainty ("state-of-the-art climate science

29 Nkonde, "Automated Anti-Blackness: Facial Recognition in Brooklyn, New York."

30 Molnar, "Technology on the Margins."

models confirm global warming"). *Reliable* means giving the same answer to the same question regardless of context.

Science fiction writer Ted Chiang asks us to think of ChatGPT as an information retrieval system that uses an approximation of what exists on the internet – in his own words, "a blurry jpeg of all the text on the Web."[31] Thus, it can fail to perform tasks for which accuracy is essential. In fact, time and again, users have been disappointed when AI tools are asked to perform logical, mathematical tasks with unique solutions or answer queries truthfully. Examples of inaccurate output have proliferated since ChatGPT turned billions of people into AI users overnight in late 2022 – non-existent case law that got some lawyers in serious trouble,[32] citations of academic articles that have never been written,[33] high-school math problems that defy the intelligence of the all-conquering technology of our times,[34] and physical and mental health advice that has at times horrified users and researchers.[35] These falsehoods have inspired a team of scholars to label LLMs "bullshit" in the sense philosopher Harry Frankfurt understood it – speech that aims to persuade without regard to truth.[36]

Disinformation, Misinformation, or Manipulation

The complicated relationship between AI and truth would have been a matter of lighthearted ridicule if generative AI were not so profoundly incorporated into search engines and newsrooms. As people are increasingly relying on AI-generated responses to queries without searching or reading any further, incorrect information has become a serious issue. To be fair, LLMs have arrived on the heels of a societal crisis of trust: There is just a lot of incorrect information, online and offline. Often, people spread such information without malicious intent (i.e., *misinformation*), but the intentional dissemination of lies and half-truths (i.e., *disinformation*) has become increasingly more common, too.

Today's AI-powered text, image, video, and sound generators exacerbate this atmosphere of misinformation and disinformation. AI-generated text responses may come across as authoritative even when they are incorrect. Most people, including experts, fail to distinguish between genuine and AI-generated photos. Some people

31 Ted Chiang, "ChatGPT Is a Blurry JPEG of the Web," *The New Yorker*, February 9, 2023 (www.newyorker.com/tech/annals-of-technology/chatgpt-is-a-blurry-jpeg-of-the-web).

32 Michael Legg and Vicki McNamara, "AI is creating fake legal cases and making its way into real courtrooms, with disastrous results," *The Conversation*, March 12, 2024 (www.theconversation.com/ai-is-creating-fake-legal-cases-and-making-its-way-into-real-courtrooms-with-disastrous-results-225080).

33 Walters and Wilder, "Fabrication and Errors in the Bibliographic Citations Generated by ChatGPT."

34 Steve Lohr, "A.I. Can Write Poetry, but It Struggles With Math," *The New York Times*, July 23, 2024 (www.nytimes.com/2024/07/23/technology/ai-chatbots-chatgpt-math.html).

35 Jacqueline Howard, "ChatGPT's responses to suicide, addiction, sexual assault crises raise questions in new study," *CNN*, June 7, 2023 (www.cnn.com/2023/06/07/health/chatgpt-health-crisis-responses-wellness/index.html).

36 Hicks, Humphries, and Slater, "ChatGPT Is Bullshit."

have already fallen victim to scams in which an AI-generated voice could not be distinguished from that of a distressed family member.[37]

AI-generated disinformation has serious implications for political campaign ads, fraud detection, and adult content, among others. What is popularly referred to as *deepfakes* manipulate unsuspecting viewers and listeners for political and financial ends or for fun. They also hurt the well-being and reputation of people depicted in those videos and images. It is not just people believing fake content that worries critics; it is feared that the widespread dissemination of deepfakes might produce an atmosphere of mistrust in which people stop believing real content.[38]

Furthermore, AI can amplify misinformation and disinformation through disseminating, not only generating, inaccurate content. Accusations of algorithmically amplified disinformation about vaccines once led US President Biden to accuse Facebook of "killing people," words that he later claimed were directed at disinformation super-spreaders.[39] Recommender systems, that is, algorithms that connect people with information and other people, amplify the dissemination of content at a speed and expanse that no earlier medium had achieved before. For example, as few as a dozen individual accounts have been found to generate up to two-thirds of misleading content on COVID-19 vaccines.[40] This leaves many more people vulnerable to disinformation than ever before.

Harm to Life, Livelihood, and Well-Being

Widespread hate speech fueled the mass murder and forcible transfer of Rohingya Muslims in Myanmar in 2016 and 2017. At the time, Facebook's leadership ignored pleas to take down disinformation and incendiary content that appeared on the news feed and Facebook groups and was amplified through the recommender system to contribute to violence against the Rohingya.[41] In December 2022, the son of Meareg Amare, a university professor who was murdered by a vigilante mob in Ethiopia following hateful and violent Facebook posts, brought legal action against Meta before Kenya's High Court. Flavia Mwangovya, Amnesty International's Deputy Regional Director of East Africa, Horn, and Great Lakes Region, alleges a direct connection between algorithms and harm: "From Ethiopia to Myanmar,

[37] Charles Bethea, "The Terrifying A.I. Scam That Uses Your Loved One's Voice," *The New Yorker*, March 7, 2024 (www.newyorker.com/science/annals-of-artificial-intelligence/the-terrifying-ai-scam-that-uses-your-loved-ones-voice).

[38] Tiffany Hsu and Steven Lee Myers, "Can We No Longer Believe Anything We See," *The New York Times*, April 8, 2023 (www.nytimes.com/2023/04/08/business/media/ai-generated-images.html).

[39] "Biden rows back on Facebook 'killing people' comment," *BBC News*, July 20, 2021 (www.bbc.com/news/technology-57901710).

[40] Erum Salam, "Majority of COVID misinformation came from 12 people, report finds," *The Guardian*, July 17, 2021 (www.theguardian.com/world/2021/jul/17/covid-misinformation-conspiracy-theories-ccdh-report).

[41] "Rohingya sue Facebook for £150bn over Myanmar genocide," *The Guardian*, December 6, 2021.

Meta knew or should have known that its algorithmic systems were fuelling the spread of harmful content leading to serious real-world harms."[42] These incidents threw into sharp relief the possibility that algorithmic amplification of misleading and hateful content could result in mass killings.

In September 2021, a massive leak of messages among Facebook and Instagram researchers made headlines. Among the notorious messages, perhaps none generated more general concern than the ones about teens' mental health. A slide from 2019 reads: "We make body image issues worse for one in three teen girls," and a presentation shows that among teens with suicidal thoughts, 3 percent of British and 6 percent of American users connect those thoughts to Instagram.[43] *The Wall Street Journal* article covering the issue quotes a young woman who searched for workout videos, and kept receiving content about ideal body types and weight loss alongside the workout material.[44] The accusation that Instagram knew about these risks and did nothing to eliminate them led to vocal accusations. A coroner's report in Britain blamed social media companies for the suicide of Molly Russell, a teenage girl.[45] The introduction of personalized chatbot friends added another layer: Sewell Setzer III, a fourteen-year-old boy, took his own life following a conversation that could be interpreted as encouraging death.[46]

Suicide prevention lays bare the contradictions of content moderation, algorithmic or otherwise, on social media platforms. In the absence of legislation, social media companies have become at once the problem and the solution. Facebook had announced an AI-powered content detection tool to discover suicidal ideation as early as February 2017, after a fourteen-year-old girl livestreamed her suicide on the platform.[47] In fact, the tool is credited with saving the life of an Argentinian woman in 2018, when first responders were alerted to her suicidal post flagged by the algorithm – a story not corroborated by Meta.[48] Research on algorithmic suicide prediction has been praised as

[42] Amnesty International Canada, "Kenya: Meta sued for 1.6 billion USD for fueling Ethiopia ethnic violence," December 14, 2022 (www.amnesty.ca/human-rights-news/kenya-meta-sued-for-1-6-billion-usd-for-fueling-ethiopia-ethnic-violence/).

[43] Georgia Wells, Jeff Horwitz, and Deepa Seetharaman, "Facebook Knows Instagram Is Toxic for Teen Girls, Company Documents Show," *The Wall Street Journal*, September 14, 2021 (www.wsj.com/articles/facebook-knows-instagram-is-toxic-for-teen-girls-company-documents-show-11631620739).

[44] Georgia Wells, Jeff Horwitz, and Deepa Seetharaman, "Facebook Knows Instagram Is Toxic for Teen Girls, Company Documents Show," *The Wall Street Journal*, September 14, 2021 (www.wsj.com/articles/facebook-knows-instagram-is-toxic-for-teen-girls-company-documents-show-11631620739).

[45] Adam Satariano, "British Ruling Pins Blame on Social Media for Teenager's Suicide," *The New York Times*, October 1, 2022 (www.nytimes.com/2022/10/01/business/instagram-suicide-ruling-britain.html).

[46] Kate Payne, "An AI chatbot pushed a teen to kill himself, a lawsuit against its creator alleges," *Associated Press*, October 25, 2024 (www.apnews.com/article/chatbot-ai-lawsuit-suicide-teen-artificial-intelligence-9d48adc572100822fdbc3c90d1456bd0).

[47] Lindsey Bever, "Facebook hopes artificial intelligence can curb the 'terribly tragic' trend of suicides," *The Washington Post*, March 1, 2017 (www.washingtonpost.com/news/the-intersect/wp/2017/02/08/why-mental-health-professionals-say-live-streaming-suicides-is-a-very-concerning-trend/).

[48] Alli McConnon, "AI Helps Identify People at Risk for Suicide," *The Wall Street Journal*, February 23, 2018 (www.wsj.com/articles/ai-helps-identify-people-at-risk-for-suicide-1519400853).

a potential counterweight to the online and offline factors behind increasingly more common expressions of suicidal intent on social media.[49] It should be noted that this line of work, especially if left to the discretion of technology companies, comes with the risks of inaccurate detection, media hype, and privacy violations.[50] In fact, an early version of an online mental health detector on Twitter, the Samaritans Radar, had to be suspended within nine days for potentially leaving users who share their difficulties candidly on the platform vulnerable to trolling and stalking.[51]

Harm to self happens in many other forms, as well. Social media platforms have been accused of not doing enough to moderate content causing eating disorders. A report by the Center for Countering Digital Hate, called Deadly by Design, finds that the algorithm behind TikTok's "For You" feed amplifies self-harm and suicide videos to what it calls "vulnerable" accounts with usernames containing *loseweight* in comparison to "standard" usernames that do not reveal a vulnerability.[52]

Algorithms are at the center of concerns around self-harm and mental health problems because recommender systems are accused of getting young and adult users addicted to social media platforms.[53] A number of US school districts sued[54] Instagram, Snapchat, TikTok, and YouTube for aggravating the youth mental health crisis through, in the words of Seattle Public Schools, "increased screen time, unfiltered content, and potentially addictive properties of social media."[55]

What aggravates content moderation woes is powerful individuals' and organizations' privileged access to online platforms. Political leaders, including those of authoritarian regimes, can get platforms to take down content in ways that ordinary citizens cannot. X's owner, Elon Musk, once admitted to complying with the Turkish government's requests for content takedowns just before the May 2023 elections to stop the platform from getting banned in that country.[56] In other words,

49 Laurie Fagan, "Ottawa researcher uses AI, Twitter to track suicide risk among students," *CBC*, May 10, 2020 (www.cbc.ca/news/canada/ottawa/mental-health-twitter-social-media-university-students-1.5558319).

50 Mason Marks, "Suicide prediction technology is revolutionary. It badly needs oversight," *The Washington Post*, December 20, 2018 (www.washingtonpost.com/outlook/suicide-prediction-technology-is-revolutionary-it-badly-needs-oversight/2018/12/20/214d2532-fd6b-11e8-ad40-cdfd0e0dd65a_story.html).

51 Karen McVeigh, "Samaritans Twitter app identifying user's moods criticised as invasive," *The Guardian*, November 4, 2014 (www.theguardian.com/society/2014/nov/04/samaritans-twitter-app-mental-health-depression).

52 The Center for Countering Digital Hate, "Deadly by Design," December 2022 (www.counterhate.com/wp-content/uploads/2022/12/CCDH-Deadly-by-Design_120922.pdf).

53 Alter, *Irresistible: The Rise of Addictive Technology and the Business of Keeping Us Hooked*; Bernstein, *Unwired: Gaining Control over Addictive Technologies*.

54 Donna St. George, "Schools sue social media companies over youth mental health crisis," *The Washington Post*, March 19, 2023 (www.washingtonpost.com/education/2023/03/19/school-lawsuits-social-media-mental-health/).

55 "Social Media Complaint Filed by Seattle Public Schools," January 10, 2023 (www.seattleschools.org/news/social-media-case/).

56 Ashley Belanger, "Musk defends enabling Turkish censorship on Twitter, calling it his 'choice,'" *Ars Technica*, May 15, 2023 (www.arstechnica.com/tech-policy/2023/05/musk-defends-enabling-turkish-censorship-on-twitter-calling-it-his-choice/).

threats to life, livelihood and well-being are not distributed uniformly across the population – those who lack direct access to the leadership of social media platforms bear the brunt of algorithmically amplified harms.

Privacy Violations

An angry man outside a Target in Minneapolis was asking a dumbfounded manager why the company was sending his teenage daughter coupons for baby clothes and cribs one day in 2012. It turned out that Target's algorithms bundled past purchases to predict what individual customers might want in the future.[57] Someone buying items related to parenting and children would be offered coupons for similar items. The algorithm can put together an eerily accurate taste profile without ever developing an intuitive understanding of childhood, parenting, or pregnancy.[58] This highlights a serious risk for algorithmically curated online platforms: The data given away by users can show up in unexpected and potentially harmful places.

Data collection in the digital age takes place under limited and uninformative consent procedures. Users give away privacy and autonomy under terms and conditions they have little understanding of, and no control over. Social media platforms monetize all sorts of data collected from users. The free versions of chatbots do not guarantee that user queries and other shared information will not be used to train models in the future. Government and business surveillance erodes privacy and autonomy even further. What is more, the infringements on personal autonomy and the issues of bias and discrimination may intersect: For example, software that claims to predict one's gender based on appearance equates gender with appearance, thereby denying autonomy in gender identity and risking biased predictions.[59]

As it will become clear in the chapters on AI governance, preserving affected individuals' data privacy, and consequently, personal autonomy, has become the leading concern of lawmakers around the world. Even though the United States, home to leading AI companies, has lagged behind in terms of federal privacy legislation, the movement for privacy and data protection legislation that started with the European Union's General Data Protection Regulation in 2016 has found resonance around the globe, including in a couple of US states.

57 Kashmir Hill, "How Target Figured Out A Teen Girl Was Pregnant Before Her Father Did," *Forbes*, February 16, 2012 (www.forbes.com/sites/kashmirhill/2012/02/16/how-target-figured-out-a-teen-girl-was-pregnant-before-her-father-did/).

58 For a similar story around sexual orientation and gender identity, see: Katie Heaney, "Facebook Knew I Was Gay Before My Family Did," *BuzzFeed*, March 19, 2013 (www.buzzfeednews.com/article/katieheaney/facebook-knew-i-was-gay-before-my-family-did).

59 Evan Selinger, "Q&A: What's the point of automated gender recognition software?" The Boston Globe, May 13, 2021 (www.bostonglobe.com/2021/05/13/opinion/qa-whats-point-automated-gender-recognition-software/).

Decline in Product and Service Quality

The 2023 word of the year, according to the American Dialect Society, was *enshittification*, a term coined by author Cory Doctorow to refer to a process of declining customer experience on online platforms.[60] Although Doctorow's original use of the term covers a much broader scope than AI products, the idea that technology companies offer a worse version of the product in their ambitious push for profit maximization resonates with critics of AI, too. "[S]hoddy or unwanted A.I. content in social media, art, books and, increasingly, in search results" has its own name: *Slop*.[61]

AI tools taking over job markets thanks to their potential to supersede human cognitive capabilities is a popular concern. The underlying assumption, that they will be at least as good as human workers, requires scrutiny, however. Some critics have argued that AI tools may provide a cheaper but low-quality alternative to humans in multiple industries.[62] Providing factual statements is an area in which even the most advanced LLMs have not produced satisfactory solutions, and the risks of bias, discrimination, hate speech, and incitement to violence are contained through heavy content moderation by humans. What is more, there is no scientific evidence that language models understand their output or reason while generating it. For all these reasons, AI-generated content, whether it be legal, scientific, medical, or logical in nature, has a good chance of being incorrect if not outright dangerous. Thus, workers may be replaced by cheaper, not necessarily better, tools, and customers may have to make do with worse versions of products they currently use.

CNET, a consumer technology news website, announced that seventy-seven of its articles had been written by an internally designed AI engine (what editor-in-chief Connie Guglielmo calls "next-generation storytelling tools"), reviewed and modified by humans between November 2022 and January 2023.[63] Soon, others found serious errors with the AI-generated texts.[64] The use of AI tools where they perform at their worst, namely delivering factually correct information, threatens to further erode trust in conventional and social media.

[60] American Dialect Society, "2023 Word of the Year Is 'Enshittification,'" January 5, 2024 (www.americandialect.org/2023-word-of-the-year-is-enshittification/).

[61] Benjamin Hoffman, "First Came 'Spam.' Now, With A.I., We've Got 'Slop,'" *The New York Times*, June 11, 2024 (www.nytimes.com/2024/06/11/style/ai-search-slop.html).

[62] Alex Hanna and Emily Bender, "'AI' Hurts Consumers and Workers – and Isn't Intelligent," *Tech Policy Press Blog*, August 4, 2023 (www.techpolicy.press/ai-hurts-consumers-and-workers-and-isnt-intelligent/).

[63] Connie Guglielmo, "CNET Is Testing an AI Engine. Here's What We've Learned, Mistakes and All," *CNET*, January 25, 2023 (www.cnet.com/tech/cnet-is-testing-an-ai-engine-heres-what-weve-learned-mistakes-and-all/).

[64] Jon Christian, "CNET's Article-Writing AI Is Already Publishing Very Dumb Errors," *Futurism*, January 22, 2023 (www.futurism.com/cnet-ai-errors); Valerie Strauss, "Lisa Marie Presley's death, AI problems and more news literacy lessons," *The Washington Post*, January 25, 2023 (www.washingtonpost.com/education/2023/01/25/lisa-marie-ai-problems-newsliteracy-lessons/).

It is plausible that LLMs and the tools they power will get progressively better. There is sufficient evidence to show that the chatbots of today have been performing much better than their predecessors from five years earlier (see Chapter 1). Throwing more money and resources at LLMs may improve model performance in the future, as well as scientific advances in algorithmic modeling. However, constant progress towards perfection remains an assumption rather than a fact. Critic Gary Marcus likens the notion that technologies, AI included, advance linearly or exponentially to expecting adults to grow at the same rate as when they were babies. In fact, there is evidence that, at least in the short run, headline-grabbing chatbots have not been getting better across all tasks: A Stanford team tracking the performance of the LLMs underlying ChatGPT between March and July 2023 finds that "the performance and behavior of both GPT-3.5 and GPT-4 varied significantly across these two releases and that their performance on some tasks has gotten substantially worse over time, while they have improved on other problems."[65]

Political Polarization, Online Radicalization, and Algorithmic Censorship

Online radicalization is arguably the most frequently mentioned malaise of the social media age. The fear that users of online platforms, especially the youth, would spiral down from innocuous communication of grievances to violent extremism has been voiced since the early days of the internet, but the 2010s brought the phenomenon to worldwide infamy. The rise and early military gains of the Islamic State were attributed to its recruitment strategy, which converted thousands of youngsters from around the world with no prior experience of war into fighters for a spectacularly brutal non-state armed actor in Iraq and Syria. Even as the horrors of Islamic State violence waned, the anxiety around online platforms gripped the world. The success of far-right groups in utilizing online chatting and posting to communicate, the aggravation of genocidal rhetoric against the Rohingya in Myanmar through Facebook groups, and the spread of disinformation on Twitter and Facebook deepened the sense of dread around online radicalization.

What makes online radicalization AI-related is the role of algorithms in recommending content and connections in online platforms. Recommender algorithms, which aim to maximize user engagement, suggest content most likely to align with a user's tastes and preferences.[66] Those who like, respond to, or repost a piece of content are likely to receive similar suggestions, which can then trigger a spiral of digging deeper and deeper into that content. Recommender systems do not only suggest content; they also suggest connections based on one's previous network of connections, tastes, and preferences. This allows users to connect with like-minded

65 Chen, Zaharia, and Zou, "How Is ChatGPT's Behavior Changing over Time?"
66 DiResta, *Invisible Rulers: The People Who Turn Lies into Reality.*

people at an amazing pace. Recommendations for content and connections are such mundane facts of our online lives that we do not even notice their presence. They have no explicit objective of radicalizing people, and for the most part, it is not what they do. However, content suggestions on potentially controversial topics may include deceptive, hateful, or violent speech in the absence of strong content moderation policies. Indeed, incendiary content tends to drive up engagement; therefore, the likelihood of being recommended such content is relatively high. The connection recommendations may likewise amplify the risk that users on the verge of joining a violent, hateful, or conspiracy-minded movement meet others who will tip them over the edge. Some users may be members of violent organizations. Others may be influencers who create incendiary content to maximize their following, and through that, ad revenues. Algorithmic amplification is so central to influencers' work that disinformation researcher Renée DiResta calls the influencer, the crowd they want to influence and the algorithms the "trinity."[67] With or without professional content creators, members of online networks may reinforce groupthink by circulating content affirming their worldviews – a phenomenon referred to as "filter bubbles" or "echo chambers."[68]

Spokespersons for social media platforms defend algorithmic content and connection recommendations on the grounds of freedom and autonomy. Accordingly, people choose what they want to experience, and the algorithm simply provides the options. Critics view algorithmic choice as generating "filter bubbles," that is, extreme self-isolation due to personalization of content, rather than enhancing autonomy, however[69] – it is worth noting that just as the research on online radicalization should be assessed with its contexts, scope conditions, and nuances, the research on whether filter bubbles exist has not produced universally applicable findings.[70]

Pew Research Center published a report called "Political Polarization & Media Habits" in October 2014.[71] It was one of the first reports to include social media alongside conventional media as a potential source of polarization in the United States. It found that liberals were more likely to unfriend someone on social media because of politics, while conservatives were more likely to hear political opinions similar to their own on Facebook. It also found that Facebook was by far the most popular platform for receiving political news. The report did not contain strong conclusions

67 DiResta: 76–77.

68 Sunstein, *Going to Extremes: How Like Minds Unite and Divide*; Pariser, *The Filter Bubble: What the Internet Is Hiding from You*; Bruns, *Are Filter Bubbles Real?*; Barberá, "Social Media, Echo Chambers, and Political Polarization."

69 Pariser, *The Filter Bubble: What the Internet Is Hiding from You.*

70 Bruns, *Are Filter Bubbles Real?*; Barberá, "Social Media, Echo Chambers, and Political Polarization."

71 Pew Research Center, "Political Polarization and Media Habits," October 2014 (www.pewresearch.org/wp-content/uploads/sites/8/2014/10/Political-Polarization-and-Media-Habits-FINAL-REPORT-11-10-14-2.pdf).

about whether social media drove polarization, but it was a pioneering effort that raised the specter of ideological echo chambers, disproportionately vocal political influencers, and a social media ecosystem where political news divided people.

Since then, a wealth of research has been published on the impact of the circulation and amplification of deceptive and incendiary content through social media platforms on political polarization and radicalization. Summarizing the entire scholarship is beyond the scope of this chapter, but here are some examples of noteworthy research. There exist justified fears that echo chambers resulting from algorithmic amplification generate a "hyper-mobilizing" environment in addition to radicalizing people who feel encouraged to act for causes they believe in – including harming others.[72] Such political polarization and radicalization can result from the efforts of a few individuals who serve as hubs of disinformation, incitement to violence, and hate speech. Some researchers argue that the normalization of violent discourse on social media has the effect of "training" ordinary people with no prior violent tendencies to express anger towards perceived others.[73]

On the other hand, recent research on polarization and radicalization tends to offer nuanced analyses of platform culture, platform regulation, and interpersonal interactions.[74] An analysis of Google searches finds that the input query is more significant in explaining the partisan bias of search results than the ideology of the user.[75] Both the overall culture of the platform and the specific subcultures influence individual decision-making. Twitter (now X) users tend to become more accustomed to expressions of moral outrage because that is the kind of behavior that is rewarded with likes and retweets. In addition to this more general reinforcement learning mechanism, individuals also conform to the norms of the social groups they are part of.[76] Hard-right social media is found to shift users' perception of participation in contentious political activity,[77] but these causal effects are not deterministic: Another study finds that the dynamics of radicalization in Germany's far-right conspiracy groups exhibit within-group variation.[78] At the individual level, there is no "type" of person, pre-determined by psychological or socioeconomic factors, that is more likely to get radicalized.[79]

72 Zack Stanton, "The Problem Isn't Just One Insurrection. It's Mass Radicalization." *Politico*, February 11, 2021 (www.politico.com/news/magazine/2021/02/11/mass-radicalization-trump-insurrection-468746).

73 Max Fisher and Amanda Taub, "How Everyday Social Media Users Become Real-World Extremists," *The New York Times*, April 25, 2018 (www.nytimes.com/2018/04/25/world/asia/facebook-extremism.html).

74 Mike Isaac and Sheera Frenkel, "Facebook's Algorithm Is 'Influential' but Doesn't Necessarily Change Beliefs, Researchers Say," *The New York Times*, July 27, 2023 (www.nytimes.com/2023/07/27/technology/facebook-instagram-algorithms.html).

75 Robertson et al., "Auditing Partisan Audience Bias within Google Search."

76 Brady et al., "How Social Learning Amplifies Moral Outrage Expression in Online Social Networks."

77 Karell et al., "'Born for a Storm.'"

78 Schulze et al., "Far-Right Conspiracy Groups on Fringe Platforms."

79 Marwick, Clancy, and Furl, "Far-Right Online Radicalization: A Review of the Literature."

One study finds that exposing Twitter users to political opinions contradicting their own does not necessarily lead to compromise; in fact, Republican users who were exposed to a bot generating progressive arguments were more entrenched in their beliefs afterwards.[80] One of the authors suggests that this may be because Twitter as a platform is not conducive to the positive, intimate connections that make compromise more likely in the long term.[81] Recent research finds that Democratic and Republican lawmakers differ on what they tweet about, what words they use, and what kinds of interactions they receive on the platform.[82] Studies of YouTube provide contradictory evidence on online radicalization. There appears to be consensus that YouTube contains a troubling number of videos supporting extremist worldviews,[83] but disagreements over whether the recommender algorithm is likely to promote this content persist. One research project finds evidence of a "radicalization pipeline," whereby users consuming far-right content end up watching increasingly more extremist videos,[84] whereas another finds that far-right content consumption is not caused by YouTube's recommender algorithm.[85] Likewise, a series of research papers presenting experiments of user engagement on Facebook and Instagram during the 2020 US election find that eliminating algorithmic content recommendations does not change political attitudes or the degree of polarization but does reduce engagement on these platforms.[86]

The social and political stakes of addressing polarization and radicalization have fueled enormous criticism of mainstream social media platforms. Company executives tend to defend their platforms by picking research findings that present them in a favorable light.[87] Meta's official policy, frequently voiced by former vice president

80 Bail et al., "Exposure to Opposing Views on Social Media Can Increase Political Polarization."
81 Christopher A. Bail, "Twitter's Flawed Solution to Political Polarization," *The New York Times*, September 8, 2018 (www.nytimes.com/2018/09/08/opinion/sunday/twitter-political-polarization.html).
82 Sarah E. Needleman, "Republicans and Democrats Even Tweet Differently," *The Wall Street Journal*, July 16, 2020 (www.wsj.com/articles/republicans-and-democrats-even-tweet-differently-11594922412).
83 Will Carless and Jessica Guynn, "YouTube continues to push dangerous videos to users susceptible to extremism, white supremacy, report finds," *USA Today*, February 12, 2021 (www.usatoday.com/story/tech/2021/02/12/youtube-channel-recommendation-white-supremacist-extremist-videos/6712787002/).
84 Ribeiro et al., "Auditing Radicalization Pathways on YouTube."
85 Hosseinmardi et al., "Examining the Consumption of Radical Content on YouTube."
86 Guess et al., "Reshares on Social Media Amplify Political News but Do Not Detectably Affect Beliefs or Opinions"; Guess et al., "How Do Social Media Feed Algorithms Affect Attitudes and Behavior in an Election Campaign?"; González-Bailón et al., "Asymmetric Ideological Segregation in Exposure to Political News on Facebook"; Nyhan et al., "Like-Minded Sources on Facebook Are Prevalent but Not Polarizing." Nonetheless, the authors report that the three-month time frame to study political attitudes is a limitation of these studies, as it cannot capture the impact of algorithms on long-term dynamics. "Changing Meta's algorithms did not help US political polarization, study finds," *The Guardian*, July 27, 2023 (www.theguardian.com/technology/2023/jul/27/meta-facebook-algorithm-2020-election).
87 Justin Hendrix and Paul Barrett, "The Meta Studies: Nuanced Findings, Corporate Spin, and Media Oversimplification," *Tech Policy Press Blog*, August 2, 2023 (www.techpolicy.press/the-meta-studies-nuanced-findings-corporate-spin-and-media-oversimplification/).

of policy and global affairs Nick Clegg, is to deny allegations of polarization and argue that societal and political factors causing polarization predate the age of social media.[88]

If polarization and radicalization is one facet of algorithms' political impact, accusations of censorship are another. Social media platforms have long marketed themselves as beacons of connectivity, creativity, and freedom. Their capacity to foster free expression and (online and offline) connectivity has earned them praise for being alternative publics. However, politicians and activists across the political spectrum frequently accuse them of censorship. Most claims of censorship do not point at AI at all, as human content moderators act on requests by individuals, organizations, and governments to take down content that violates a social media platform's terms and conditions or ethical principles. However, algorithms have also played a part in sifting through content to find violators.

According to some, algorithms also render certain content practically invisible. A *shadow ban* happens when an online platform reduces the visibility of a post without deleting it. Accusations of shadow-banning go back to at least 2012, when Reddit was suspected of banning a link to a Gawker article.[89] Donald Trump's accusation, in July 2018, that Twitter was shadow-banning him brought the issue to national prominence in the United States, but the skepticism cuts across political cleavages: Content creators accused TikTok of removing Black Lives Matter content in the midst of the George Floyd protests, for example. Instagram has long been criticized for making sexually suggestive images less visible. TikTok has been accused of implementing shadow bans on people its algorithms deem unattractive. More recently, accusations of politically motivated shadow-banning were made against the government of Narendra Modi in India.[90] Social media companies either deny such accusations or explain suspicious incidents away as mere glitches; therefore, without access to the proprietary data and algorithms or an explicit admission by people working at these companies, the veracity of accusations cannot be ascertained, but their popularity across the political spectrum has put free-speech advocates in the difficult position of defending their principles while avoiding the impression of carrying water to conspiracy theories.

Accusations of censorship, shadow bans and arbitrary removals lay bare two contradictory premises with which today's online platforms claim to operate: On the one hand, they are private service providers that may choose to refuse service to

88 Mike Isaac, "Whistle-Blower to Accuse Facebook of Contributing to Jan. 6 Riot, Memo Says," *The New York Times*, October 2, 2021 (www.nytimes.com/2021/10/02/technology/whistle-blower-facebook-memo.html).

89 Ephrat Livni, "What is 'Shadow Banning'?" *The New York Times*, January 13, 2023 (www.nytimes.com/interactive/2023/01/13/business/what-is-shadow-banning.html).

90 Shan Li, and Salvador Rodriguez, "India's Rahul Gandhi Says His Twitter Following Was Squashed by Modi Government," *The Wall Street Journal*, January 26, 2022 (www.wsj.com/articles/indian-opposition-figure-rahul-gandhi-says-his-twitter-following-was-restricted-11643207184).

anyone; on the other, they provide free and open services.[91] Platforms' spokespersons insist that they foster communities, but in truth, their service facilitates the ephemeral gathering of online users at best. The current organization of people and information on social media platforms breeds cynicism, as alienated users imagine they are facing a centralized and ill-intentioned force aiming to derail their message, rather than a platform that operates on "practiced, selective indifference, guided by growth and advertising."[92]

Job Replacement

The Industrial Revolution automated countless tasks requiring physical effort, thereby rendering the labor of humans and some animals, like horses, superfluous. One hypothesis about the future of work is that AI will perform cognitive tasks better than humans, thereby making their labor unnecessary. Techno-optimists hail the reduction in work hours, and the replacement of tedious tasks by creative ones. Reflecting on the Industrial Revolution, the optimist sees in technological change a brief period of disruption followed by the mushrooming of new jobs that will keep people busy, gainfully employed, and who knows, even satisfied. The hope, then, is that AI will end up doing the same in the twenty-first century by generating new sectors and jobs that we can hardly imagine today. A somewhat more nuanced version of the optimistic scenario is that AI will complement, rather than replace or liberate, human labor. Accordingly, AI's disruption of the labor market will result in future jobs that will require novel kinds of human training, experience, creativity and judgment.[93]

The more pessimistic scenario is, of course, the replacement of human jobs by machines.[94] Accordingly, employers would have every incentive to save on wages and benefits. What is more, if AI manages to perform tasks up the value chain, then the incentive to keep human workers disappears for most jobs. Thus, instead of being asked to perform creative tasks in short, rewarding work days, many will have to suffer mass unemployment and irrelevance. A similar scenario is underemployment rather than unemployment: Employers will treat employees as an ancillary

[91] In fact, some conservative lawyers and commentators in the US argue that online platforms, such as phone, mail, or airline companies, should be regulated under "common carriage" law. Brian Fung, "Are social media platforms like railroads? The future of Facebook and Twitter could depend on the answer," *CNN Business*, June 8, 2022 (www.cnn.com/2022/06/08/tech/common-carriage-social-media/index.html).

[92] John Herrman, "Twitter's Misguided Quest to Become a Forum for Everything," *The New York Times*, August 27, 2018 (www.nytimes.com/2018/08/15/magazine/twitters-misguided-quest-to-become-a-forum-for-everything.html).

[93] David Autor, "AI Could Actually Help Rebuild the Middle Class," *Noema*, February 12, 2024 (www.noemamag.com/how-ai-could-help-rebuild-the-middle-class/).

[94] Brian Merchant, "The AI jobs crisis is here, now," *Blood in the Machine* (blog), May 2, 2025 (www.bloodinthemachine.com/p/the-ai-jobs-crisis-is-here-now).

labor force with precarious jobs and modest compensation. In a way, AI will generalize the precariousness of work in today's gig economy to the entire labor force. The disruption of today's labor market, which consists of workers with full-time jobs and benefits, and those trying to make a living with no job security, will mean that most workers will see their jobs collapse into the latter category in the future.

Widespread AI-driven unemployment and underemployment have not happened yet. It seems that the integration of AI technologies into workplace productivity tools is moving along slowly. However, some sectors have been feeling the strain already. First among them are visual artists who see customers leave them for cheaper AI-generated visuals.[95] Another group at risk are service-sector workers, for example call-center employees, whose tasks are in part automated with the use of chatbots. These workers still have plenty of work to do, but they report that their job has become a lot more difficult, as chatbots manage to solve relatively straightforward customer demands, directing frustrated customers with complicated problems to human operators. Even if massive unemployment is not felt as a risk, the loss of reasonably well-paying jobs in some industries, therefore, is a realistic scenario.[96]

SYSTEMIC PROBLEMS AGGRAVATED BY AI

Environmental Degradation

The electricity and water use, and the consequent carbon footprint, of training large AI models has caught academics' and journalists' attention in recent years.[97] Data-intensive AI systems use enormous amounts of data storage space and compute power to accomplish their goals. The more intensive the underlying model, the more resource-intensive it gets. It is estimated that a natural language processing model using transformers and a neural architecture search uses the equivalent of what five cars do in their lifetime.[98] The advent of LLMs has aggravated the energy-use problem of AI companies significantly – to the point that Microsoft, Google, and Amazon recently announced plans to purchase nuclear energy to meet the demand.[99] According to a statistic on OpenAI's website, the amount of

95 Sarah Shaffi, "'It's the opposite of art': why illustrators are furious about AI," *The Guardian*, January 23, 2023 (www.theguardian.com/artanddesign/2023/jan/23/its-the-opposite-of-art-why-illustrators-are-furious-about-ai).

96 Emma Goldberg, "'Training My Replacement': Inside a Call Center Worker's Battle With A.I.," *The New York Times*, July 19, 2023 (www.nytimes.com/2023/07/19/business/call-center-workers-battle-with-ai.html).

97 Luccioni, "The Mounting Human and Environmental Costs of Generative AI."

98 Strubell, Ganesh, and McCallum, "Energy and Policy Considerations for Deep Learning in NLP."

99 Mark Peplow, "How the US tech industry is shaping the transition to green energy," *Nature*, March 19, 2025 (www.nature.com/articles/d41586-025-00743-7).

compute-power used in the largest AI training runs has increased 300,000 times between 2012 and 2023.[100] What is more, every step of the machine learning pipeline contributes to environmental degradation.[101] A recent study finds that the increasing demand for AI data center power may result in forty-six to eighty-two terawatt-hours of electricity consumption, which is comparable to the annual energy consumption of countries such as Switzerland, Austria, and Finland.[102]

DeepSeek, a Chinese AI company, shocked American Big Tech companies by achieving comparable evaluation benchmark success as their LLMs at a fraction of the energy use. This has rekindled the hope that AI technologies of the future could be resource-efficient, more for businesses' interest in cutting down costs than their respect for the environment. While this should definitely be hailed as a possibility, environmentally sustainable – or minimally harmful – AI is still an aspiration rather than reality.

Exploitation of Labor

In February 2022, journalist Billy Perrigo published "Inside Facebook's African Sweatshop" in *Time* magazine, detailing the human labor that went into digital platforms. For all the talk of automating content moderation decisions, social media companies like Meta rely on humans to flag illegal or banned images and videos, including trauma-inducing suicide, murder, rape, and child abuse content. In fact, in 2020, Meta (then Facebook) agreed to pay $52 million for the mental health treatment of some of its US-based content moderators. Content moderation jobs, in addition to being extremely unpleasant, pay little. Large companies use subsidiaries around the world to employ people for as little as $2 an hour, with no additional benefits or mental health support. When Daniel Motaung, a content moderation worker employed by Sama, a Kenyan subsidiary of major American tech companies, tried to organize fellow underpaid workers for a strike, he was promptly fired.[103]

The *Time* article speaks to a broader phenomenon: Today's data-intensive economy runs on the physical and cognitive labor of workers whose jobs have become increasingly more precarious over the past decade.[104] The *gig workers* of the modern economy drive ride-sharing cabs and delivery trucks, pick up and deliver food, tag and analyze data, and do much more. Despite the fact that their precarious labor is what keeps some sectors of the data-driven economy running, they are not

[100] www.openai.com/research/ai-and-compute
[101] Wu et al., "Sustainable AI."
[102] De Vries-Gao, "Artificial Intelligence."
[103] Billy Perrigo, "Inside Facebook's African Sweatshop," *Time*, February 14, 2022 (www.time.com/6147458/facebook-africa-content-moderation-employee-treatment/).
[104] Neff, *Venture Labor Work and the Burden of Risk in Innovative Industries.*

remunerated with fixed salaries or benefits, and the continuation of their employment is not guaranteed. Courts, especially in the US, have not been sympathetic to their demands to be treated as employees rather than contractors.[105] This layer of exploitation is a systemic and somewhat less visible harm arising from today's AI.

Market Concentration

It's not uncommon to read technology evangelists praising today's AI industry as the "startup revolution," but the truth is, the research infrastructure and financial investment are concentrated in the hands of a few businesses. Google, Amazon, and Microsoft have collectively invested two-thirds of the $27 billion raised for AI startups.[106] The cloud services offered by these three companies make up about two-thirds of the cloud computing market, as well.[107] What is more, Big Tech companies control not only the funding and the physical infrastructure, but increasingly, the academic landscape: Every Big Tech company has at least one member in the organizing committee of the NeurIPS, the main machine learning conference. Google and Microsoft in particular play an oversized role in influencing the AI research agenda.[108]

Big Tech companies do not only dominate through market share; they also bundle services and products. In fact, antitrust concerns in the EU and the US focus on allegations that large platform companies take undue advantage of their services in one domain to weed out competition in another. For example, a smartphone company using its online store to promote its own applications at competitors' expense would raise legal questions about illegal bundling. Even though antitrust concerns are not exclusive to AI companies, the prominence of algorithmically curated recommendations in shaping customer choice and the bundling of AI tools with online search platforms and productivity software have heightened the scrutiny of AI-powered products and services, especially in the EU[109] and the US.[110]

[105] Spier, "The Politics of Platform Technologies"; Benjamin, *Viral Justice: How We Grow the World We Want*: Chapter 4.

[106] Cecilia Rikap, "Dynamics of Corporate Governance Beyond Ownership in AI," *Common Wealth*, May 15, 2024 (www.common-wealth.org/publications/dynamics-of-corporate-governance-beyond-ownership-in-ai).

[107] Cecilia Rikap, "Dynamics of Corporate Governance Beyond Ownership in AI," *Common Wealth*, May 15, 2024 (www.common-wealth.org/publications/dynamics-of-corporate-governance-beyond-ownership-in-ai).

[108] Cecilia Rikap, "Dynamics of Corporate Governance Beyond Ownership in AI," *Common Wealth*, May 15, 2024 (www.common-wealth.org/publications/dynamics-of-corporate-governance-beyond-ownership-in-ai).

[109] Siladitya Ray, "EU Fines Apple $570 Million And Meta $228 Million For Digital Market Rules Violations," *Forbes*, April 23, 2025 (www.forbes.com/sites/siladityaray/2025/04/23/eu-fines-apple-570-million-and-meta-228-million-for-digital-market-rules-violations/).

[110] See, for example, *United States v. Google LLC* (2023).

UNDERSTANDING THE CAUSES OF AI RISKS AND HARMS

Data Bias

"Garbage in, garbage out" is a generally agreed-upon slogan in the data science community. If the training dataset is of low quality, the resulting output will not get better no matter how sophisticated the data analysis methods may be. Data quality has turned out to be a particularly taxing problem in the digital age, when just about anything is data but not necessarily *good* data.

But what constitutes good data? For scientific methods using experiments and surveys, samples drawn from a sufficiently large and randomly or quasi-randomly selected subcategory of the target population would qualify as good data. It goes without saying that the features of the collected data should be relevant for the real-world issue at hand: To put it simply, if the goal is to identify cat and dog photos accurately, the dataset should contain dog and cat photos; if the goal is to model a natural language, the dataset should present as full a representation of that language as possible; and if the goal is to estimate the factors motivating customers to purchase a certain product, the relevant variables explaining customer behavior should be present in the dataset. In addition, if the data claim to measure human characteristics, preferences, decisions, or behavior, the dataset should contain a truthful representation of these real-world phenomena. Finally, the extraneous features in the dataset – what is referred to as the "noise" – should be kept at a minimum.

All observational data, that is to say, data generated under real-world conditions rather than an experimental setting, deviate from this idealized model of representative, relevant, noise-free, and accurate data to some extent. Digital data present exceptionally intractable problems for representativeness because many datasets measuring humans come from individuals with internet access, and self-selecting into certain characteristics, preferences, decisions, or behavior. The exclusions may or may not deepen real-world inequalities depending on the goals of algorithmic modeling: For example, if the end goal is to sell a product more effectively to customers who are already frequent users of an online marketing platform, perhaps the absence of data on people without access does not present a major drawback, but if the goal is to deliver healthcare effectively to an entire population, then the consequences of the digital divide, manifested in the dataset, threaten equal access to healthcare.

What are the sources of bias and discrimination in AI? By far the most popular answer to the question has been the data. Training datasets that reflect the historic underrepresentation of women, sexual minorities, people of color and persons with disabilities in the public sphere, or that contain, implicitly or explicitly, society's biased attitudes towards these groups, end up reproducing bias and discrimination. Unrepresentative datasets make it less likely for employees to detect bias in their datasets. For example, Deborah Raji notes that Clarifai, an image-recognition startup she worked at, had been using a combination of G-rated and pornographic images it scraped from the internet. The relative underrepresentation of Black people in the G-rated images in comparison to the pornographic ones, however, meant that algorithms trained to detect pornography picked up Black people disproportionately and inaccurately.[111]

When businesses that have not interviewed or hired women in the past use past data to train algorithms, they effectively use those algorithms not to hire women in the present. The crystallization of racialized socioeconomic hierarchies in US postal codes ends up criminalizing Black people in every dataset that uses postal codes as a relevant feature. The underrepresentation of people of color leads to faulty facial recognition matches. The hyper-sexualization of girls and women of color in text and image datasets produces prejudiced and demeaning search results. Image datasets, no matter how large they claim to be, leave out objects, humans, and through them identities, experiences and values. The overall racism and sexism of some online communities, whose past conversations train LLMs, suffice for chatbots, with no prior bias of their own, to generate incredibly offensive content in a matter of hours. It is worth mentioning that bias creeps into datasets even when information about sensitive characteristics is excluded. For example, COMPAS's much-criticized crime prediction algorithm does not use race as a variable,[112] but race may have been inferred from other variables – for example, the postal code, which serves as a proxy for race in the context of highly segregated US cities.

Finally, the assumption that digital datasets offer an accurate representation of characteristics, preferences, decisions and behavior needs to be rethought. In some cases, the assumption is uncontroversial: If I am purchasing a product, it means that I expect, at least for the time being, that it will be useful to me. Yet, people may falsify their characteristics and preferences on online platforms to anonymize their identity, present themselves as interesting or attractive or, less innocuously, scam others. What is more, choices do not always fit the neat categories of truthful or mendacious. People tend to fall for groupthink or the "herd instinct." For example, minor manipulations of online customer ratings nudge individuals to agree with what they view as the dominant opinion – especially if that opinion is a positive one.[113]

Can AI-driven *feature engineering*, that is, selecting relevant aspects of datasets to improve model accuracy, solve data problems? A dataset should contain information about individual education level as a feature to be able to predict income, for

[111] Cade Metz, "Who Is Making Sure the A.I. Machines Aren't Racist?" *The New York Times*, March 15, 2021 (www.nytimes.com/2021/03/15/technology/artificial-intelligence-google-bias.html).

[112] Sam Corbett-Davies, Emma Pierson, Feller, Avi, and Goel, Sharad, "A computer program used for bail and sentencing decisions was labeled biased against blacks. It's actually not that clear," *The Washington Post*, October 17, 2016 (www.washingtonpost.com/news/monkey-cage/wp/2016/10/17/can-an-algorithm-be-racist-our-analysis-is-more-cautious-than-propublicas/).

[113] Aral, "The Problem With Online Ratings."

example. Most training datasets have been generated without prior feature engineering. The scientific logic of including the relevant variables is not built into them. One way to get around this problem is finding as much data as possible, for example by merging multiple datasets when possible, and hoping that AI algorithms would work their magic, or in less enigmatic terms, outperform humans by picking up relevant information from unexpected data features in large datasets and leaving out the "noise," that is, irrelevant features. Humans can of course help by preprocessing the data, that is to say, sifting through some of the potential noise to facilitate the algorithmic processing of relevant information.

These strategies definitely work some of the time, but the AI magic is not to be trusted: Algorithms may fail to draw meaningful insights in the absence of relevant features or pick up features they should not. An algorithm that aims to distinguish photos of wolves from those of huskies may end up failing its mission by picking up on the snow that usually accompanies husky photos.[114] The spectacular success and equally spectacular failure of Google Flu Trends in predicting flu (Chapter 2) shows that the absence of a scientific feature selection protocol can take its toll on accuracy, sooner or later. Research papers that claim to predict criminality or sexual orientation from photos of faces have been long criticized for picking up on confounding variables or inferring causation from correlation.[115] While the failure to offer an adequate causal explanation cuts much deeper than data problems, what is in part responsible for scientifically unsound research is the tendency to believe that algorithms will find meaningful insights in large enough datasets regardless of the fit between the question at hand and data features. Thus, magic that defies human understanding may not be so magical or useful after all.

All in all, faulty data may account for some, but by no means all, of the failures of today's AI. As the following sections make clear, however, fixing datasets is neither easy nor sufficient to address risks and harms.

Limitations of Algorithms

There is no denying that bringing together vast datasets and compute-power with statistics, calculus, linear algebra and social network theory has opened up enormous possibilities since the early 2010s. However, no matter how advanced, algorithms have built-in limitations that need to be scrutinized. It is wrong to expect algorithms to magically fix data problems. As the previous subsection makes clear, unrepresentative datasets containing built-in biases cannot be rectified through algorithms alone. Likewise, algorithms can facilitate the work of identifying and taking down disinformation or violent and hateful speech, but content moderation is primarily a human job.

114 Bergstrom and West, *Calling Bullshit: The Art of Skepticism in a Data-Driven World*: 167.
115 Bergstrom and West.

It is not only that algorithms cannot solve all problems; they aggravate problems, too. Algorithms can amplify, and not merely reflect, bias in data. For example, recent reporting shows that the creation of new samples through generative AI can amplify human bias. Diffusion Bias,[116] a research project hosted by Hugging Face, a company that offers machine learning solutions, allows users to compare visual output from different visualization generation models (Stable Diffusion 1.4, Stable Diffusion 2, and Dall-E 2) when selected profession names, and optionally adjectives, are entered. The results suggest not only a reflection of human bias in hiring, but actually an amplification of it. For example, the query "lawyer" returns a slate of nine men out of nine in each of the three models. Considering the fact that women make up around 40 percent of legal professionals in the United States, the zero percent women's representation in visualization generation models is much worse than the real-world inequality in numbers. Similarly, recommender systems that aim to maximize user engagement (and through that, ad revenues) have long been accused of amplifying hateful and violent content above and beyond what would have existed without such amplification.

Statistical techniques offer ways to quantify the error, that is, the mismatch between an abstract model for estimating, classifying and predicting a real-world phenomenon, and the data collected about that phenomenon. Minimizing error is what keeps theoretical statisticians and practitioners up at night. At the end of the day, however, zero error is not possible. In fact, a model capable of generating meaningful insights beyond the dataset it trains on should contain some error. Thus, the statistics underlying most ML models requires humans to decide on an acceptable error rate. Beating random luck – for example, performing better than a coin toss in a binary classification task – is of course the absolute bare minimum. Most researchers and businesses hoping to develop useful technologies want to perform better than human evaluators. The acceptable error rate should be much lower for some tasks, however: Tests for certain illnesses and disorders, for example, should be accurate at such high levels to render them almost error-free. In other words, human societies will always have to choose how much AI error with which they can live. How often are we willing to accept an algorithm mistaking a dog for a cat? A false statement for a truthful one? An innocent person for a criminal? A civilian for a combatant? There is no correct technical answer to these questions, but what is certain is that AI developers today find themselves navigating these complex moral questions around scientific error.

Furthermore, classification tasks introduce different error types – false positives and false negatives, to be precise. With a given dataset and algorithm, reducing the rate of one error type typically requires increasing the rate for another. Medical tests prefer as few false negatives as possible, because mistaking a person who is well for

[116] www.huggingface.co/spaces/society-ethics/DiffusionBiasExplorer

one who is sick causes minor and reparable harm compared to sending a sick person home without a diagnosis or treatment. A spam filter is likely to follow the opposite approach: Flagging an important email as spam can be much more harmful than letting spam emails slip every once in a while.

Not all error-minimization decisions are straightforward, however. Should a social media platform prioritize taking down speech that incites violence or giving unimpeded access to its users? Perhaps the intuitive answer is "both," but algorithmic content moderation may take down innocent content or retain violent speech. The scrutiny of online platforms prioritizes false negatives, that is, content that should be taken down but is not, because investors, advertisers and users are likely to be uncomfortable with content that recruits terrorists, ask people to commit suicide, etc. However, false positives, that is, content that is falsely removed, or "unglamorous mistakes" in the words of *The New York Times* reporter Shira Ovide, constitute another major shortcoming of automated content moderation.[117]

Furthermore, error minimization can be a profoundly political issue. Judges, prosecutors and law-enforcement agents using crime-prediction software are likely to support minimizing false negatives, that is, undetected criminals. People likely to be falsely accused of criminal conduct would prefer minimizing false positives, that is, wrongful arrests and indictments. Again, improvements in data quality and algorithms can alleviate these problems, but ultimately, there is no technical solution with universal acclaim.

Human Decisions

The limitations of data collection and analysis methods should not detract from the role of human decisions in deepening AI-related risks and harms. The fact that algorithms are mathematical formulations optimizing for given goals is both a source of their usefulness and a weakness. An algorithm meant to maximize ad revenue does not necessarily minimize the risk of self-harm to end-users; the list of statistically plausible responses to a chatbot prompt probably contains many falsehoods; and a crime prediction algorithm meant to be sold to law-enforcement agencies is unlikely to prioritize the interests of the wrongfully accused. This means that socially desirable goals may never be achieved through algorithms alone. Despite enormous progress in LLMs, for example, there exists no publicly available technique to validate the veracity of chatbot output. What is popularly called chatbot *hallucinations* happen because no feature of LLMs offers a way to distinguish between true and false.[118]

[117] Shira Ovide, "Facebook's Unglamorous Mistakes," *The New York Times*, January 19, 2022 (www.nytimes.com/2022/01/19/technology/facebook-moderation-mistakes.html).

[118] Gerrit De Vynck, "ChatGPT 'hallucinates.' Some researchers worry it isn't fixable," *The Washington Post*, May 30, 2023.

Just as the determination of acceptable error rates is a political question, the determination of what goals algorithms should serve reflects power relations in a society. The same underlying technology, say image classification through pattern recognition, can detect a cancerous cell or surveil political dissidents. Algorithms can save workers time from tedious tasks, but whether that will lead to a shorter and more creative workday or massive unemployment or underemployment is something that human societies will end up deciding. If the trend of corporate control in technology governance persists, then a small number of powerful individuals will make those decisions.

In *Algorithms of Oppression*, Safiya Noble makes it clear that the sexism and racism of online search results have their origins in active decisions, made by technology companies, about what to include or exclude on their pages. As they want to maximize engagement, they do not mind promoting offensive content. Furthermore, she argues, the male gaze, always present in the male-dominated technology industry, is responsible for these decisions.[119] In their critique of arguably the largest image dataset at the time, Crawford and Paglen go above and beyond data quality issues to suggest that the classification and categorization of images, including those of people, are inherently political acts that inevitably introduce criteria of inclusion and exclusion.[120] Those criteria do not get formed randomly or in a vacuum, of course; they reflect historically constructed stereotypes.

Key human decisions involve more than how algorithms are constructed and interpreted. In fact, despite talk of full automation in the technology industry, content moderation on digital platforms involves heavy human input. Facebook is said to have employed around 15,000 human content moderators. Much of YouTube's content moderation falls on underpaid people from the developing world who find themselves sifting through thousands of disturbing videos every day. Even the more autonomous-sounding recommender systems are constantly tweaked – in the words of platform governance researcher Robyn Caplan, "algorithms equal editors."[121]

All these critiques converge on one overarching message: Even if technology introduces uniquely technical opportunities and challenges at times, ultimately the challenges cannot be understood in isolation from the histories of socioeconomic, political and cultural inequality and injustice that precede and encapsulate today's technological developments. This is why some of the leading research in AI risks and harms consists of genealogies, historiographies and ethnographies of surveillance, facial recognition, emotion recognition, image classification and categorization, the material infrastructure of computing, and labor-market considerations for various subclasses of technology workers.

119 Noble, *Algorithms of Oppression: How Search Engines Reinforce Racism*: 57–59.

120 Kate Crawford and Trevor Paglen, "Excavating AI: The Politics of Images in Machine Learning Training Sets" (www.excavating.ai).

121 Farhad Manjoo, "Facebook's Bias Is Built-In, and Bears Watching," *The New York Times*, May 11, 2016 (www.nytimes.com/2016/05/12/technology/facebooks-bias-is-built-in-and-bears-watching.html).

Demographic Uniformity in the Technology Industry

Even though women led early computer science research and development in the United Kingdom,[122] the profession has been dominated by men since the mid-1980s. The percentage of women in computer science majors has hovered slightly under 20 percent throughout the 2010s in the US.[123] The AI sector reflects these trends: In 2022, women made up thirty percent of the AI workforce – slightly up from twenty-six percent in 2016.[124] Further aggravating women's under-presentation is the fact that they are less likely to be represented in C-suite positions than entry-level ones across industries.[125]

Computer science professor John MacCormick cautions against racial bias in facial recognition by reflecting on an image extraction system he had worked on as a graduate student in 1998: He remembers the anxiety he felt while showcasing the system to Japanese company executives, realizing that the images that he had casually collected on his digital camera to train the algorithm only contained faces of white people, his own included.[126] Fast forward to 2015, when computer scientist Timnit Gebru shares her experience at the AI workshop in Barcelona, when she counted in the crowd six Black people, all men, other than herself.[127] So much changed in the intervening decades, but the demographic uniformity in the technology industry and the attending biases remained more or less constant.

The combination of gender and racial disparities in education, hiring and retention is sometimes referred to as AI's "white guy problem."[128] In addition to the intrinsic injustice of denying access to lucrative employment opportunities, the lack of demographic diversity is said to aggravate the biases in AI systems.[129] For example, the original "Gender Shades" article that documents bias in facial analysis algorithms and datasets finds that benchmark datasets IJB-A and Adience overrepresent males with lighter skin, underrepresent females with darker skin, and underrepresent

[122] Hicks, *Programmed Inequality: How Britain Discarded Women Technologists and Lost Its Edge in Computing*.

[123] Steve Henn, "When Women Stopped Coding," *Planet Money (NPR)*, October 21, 2014 (www.npr.org/sections/money/2014/10/21/357629765/when-women-stopped-coding).

[124] World Economic Forum, "Global Gender Gap Report 2023": 7.

[125] World Economic Forum, "Global Gender Gap Report 2023": 41.

[126] John MacCormick, "I unintentionally created a biased AI algorithm 25 years ago – tech companies are still making the same mistake," *The Conversation*, May 9, 2023 (www.theconversation.com/i-unintentionally-created-a-biased-ai-algorithm-25-years-ago-tech-companies-are-still-making-the-same-mistake-203734).

[127] Cade Metz, "Who Is Making Sure the A.I. Machines Aren't Racist?" *The New York Times*, March 15, 2021 (www.nytimes.com/2021/03/15/technology/artificial-intelligence-google-bias.html).

[128] Crawford, "Artificial Intelligence's White Guy Problem."

[129] Toby Walsh, "Why we need to start preparing for our robotic future now," *UNSW – Sydney Newsroom*, November 7, 2017 (www.unsw.edu.au/newsroom/news/2017/11/why-we-need-to-start-preparing-for-our-robotic-future-now).

individuals with darker skin in general.[130] The article does not explain why those datasets contain bias, and it may or may not be the case that demographic uniformity in the industry is the chief reason for data bias, but it is safe to argue that the relatively uniform group of developers and users of the datasets simply failed to notice bias or take it seriously enough to rectify it.

The travails of alerting technology companies to bias reveal a profound discrepancy between portrayals of data and algorithms as immune to human bias and the realities of bias arising from human decisions at every stage of AI development. Background diversity is thus regularly voiced as a potential solution to AI bias, at least in part.[131] Perhaps even a hypothetically diverse workplace cannot address all the risks and harms arising from business incentives and models that rely on the amplification of those risks and harms, but the inclusion of more voices, especially those of the historically disadvantaged communities, can work to question, negotiate with, and ultimately transform those incentives and models.

CONCLUSION

This chapter tracks down academic and media descriptions of potential risks and actual harms targeting individuals and communities as a result of the development and use of AI tools.[132] Some of the harms, such as bias and discrimination in hiring, education, banking and law enforcement, are associated with automated decision-making systems. Others, such as deepfakes, are features of LLM-powered chatbots and visualization tools. Most of the harms are immediate while a few predicted risks, like massive unemployment, are yet to be seen. While it would be unfair to argue that AI single-handedly causes political polarization and radicalization, recommender systems and AI-generated content intersect with an information ecosystem in crisis to aggravate the decline in civic democratic discourse. The scholarly evidence summarized in this section suggests that online radicalization is a serious threat even if it does not happen deterministically. Collectives with a wide range of worldviews and goals indeed employ strategies to recruit online, and many individuals who would not have otherwise advocated, much less joined, violent, hateful and mendacious causes end up doing so. Online platforms enable the spread of disinformation and inciting speech, while algorithms tailor curated content to individuals and small groups in ways that would not have been possible with conventional telecommunications. However, it is also true that online radicalization depends crucially on

[130] Buolamwini and Gebru, "Gender Shades: Intersectional Accuracy Disparities in Commercial Gender Classification": 5.

[131] Kriti Sharma, "How to keep human bias out of AI," *TED Talks*, April 12, 2019 (www.youtube.com/watch?v=BRRNeBKwvNM).

[132] A number of academic and journalistic projects keep track of AI risks and harms. For the AI Incident Database, see: incidentdatabase.ai; for AI Hallucination Cases, see: www.damiencharlotin.com/hallucinations/.

scope conditions, such as platform governance, offline political polarization, etc. All in all, there is no doubt that algorithmically curated content recommendations may expose vulnerable users to inaccurate, violent and hateful content, and may radicalize some. Where scholars disagree on is whether such content drives radicalization and polarization once all other personal, societal and platform-specific factors are accounted for.

Many harms are manifestations of profound social, political, economic and cultural inequalities, injustices and failures that AI tools reproduce, amplify, and normalize. And ultimately, none of the harms and risks are purely technical in nature. Rather, intricate technical challenges intersect with decisions made by corporate leaders, governments, legal professionals and software engineers to create the massive list of problems associated with today's AI.

Is AI racist? Sexist? Ableist? An avid reader of popular AI journalism must have come across these questions dozens of times. It is a simplistic formulation that serves to dilute the relationship between the development of AI technologies and systems of oppression based on race, gender and ability status rather than scrutinize them. Of course, algorithms, computers and sensors do not have belief systems and attitudes, much less racist, sexist, or ableist ones. Yet, arguing that mathematics and machines are not biased fails to understand the forces at play that reproduce bias and discrimination in employment, housing, education, banking and law enforcement in the age of algorithms. All the risks and harms presented in this chapter stem from the creation and distribution of power, wealth, opportunities and information to inherently limited and flawed technologies designed to satisfy narrow market interests in already unequal societies.

The risks and harms covered in this chapter set the stage for the promises and challenges of governing AI through technical solutions, business self-regulation, and law and policy. No matter what governance toolkit is used, one thing should be clear: AI governance requires hard conversations and decisions about the role of technology in unequal societies where existing political and social institutions to safeguard fundamental rights and access to information are in crisis. While some technical fixes are possible and necessary, there are no technical or objectively correct answers to questions around bias and discrimination, AI inaccuracies, product quality, privacy violations, online polarization, and so on. Theoretically, a technology like AI can produce positive or negative impact for everyone, but in practice, the winners and losers of today look a lot like the winners and losers of yesterday. If those who have been historically excluded from economic and political decision-making are excluded again, AI governance will at best scratch the surface of problems it aims to address.

4

Technical Solutions to AI Risks and Harms

In July 2023, the Biden White House announced eight commitments that leading AI companies agreed to uphold voluntarily. In a nutshell, the commitments included internal and external testing of AI systems, information-sharing with stakeholders, investing in cybersecurity and guarantees against insider threats, facilitating third-party discovery and reporting of vulnerabilities, informing users about AI-generated content, reporting the strengths and weaknesses of AI systems, promoting research on the risks of AI systems, and developing and deploying AI systems to address society's greatest challenges.[1] In addition to boilerplate promises to do the right thing, the list of commitments reflected the conviction that technical solutions, such as testing, vulnerability discovery, and watermarking, would provide adequate solutions to the problems created by today's AI. Soon after, twenty leading tech companies committed to fighting election interference in anticipation of the 2024 US presidential race – and not surprisingly, the voluntary commitment was replete with references to developing technologies to address disinformation.[2]

The belief that technology is the remedy to its own ills is widespread. The initiatives that devote themselves to AI for social good, algorithmic bias detection, de-biasing, testing, and more have mushroomed since the mid-2010s. Businesses, universities, and even governments organize hackathons – time-bound competitions to detect and fix errors – that bring together computer programmers to improve the efficiency and accuracy of AI systems and to enhance their ability to serve social, economic, and environmental goals. Some of the technical solution ideas are contained within the industry, business, or team responsible for the shortcomings of the earlier versions of that specific technology. Another model that has become

1 Kevin Roose, "How Do the White House's A.I. Commitments Stack Up?" *The New York Times*, July 22, 2023 (www.nytimes.com/2023/07/22/technology/ai-regulation-white-house).

2 Sheila Dang and Katie Paul, "OpenAI, Meta and Other Tech Giants Sign Effort to Fight AI Election Interference," *Reuters*, February 16, 2024 (www.reuters.com/technology/openai-meta-other-tech-giants-sign-effort-fight-ai-election-interference-2024-02-16/).

increasingly more prominent is for one business to fix the problems created by another's products or services.

This chapter introduces (1) AI for social good, (2) human-in-the-loop solutions, (3) de-biasing, (4) AI-generated text, image, and voice detection, and (5) testing as potential technical solutions. This is a non-exhaustive list that nonetheless includes the solution concepts most frequently discussed in academic scholarship and journalism. This chapter lays out the theoretical rationale for advocating for such solutions, as well as the evidence for how well they work. The technical solutions proposed in this chapter claim to address one, some, or all of the problems discussed in Chapter 3. Typically, they are expected to improve accuracy, reliability, efficiency, or transparency in a domain of application. AI for social good is a generic category that has historically been used for fairness, accountability, and transparency research, as well as improvements to product quality. Thus, AI for social good addresses all potential AI risks and harms but is particularly well-suited for tackling bias and maintaining product and service quality. Human-in-the-loop solutions, which introduce human supervision and control to otherwise-automated processes, are similarly generic in that they address multiple risks and harms. They have been proposed as a corrective to fully automated decision-making systems. De-biasing seeks to rectify bias and discrimination. AI-producing businesses themselves are the primary intended audience for de-biasing tools, but non-profits and government agencies may also invest in de-biasing as a way to hold businesses in check. The detection of AI-generated text, image, and voice may empower consumers indirectly by allowing AI-producing businesses, if they so choose, to label AI-generated content. Finally, testing is a general-purpose tool: Adversarial testing before and after deployment can improve the accuracy, reliability, and security of AI systems.

Do technical solutions work? Most commentators would agree that such solutions cannot fix everything by themselves. It is important to understand how and how well they work in the context of today's AI risks and harms. The evidence presented in this chapter suggests that technical solutions make important contributions on a tool-by-tool basis, but have little impact on the society-wide effects of AI systems. There is no evidence that major issues like climate change or political disinformation can be resolved through technical fixes. Incentivizing tech-for-good projects will make the world a better place, one tiny issue at a time, but relying solely on such projects for social, economic, and political progress is an illusion.

TECHNICAL SOLUTIONS: PROPONENTS AND CRITICS

Technical solutions are thoughtful and sophisticated interventions that eliminate or mitigate the risks and harms that existing technologies pose, or that tackle broader social problems.[3] The history of technology is replete with innovations overcoming

[3] Abebe et al., "Roles for Computing in Social Change."

the shortcomings of earlier ones. The conviction that well-intentioned inventors can solve society's problems, caused by technology or otherwise, has vocal supporters in today's computer-driven technological landscape, too. Arguably, none has advocated techno-solutionism as systematically and persuasively as Orly Lobel. Writing at a time of growing skepticism toward technology companies and their leadership, her 2022 book, *The Equality Machine*, argues that the detection of inequalities is one of the major contributions of data collection and analysis to the striving for equality.[4] She acknowledges the countless injustices preceding the advent of algorithms that nonetheless ended up getting replicated through them. Rather than blame algorithms for all that is wrong with contemporary society, however, Lobel argues that technology-driven solutions have begun to address and reverse injustices – hence the term *equality machine*. She introduces "coding ninjas," "bots for pay equity," "hagglebots" that negotiate for a fair wage, "upstander" bots that call out users for discriminatory speech on online platforms, and MonsterMatch, an educational tool that allows users to pick and chat with potential dates using monster avatars, and informs them about how their choices influence their future dating profile,[5] as data-driven solutions deliberately designed to rectify inequalities, algorithmically generated or otherwise. "Smoke detector" AI analyzes public online content to present early warnings of sexual harassment, and some kinds of insurance software check for potential sexual harassment in company correspondence.[6]

The defense of technical solutions aligns closely with the market logic.[7] Solving society's problems with technology may favor capitalist innovation because the push for equality and justice may be good for business. Consumers want safe and reliable products, and businesses want satisfied customers to maximize their profits. Making the most of a society's talent pool requires overcoming hurdles to diversity in recruitment and hiring. Thus, it may be argued, doing the right thing is good business.

Furthermore, technology producers' and investors' interests and personal values may motivate them to develop and deploy products that make a dent in gender and racial inequality. As an increasing number of women and people of color – identities that had been underrepresented in the technology sector – join the workforce, the push for change may be irresistible. Established businesses may build equality into their practices or collaborate with up-and-coming small businesses to get their biases rectified.

Critics are quick to point out the potential flaws in relying on the technology sector alone for positive change. First, most tech workers, and almost all tech executives and investors, still tend to come from a limited pool of gender and racial backgrounds. Furthermore, the business case for doing the right thing comes with

4 Lobel, *The Equality Machine: Harnessing Digital Technology for a Brighter, More Inclusive Future*.

5 Rachel Kraus, "A Dating App for Literal Monsters Exposes the Bias in our Swipes," *Mashable*, May 22, 2019 (www.mashable.com/article/monstermatch-dating-app-algorithm-bias).

6 Lobel, *The Equality Machine: Harnessing Digital Technology for a Brighter, More Inclusive Future*: 104–106.

7 See Gry Hasselbalch's presentation at *EUNIC DX / AI Week: The Geopolitics of AI Technologies*.

qualifiers – as Chapter 5 illustrates. As the disbanding of multiple trust and safety teams in the tech industry in early 2023 shows, the business case for social justice rests on shaky ground, as doing the right thing may be considered a lesser worry in a crisis moment. What is more, it remains debatable whether technology companies that aim to rectify others' wrongs manage to produce veritable change. The explosion of interest in technology for social good or technology to fix technology's own shortcomings is laudable, but to what extent have these initiatives delivered? In what follows, I describe and analyze a list of technical fixes to AI-related risks and harms.

PROPOSED TECHNICAL SOLUTIONS

AI for Social Good

AI for social good projects combine the technical competencies required for building AI tools with an awareness of social problems caused by nature or humans. Such projects include, but are not limited to, earthquake response, weather forecasting, agricultural productivity, drug discovery, deciphering of ancient texts, and algorithmic fairness in automated decision-making systems. Even though many publicly minded projects were hatched in universities, for-profit businesses have increasingly assumed leadership in the AI for social good field, as they can afford the initial investments and recruit top talent. For example, AI tools that claim to enhance equality and fairness in hiring and promotion are almost exclusively developed by businesses to be sold to other businesses.

Members of the Fairness, Accountability, and Transparency in Machine Learning (FAT/ML, later FAccT) community have been active at least since the early 2000s.[8] Their self-stated goal is to detect issues of bias and discrimination, due process, and understandability.[9] The first FAT/ML workshop was conceived in 2014 toward that end.[10] Since 2018, the annual conference has been organized by the Association for Computing Machinery. As the conference website states, providing technological solutions is only one component of the overall goal of addressing problems caused by algorithmic decision-making; toward that end, the conference invites scholars from law, social sciences, and humanities in addition to computer science.[11]

Soon after the first FAT/ML workshop, Black in AI convened as a meeting hub for Black AI researchers who had been underrepresented in the Neural Information Processing Systems (NeurIPS) conference, the profession's leading event.[12] The

[8] For a list of the early scholarship in this field, see www.fatml.org/resources/relevant-scholarship

[9] www.fatml.org

[10] Karen Hao, "Inside the Fight to Reclaim AI from Big Tech's Control," *MIT Technology Review*, June 14, 2021 (www.technologyreview.com/2021/06/14/1026148/ai-big-tech-timnit-gebru-paper-ethics).

[11] www.facctconference.org

[12] Tom Simonite, "What really happened when Google ousted Timnit Gebru," *Wired*, June 8, 2021 (www.wired.com/story/google-timnit-gebru-ai-what-really-happened/).

push to reflect on the social and political implications forced NeurIPS to require presenting authors to include in their papers a statement on the broader societal impact of their work in 2020 – a requirement that was lifted in 2021 in favor of a negative societal impact checklist. Since then, alternative formulations of impact statements have been suggested,[13] while the overall impact of existing statements on the nature of research remains to be seen.

AI research and development itself can be interpreted as the technical solution par excellence. Some ongoing projects seek to collect better data and improve the accuracy of past algorithms, thereby contributing not only to efficiency but also to socially desirable outcomes. *AI for social good* (AI4SG) and its cousins, *machine learning for social good* (ML4SG) and *data science for social good*, have become catchphrases for academic and industry initiatives hoping to improve lives and livelihoods through data and algorithms. The three terms have appeared in a total of 136 papers admitted to the *arXiv* repository between January 2015 and April 2025. AI for social good has been institutionalized in academic, business, and even public-sector settings.[14]

There is no limit on what kinds of projects are undertaken as part of AI4SG. Some align themselves with existing frameworks, like the United Nations Sustainable Development Goals, while most projects work with self-definitions of what is good for poverty reduction, physical and mental health, animal well-being, accessibility, reduction of algorithmic bias, productivity in agriculture, access to education, and more.[15]

Some of the most prominent examples of the use of AI for social good come from efforts to promote gender equality in the workplace and beyond.[16] Code Like a

[13] Khari Johnson, "NeurIPS Requires AI Researchers to Account for Societal Impact and Financial Conflicts of Interest," *VentureBeat*, February 24, 2020 (www.venturebeat.com/ai/neurips-requires-ai-researchers-to-account-for-societal-impact-and-financial-conflicts-of-interest/); Ashurst et al., "AI Ethics Statements – Analysis and Lessons Learnt from NeurIPS Broader Impact Statements"; Liu et al., "Examining Responsibility and Deliberation in AI Impact Statements and Ethics Reviews."

[14] To give a few examples: the Association for the Advancement of Artificial Intelligence has been hosting an AI4SG conference since 2019; National University of Singapore has an AI4SG lab; Carnegie Mellon University has an ML4SG initiative as well as a Data Science for Social Good fellowship; the University of Chicago funds a fellowship with the same name; San José State University has been developing an AI4SG curriculum; the University of Auckland has a Centre for Machine Learning for Social Good; the University of Washington has a Data Science for Social Good summer program; Google provided the Asia Pacific AI for Social Good Research Network with funding, established AI for social good labs in India, and held the AI for Social Good Workshop in 2021 and 2022 for academics and NGOs in North, Central and South America; major corporations such as Microsoft, Intel, and IBM have established AI for social good teams; and in June 2023, China announced an initiative to support AI4SG initiatives around the world called the World Internet Conference Artificial Intelligence for Social Good Action Plan.

[15] Lavista Ferres and Weeks, *AI for Good: Applications in Sustainability, Humanitarian Action, and Health*.

[16] Te-Ping Chen, "Women Founders of AI Startups Take Aim at Gender Bias," *The Wall Street Journal*, September 29, 2020 (www.wsj.com/articles/women-founders-of-ai-startups-take-aim-at-gender-bias-11601388625).

Girl,[17] an Australia-based company founded in 2015, provides girls and women with resources to "enter and flourish" in the world of coding. AI is used to address bias in recruitment in a number of industries.[18] Although every company's approach to AI-assisted recruitment is different, the goals converge to making recruitment faster and more successful by using efficient methods for collecting, processing, and analyzing data on job candidates. The additional sales pitch is to make the recruitment process free of discrimination by minimizing human bias and rectifying potential sources of machine bias. Toward those ends, companies such as Blendoor, HireVue, and Entelo specialize in candidate selection, interviewing, and bias mitigation. Textio aims to ensure workplace equality by taking bias out of the language of job specifications and performance reviews. For companies volunteering to improve pay gaps, a number of pay equity and compensation management vendors, such as Syndio, Trusaic, ADP, and PayAnalytics, offer AI-powered tools. Algorithms can reduce information gaps, too. Glassdoor's Know Your Worth provides potential employees with an estimate of compensation they may expect to receive.[19]

Countering accusations of racial bias and discrimination motivates non-profit and for-profit AI producers. It has been shown that large language models (LLMs) tend to underrepresent texts about, and dialects of, marginalized groups.[20] A team from Morgan State University recently teamed up with Latimer.ai to create an LLM to ensure historically accurate and unbiased interactions for people of color.[21] In addition, workplace risk assessment and misconduct detection software map incoming reports onto predefined patterns of harassment and misconduct; in other words, for their algorithms to work, a sufficient number of similar cases must have already happened and been incorporated into the dataset.[22] Botler uses LLMs to detect instances of misconduct in confidential descriptions of allegations.[23] The goal is to provide victims with a non-adversarial platform. The testimonials on the platform's website suggest that the victims go on to seek settlements with employers once misconduct allegations are detected by AI.

17 www.codelikeagirl.com

18 Hannah Kuchler, "Beware AI Programs Recruiting Staff in Their Own Image," *Financial Times*, September 26, 2017 (www.ft.com/content/a5982330-75f6-11e7-a3e8-60495fe6ca71); Kate Bussman, "How to Nail a Job Interview with a Robot (Yes, These Exist)," *The Telegraph*, October 30, 2022 (www.telegraph.co.uk/education-and-careers/2022/10/30/how-nail-job-interview-robot-yes-exist/).

19 Lauren Weber, "Glassdoor's New Tool Helps With Pay Comparisons," *The Wall Street Journal*, October 15, 2016 (www.wsj.com/articles/glassdoors-new-tool-helps-with-pay-comparisons-1477404139).

20 Welbl et al., "Challenges in Detoxifying Language Models."

21 "Morgan State Announces Collaboration in 'The Pursuit of Unbiased AI,'" *The Daily Record*, January 31, 2024 (www.thedailyrecord.com/2024/01/31/morgan-state-announces-collaboration-on-racially-inclusive-ai-project/).

22 de Haan, "Preventing #MeToo: Artificial Intelligence, the Law, and Prophylactics."

23 botler.com; also see Zosia Bielski, "Stepping Up: Woman Who Was Stalked Uses Her Own Experience to Develop AI-Powered App to Provide Information for Other Victims," *The Globe and Mail*, October 15, 2020 (www.theglobeandmail.com/canada/article-stepping-up-woman-who-was-stalked-uses-her-own-experience-to-develop).

Technical interventions that redefine the metrics of algorithmic success can improve substantive outcomes. For example, researchers at Stanford University have developed the Multiaccuracy Boost algorithm, which seeks to maximize not only the overall accuracy metric but also the highest accuracy for every subpopulation.[24] Another way in which the risks and harms arising from AI can be mitigated or eliminated is to reverse-engineer algorithmic processes. For example, a team of researchers from the American Civil Liberties Union, Carnegie Mellon University, Idaho Justice Project and the University of Pennsylvania developed an algorithm to predict the likelihood that a criminal defendant would be unfairly treated by algorithmic risk assessment systems.[25] The project turns the tables on the use of algorithms in the justice system, as it puts under the spotlight not the criminal defendants, but the system that judges their likelihood of committing crime. Another project proposes to reverse the legacies of structural racism in the US housing market through "reparative algorithms" that account for historical discrimination patterns.[26]

All in all, the sky's the limit when it comes to imagining AI technology to make the world a better place. Many of the ideas discussed in this section have already begun to make an impact. Nonetheless, as it will become in the rest of this chapter, the gap between imagining technical solutions and implementing them should be taken into account while assessing their overall efficacy.

Human-in-the-Loop Solutions

The realization that complex algorithmic tasks cannot be automated accurately and safely has kindled interest in human input and oversight throughout the lifecycle of AI products. Numerous examples of algorithmic bias and discrimination in hiring, banking, education, and law enforcement have prompted scrutiny of automated decision-making systems. Many argue that humans should consider algorithmic output a component of their decision process instead of relying on it.

The importance of human control at various stages of AI design and development prior to the final output is increasingly recognized as well. To give an example: To avoid instances of gender stereotyping in voice assistants and chatbots, which tend to replicate conversational styles associated with traditional gender roles, like self-deprecating or flirtatious responses, some technology companies hire writers who nudge these assistants toward setting boundaries against abusive, harassing, and insulting users.[27] Other companies are focused on the design process to ensure that

24 Lobel, *The Equality Machine: Harnessing Digital Technology for a Brighter, More Inclusive Future*: 28.

25 Meyer et al., "Flipping the Script on Criminal Justice Risk Assessment: An Actuarial Model for Assessing the Risk the Federal Sentencing System Poses to Defendants."

26 So et al., "Beyond Fairness."

27 Jacqueline Feldman, "A Human Wrote This," *Statorec* (blog), 2023 (www.statorec.com/a-human-wrote-this-by-jacqueline-feldman/).

tools like chatbots are aligned with gender equality.[28] To give another example from the world of so-called autonomous vehicles: Human backup drivers are required to assume control in case the autonomous component fails in most jurisdictions.

De-Biasing

The origins of de-biasing are in cognitive psychology research that identifies the sources of human bias. Lists of best practices to tackle bias and discrimination in contexts as varied as the workplace, courtroom, dating, etc., have been published in bestsellers, like Pragya Agarwal's *Sway*, Jessica Nordell's *The End of Bias: How We Change Our Minds*, and Malcolm Gladwell's *Blink*. De-biasing in the AI context refers to the elimination of bias and discrimination in automated decision-making.[29]

De-biasing has generated enthusiasm in the AI development community as part of an ongoing academic research agenda in universities and corporations. The FAccT community dedicates annual conferences to novel research on de-biasing techniques. To date, IBM's Watson OpenScale, with its strategies that identify bias (*passive debiasing*) and change the model in real time to prevent bias (*active debiasing*), is the highest-profile de-biasing tool.[30] IBM released AI Fairness 360, an open-source software toolkit to detect and remove bias in ML models, in 2018.[31] A number of smaller companies have announced de-biasing tools, too: Abacus.AI de-biases datasets,[32] Zest AI uses "adversarial de-biasing" to look for patterns of bias in historical data to readjust the model,[33] Herophilus identifies confounding variables in ML models,[34] and Facteus, a financial data firm, has launched the "Debiasing Transactional Alternative Data to Maximize Population Representativeness" project in collaboration with NYU.[35] Applied Research Associates received a patent grant for their project "Identifying False Positive Data Within a Set of Blast Exposure

[28] Josie Young, "Why We Need to Design Feminist AI," *TED Talk*, December 2018 (www.ted.com/talks/josie_young_why_we_need_to_design_feminist_ai).

[29] For an informative summary of de-biasing techniques, see Lara Nguyen, "Debiasing Machine Learning," *Medium*, August 7, 2022 (www.medium.com/@laranguyen/debiasing-machine-learning-94cc32d3f2cc).

[30] www.ibm.com/docs/en/cloud-paks/cp-data/4.6.x?topic=results-reviewing-debiased-transactions

[31] www.ibm.com/opensource/open/projects/ai-fairness-360/

[32] Frederic Lardinois, "RealityEngines AI Becomes Abacus.AI and Raises $13M SeriesA," *TechCrunch*, July 14, 2020 (www.techcrunch.com/2020/07/14/realityengines-ai-becomes-abacus-ai-and-raises-13m-series-a).

[33] Michael Totty, "How to Make Artificial Intelligence Less Biased," *Wall Street Journal*, November 3, 2020.

[34] "Herophilus Publishes General Method for Detecting Relevant Signals in Machine Learning Analysis of Complex Biological Datasets," *Business Wire*, February 28, 2022 (www.businesswire.com/news/home/20220228005373/en/Herophilus-Publishes-General-Method-for-Detecting-Relevant-Signals-in-Machine-Learning-Analysis-of-Complex-Biological-Datasets).

[35] "Facteus Collaborates with New York University to Bring Unique Alternative Financial Data to the Courant Institute," *Business Wire*, March 23, 2021 (www.businesswire.com/news/home/20210323005565/en/).

Data" in 2023.[36] Thus, it is safe to argue that algorithmic bias has prompted the development of a cottage industry of de-biasing.

Broadly speaking, de-biasing strategies can be data-centered or model-centered.[37] Responding to criticisms that AI algorithms are often trained on data that replicate the historical patterns of exclusion in society in general and the technology sector in particular, data-centered de-biasing strategies focus on improving the representativeness of training datasets. Taking their cue from survey methods, which have a long history of rectifying representation problems, these strategies focus on increasing the amount and representativeness of data, and processing existing data in bias-reducing ways.

Prioritizing data-centered strategies has been criticized for not paying sufficient attention to the underlying algorithms, which has prompted the development of model-centered de-biasing strategies. Such strategies may focus on feature engineering, tweaking the model to reduce the likelihood of bias, de-biasing numerical representations of textual data,[38] and in-processing interventions that aim to reverse-engineer the algorithm to identify sources of bias.[39] All in all, model-centered de-biasing takes data problems for granted and seeks ways to minimize them.

AI-Generated Text, Image, and Voice Detection

Once OpenAI's latest chatbot, ChatGPT, made the headlines in late 2022, efforts to identify chatbot-generated text, image, and voice have stepped up, too. Technical solutions focus either on the supply side (i.e., allowing producers to voluntarily label AI-generated content) or the demand side (i.e., detecting AI-generated content before they reach unsuspecting end-users).

The education sector has responded to the increasing risk of chatbot-enabled cheating and plagiarism with panic. In response, companies announced new models of anti-plagiarism software right away. OpenAI itself released a classifier to detect AI-generated text, all the while admitting that its accuracy rate was quite low.[40]

36 "ARA Receives Patents for Processing of Body-Mounted Blast Overpressure Sensor Data," *ARA News*, July 16, 2024 (www.ara.com/news/ara-receives-patents-for-processing-of-body-mounted-blast-overpressure-sensor-data).

37 Subbarao Kambhampati, "Why are Artificial Intelligence Systems Biased?" *The Hill*, July 20, 2020 (www.thehill.com/opinion/cybersecurity/506924-why-are-artificial-intelligence-systems-biased/); Natalie Huet, "Gender Bias in Recruitment: How AI Hiring Tools are Hindering Women's Careers," *EuroNews*, March 8, 2022 (www.euronews.com/next/2022/03/08/gender-bias-in-recruitment-how-ai-hiring-tools-are-hindering-women-s-careers).

38 Hooker, "Moving Beyond 'Algorithmic Bias Is a Data Problem'"; Bolukbasi et al., "Man Is to Computer Programmer as Woman Is to Homemaker?"

39 Haniyeh Mahmoodian, "Using Adversarial Debiasing to Reduce Model Bias," *Towards Data Science*, April 21, 2020 (www.towardsdatascience.com/reducing-bias-from-models-built-on-the-adult-dataset-using-adversarial-debiasing-330f2ef3a3b4).

40 Kyle Wiggers, "OpenAI Releases Tool to Detect AI-Generated Text, Including from ChatGPT," *TechCrunch*, January 31, 2023 (www.techcrunch.com/2023/01/31/openai-releases-tool-to-detect-ai-generated-text-including-from-chatgpt/).

Predictably, the zeal to crack down on plagiarism resulted in a serious questioning of the underlying technology after a university professor falsely accused some students of cheating.[41] A study of sixteen AI-generated content detectors finds that three of them, namely Copyleaks, TurnItIn, and Originality.ai, produce comparatively accurate and unambiguous results on average, and versions of detectors that require registration and payment are only slightly more accurate than others.[42] A recent report suggests that AI-text detection tools do not work as successfully as advertised: A study of fourteen tools finds that their accuracy in identifying ChatGPT-produced text is 74 percent (compared to 96 percent in detecting text written by humans), and the accuracy falls to 42 percent for slightly tweaked text.[43]

Detecting AI-generated images reached panic levels in 2023, when deepfake images and videos of politicians and non-consensual sexually explicit deepfakes of celebrities began to circulate on social media platforms, but researchers have been working on detection technology for longer. DeepFake-o-Meter, developed by a University at Buffalo team, is said to detect deepfakes in portrait photos with 94 percent accuracy.[44] Another exciting field of research is watermarking, which refers to the embedding of difficult-to-remove elements in AI-generated text, image, or voice output to authenticate its fabricated origins. A familiar example of the watermark is the "Getty Images" script across stock photos. The ideal watermark in AI applications would be imperceptible and "resilient to simple manipulations like cropping, resizing, color adjustment and converting digital formats."[45] In August 2023, Google DeepMind launched SynthID,[46] a tool that allows users to embed digital watermarks in AI-generated content, as a supply side solution. In October 2023, Meta AI announced Stable Signature, a watermarking method for AI-generated images.[47] In February 2024, OpenAI announced the use of watermarking in DALL-E images.[48]

41 Pranshu Verma, "A Professor Accused His Class of Using ChatGPT, Putting Diplomas in Jeopardy," *The Washington Post*, May 18, 2023 (www.washingtonpost.com/technology/2023/05/18/texas-professor-threatened-fail-class-chatgpt-cheating/).

42 Walters, "The Effectiveness of Software Designed to Detect AI-Generated Writing."

43 Rhiannon Williams, "AI-Text Detection Tools Are Really Easy to Fool," *MIT Technology Review*, July 7, 2023 (www.technologyreview.com/2023/07/07/1075982/ai-text-detection-tools-are-really-easy-to-fool).

44 Hu, Li, and Lyu, "Exposing GAN-Generated Faces Using Inconsistent Corneal Specular Highlights."

45 Hany Farid, "Watermarking ChatGPT, DALL-E and Other Generative AIs Could Help Protect against Fraud and Misinformation," *The Conversation*, March 27, 2023. (www.theconversation.com/watermarking-chatgpt-dall-e-and-other-generative-ais-could-help-protect-against-fraud-and-misinformation-202293).

46 www.google/technologies/synthid/

47 www.ai.meta.com/blog/stable-signature-watermarking-generative-ai/

48 Emilia David, "OpenAI is adding new watermarks to DALL-E 3," *The Verge*, February 6, 2024 (www.theverge.com/2024/2/6/24063954/ai-watermarks-dalle3-openai-content-credentials).

Testing

Beyond the routine practice of quality-testing products, AI companies can be expected to test their products for AI-related risks and harms. Those tests can be conducted internally by company teams or externally by independent researchers or regulators. An idea that has gained traction in the early 2020s is red-teaming, which refers to the detection of failures and vulnerabilities by team members who take on the role of hypothetical outsiders who accidentally or malignantly break or corrupt a computer system. Red-teaming can involve penetration testing to identify technical vulnerabilities, as well as social engineering tests to assess human operators' susceptibility to manipulation.

To give some examples: OpenAI uses red-teaming to understand and mitigate immediate risks.[49] In fact, ChatGPT was tested in a red-teaming process, which revealed that it could be used "to make bioweapons, synthesize bombs, or buy ransomware on the dark web."[50] Meta announced that the Large Language Model Meta A (LLaMa) had gone through testing for inaccuracy, offensive material, and content promoting terrorism, child sex abuse, and discrimination.[51] Google's Bard reportedly went through red-teaming to avoid offensive remarks in multiple languages.[52] On August 12–13, 2023, the Generative Red Team Challenge was held as part of the DEF CON hacker convention.[53]

Another approach to testing is algorithmic auditing (also known as AI auditing),[54] which refers to the assessment of algorithmic models for accuracy, performance, fairness, and other desirable goals. Such audits can take place at one stage of product design and development or at multiple stages, and can be carried out by internal teams as well as external entities, such as auditing firms, government researchers, or academics. It is argued that a comprehensive assessment should include insights from law, social sciences, engineering, philosophy, and business practice, in addition to technical specifications.[55] A study of algorithmic audits finds that civil society audits and journalistic investigations often produce significant impact, often

49 www.openai.com/blog/red-teaming-network; David Elliott, "AI: Will Governance Catch Up with the Tech in 2024?" *World Economic Forum* (blog), March 1, 2024 (www.weforum.org/agenda/2024/03/ai-advances-governance-2024/).

50 Will Knight, and Khari Johnson, "Now That ChatGPT Is Plugged In, Things Could Get Weird," *Wired*, March 28, 2023 (www.wired.com/story/chatgpt-plugins-openai/).

51 Gerrit De Vynck and Naomi Nix, "Facebook to Make its AI Free to Use, Expanding Access to Powerful Tech," *The Washington Post*, July 18, 2023 (www.washingtonpost.com/technology/2023/07/18/facebook-meta-ai-llama/).

52 Sam Schechner, "Google's Bard AI Chatbot Adds More Languages to Take On ChatGPT," *The Wall Street Journal*, July 13, 2023 (www.wsj.com/articles/googles-bard-ai-chatbot-adds-more-languages-to-take-on-chatgpt-a2acfc5b).

53 Will Oremus, "Meet the Hackers Who Are Trying to Make AI Go Rogue," *The Washington Post*, August 8, 2023 (www.washingtonpost.com/technology/2023/08/08/ai-red-team-defcon/).

54 Hirsch et al., *Business Data Ethics: Emerging Models for Governing AI and Advanced Analytics*.

55 Mökander, "Auditing of AI."

through legal action, while academic audits tend to have unclear mechanisms to produce impact. Furthermore, stakeholder engagement and a willingness to consider structural factors, such as the uneven distribution of power and risks, improve an audit's impact.[56]

ASSESSING WHAT TECHNICAL SOLUTIONS CAN OR CANNOT DO

The use of AI for equality and fairness to overcome natural, human-made, and technological challenges is sometimes criticized for failing to live up to the hype. Proposed technical solutions, insofar as they use technologies similar to the ones they hope to fix, raise novel objections. For example, recruitment company HireVue had to stop using facial recognition technology after the Electronic Privacy Information Center filed a complaint with the Federal Trade Commission in 2019.[57] In 2022, the Center for Democracy and Technology released an assessment report of HireVue's commitment to explainable AI, finding that the recruitment platform indeed delivers on a number of non-discrimination and transparency metrics, while failing in others.[58] More recently, HireVue was sued by a candidate for a CVS Pharmacy job, who claimed that the AI platform's interview amounted to a lie detector, the use of which is forbidden under Massachusetts labor law[59] – the lawsuit was settled in August 2024.

The troubles of AI-assisted employment are not unique to one company. The likelihood of perpetuating existing gender and race bias, not doing enough to safeguard the rights of persons with disabilities, committing privacy violations, and filtering out non-conventional yet competent candidates have all been raised as potential shortcomings of AI-assisted recruiting.[60] Journalist Hilke Schellmann's years-long interview and participant-observation research on employment algorithms finds opaque and routinely erroneous practices that amount to surveillance, privacy violations, and, in many cases, discriminatory outcomes.[61]

There is no doubt that humans should play key roles in control, oversight, and responsibility. There is hardly any technology that can be deployed fully autonomously in a safe way. Thus, human-in-the-loop solutions raise objections not for

56 Birhane et al., "AI Auditing."

57 Jeremy Kahn, "HireVue Drops Facial Monitoring Amid A.I. Algorithm Audit," *Fortune*, January 19, 2021 (www.fortune.com/2021/01/19/hirevue-drops-facial-monitoring-amid-a-i-algorithm-audit/).

58 Matt Scherer, "HireVue 'AI Explainability Statement' Mostly Fails to Explain What it Does," *Center for Democracy & Technology*, September 8, 2022 (www.cdt.org/insights/hirevue-ai-explainability-statement-mostly-fails-to-explain-what-it-does/).

59 Allison Dunn, "CVS Health Accused of Using AI 'Lie Detector Screening' without Notice," *BenefitsPRO*, July 7, 2023 (www.benefitspro.com/2023/07/07/job-candidate-accuses-cvs-health-of-using-ai-powered-lie-detector-screening-without-proper-notice-412-150996).

60 Anna Helhoski, "AI Could Prevent Hiring Bias – Unless It Makes It Worse," *NerdWallet*, June 12, 2023 (www.nerdwallet.com/article/finance/ai-hiring-decisions).

61 Hilke Schellmann, *The Algorithm: How AI Decides Who Gets Hired, Monitored, Promoted & Fired & Why We Need to Fight Back Now*.

what they accomplish, but rather the mindset they can inadvertently cultivate: Relying on humans at the ultimate instance may produce a false sense of comfort in the face of algorithmic risks and harms. The protections they afford can be insufficient when companies and governments sidestep them. What is more, putting the emphasis on the responsibility of frontline human operators runs the risk of ignoring broader system-level failures.[62] For example, after an autonomous Uber driver killed a pedestrian in 2018, its human backup driver – a gig worker – was the only person to get into legal trouble.[63]

How well does de-biasing work? The scant empirical evidence on the real-world achievements and shortcomings of de-biasing suggests a complex picture. Deborah Raji and Joy Buolamwini have conducted two studies to assess gender and racial bias in facial recognition models. The first study identifies the overall error for the IBM, Microsoft, and Megvii (Face++) models as of May 2017, while the second one compares the initial error rates to those of the companies' improved models in August 2018 and introduces the Amazon and Kairos models. The results indeed show reductions in error for the original models.[64] It also shows Amazon and Kairos producing high error rates at the time – the CEO of Kairos later claimed to have improved the accuracy of their models.[65]

However, not all evidence points to progress through de-biasing. Amazon's hiring algorithm, which favored candidates with stereotypically male-associated characteristics, reportedly continued biased recommendations even when the obvious gender markers were removed.[66] The corpus of Common Crawl was found to contain hate speech and sexually explicit content even after filtering procedures.[67] Similarly, bias in crime recidivism algorithms continued after years of close media scrutiny and consequent efforts to de-bias.[68] An additional paradox in data-centered de-biasing is that the additional data required to de-bias likely come from the same vulnerable populations that the de-biasing work seeks to help. Thus, the ethical challenges of ensuring data privacy and legal requirements to keep data on protected categories off-limits constrain this line of work.[69]

62 Green and Kak, "The False Comfort of Human Oversight as an Antidote to A.I. Harm."

63 Lauren Smiley, "'I'm the Operator': The Aftermath of a Self-Driving Tragedy," *Wired*, March 8, 2022 (www.wired.com/story/uber-self-driving-car-fatal-crash/).

64 Raji and Buolamwini, "Actionable Auditing Revisited – Investigating the Impact of Publicly Naming Biased Performance Results of Commercial AI Products."

65 Natasha Singer, "Amazon Is Pushing Facial Technology That a Study Says Could Be Biased," *The New York Times*, January 24, 2019 (www.nytimes.com/2019/01/24/technology/amazon-facial-technology-study.html).

66 Vivienne Ming, "Human Insight Remains Essential to Beat the Bias of Algorithms," *Financial Times*, December 4, 2019 (www.ft.com/content/59520726-d0c5-11e9-b018-ca4456540ea6).

67 Luccioni and Viviano, "What's in the Box?"

68 Dressel and Farid, "The Accuracy, Fairness, and Limits of Predicting Recidivism."

69 Andrus et al., "What We Can't Measure, We Can't Understand"; Van Bekkum and Zuiderveen Borgesius, "Using Sensitive Data to Prevent Discrimination by Artificial Intelligence."

Critics of de-biasing do not argue that efforts to improve data quality and/or algorithms fail completely. Rather, the crux of the argument is that the technological, the human, and the social are interdependent elements of de-biasing work,[70] which is why reducing complex social phenomena to technical fixes falls short of what needs to be done for safe and responsible technology. For example, registering her disagreement with then head of Google's AI research Jeff Dean's interpretation of why Bender et al.'s "Stochastic Parrots" research fell short of Google's research standards, Layla Al Asri writes, "This statement immediately irked me because it brushes off the fundamental issue of the content of the training data as just another technical issue."[71] Cognitive scientist Abeba Birhane argues that using de-biasing while ignoring deeply ingrained historical injustices will not do more than "scratch the surface."[72] An additional argument, not against de-biasing as such but against the optimism that de-biasing solutions scale, is that since fairness metrics are case-specific, de-biasing solutions that apply in one context may not be transferable.[73]

Detecting AI-generated content has proven exceptionally difficult. Using plagiarism detection software to catch offenders of academic integrity requires awareness of the limitations of pattern-matching and classification algorithms. Given that false positives (i.e., human writing wrongly flagged as AI-generated) and false negatives (i.e., undetected AI-generated content) are always possible,[74] overreliance on algorithms can result in embarrassment for teachers eager to catch AI-generated content. What is more, errors of algorithms are not randomly distributed: Unusual phrasing is more likely to be flagged as AI-generated, which puts non-native speakers at greater risk of being wrongly accused of plagiarism.[75]

AI-generated text detection is not the only proposed solution. School districts, universities, and individual instructors have been experimenting with bans on the use of chatbots, switching from take-home essay assignments to in-class, handwritten or oral ones, and enforcing an honor code to not use chatbots for schoolwork.[76] It is questionable whether bans are feasible, and as importantly, desirable: Chatbots may

70 Celis, "Debiasing the Algorithm."

71 Layla El Asri, "The ML Community Needs a Provisional Morality," *Speaking Machines Blog*, December 5, 2022 (www.speakingmachines.com/blog/2020/12/5/the-ml-community-needs-a-provisional-morality).

72 Joe Humphreys, "Who Is More Racist, Sexist and Biased: You or Your Computer?: Cognitive Scientist Abeba Birhane Is among a Growing Number of Professionals Sounding the Alarm about Algorithmic Prejudice," *Irish Times*, November 19, 2020 (www.irishtimes.com/culture/who-is-more-racist-sexist-and-biased-you-or-your-computer-1.4408555).

73 Celis, "Debiasing the Algorithm."

74 Bethan Staton, "Universities express doubt over tool to detect AI-powered plagiarism," *Financial Times*, April 3, 2023 (www.ft.com/content/d872d65d-dfd0-40b3-8db9-a17fea20c60c).

75 Liang et al., "GPT Detectors Are Biased against Non-Native English Writers."

76 Kalley Huang, "Alarmed by A.I. Chatbots, Universities Start Revamping How They Teach," *The New York Times*, January 16, 2023 (www.nytimes.com/2023/01/16/technology/chatgpt-artificial-intelligence-universities.html).

create opportunities for learning that blanket bans threaten to curtail.[77] Thus, the solution to chatbot-enabled cheating and plagiarism is neither blanket prohibition nor AI-generated content detection: Careful course and syllabus design can alleviate, if not eliminate, the problem.[78]

AI watermarking is not a panacea, either, as it is not immune to tactics of evasion. A hack as simple as the removal of metadata may destroy valuable information to detect AI-generated content. Seventeen of the twenty-three researchers interviewed by an *Economist* survey believe that AI-generated fakes will be undetectable in the future. The article introduces more robust technologies than the ones publicly available today, such as Tree-Ring watermarking, to suggest a way forward, but warns that even those advanced techniques have not proven failproof against AI-generated fakes.[79]

So far, red teams have been useful in diagnosing problems. The report from the 2023 DEF CON convention suggests that today's AI chatbots tend to stick to the guidelines given to them but are susceptible to inaccuracies. According to researcher and entrepreneur Rumman Chowdhury, this means "AI companies and their critics and regulators should perhaps focus less on elaborate prompt hacks and more on how chatbots might confirm or amplify users' own biases and misconceptions."[80] What remains to be seen is whether the detection of problems will prompt the developers of AI tools to address them.

CONCLUSION

Without a doubt, AI for social good projects, human-in-the-loop solutions, debiasing, AI detection, and testing bring out researchers' and developers' aspirations to improve today's AI, and by doing that, to make the world a better place. I believe the right question to ask is not "do they work?" as they almost always contribute in some measure. The more appropriate question is "how transformative are they?" Evidence shows that AI for social good projects at their best move the needle by prompting change in one product, company, or issue area at a time. Human-in-the-loop solutions and testing will be key components of any AI development. De-biasing has proven technically difficult, but multiple teams have achieved

77 Joanna Stern, "ChatGPT Wrote My AP English Essay–and I Passed," *The Wall Street Journal*, December 21, 2022 (www.wsj.com/articles/chatgpt-wrote-my-ap-english-essayand-i-passed-11671628256).

78 "AI Detectors Don't Work. Here's What to Do Instead," *MIT Management STS Teaching & Learning Technologies* (www.mitsloanedtech.mit.edu/ai/teach/ai-detectors-dont-work/).

79 "Many AI Researchers Think Fakes Will Become Undetectable," *The Economist*, January 17, 2024 (www.economist.com/science-and-technology/2024/01/17/many-ai-researchers-think-fakes-will-become-undetectable).

80 Will Oremus, "Hackers Competed to Find AI Harms. Here's What They Found," *The Washington Post*, April 4, 2024 (www.washingtonpost.com/politics/2024/04/04/hackers-competed-find-ai-harms-heres-what-they-found/).

satisfactory results. AI detection appears to be the one technical solution category facing the greatest difficulties so far.

For all their contributions, however, technical solutions have not managed to eliminate or mitigate AI risks and harms, let alone tackle systemic social and political problems. What are the obstacles? First, good ideas do not always result in good tools because not every proof of concept gets adopted for production. Online academic preprint repositories like arXiv list dozens of well-meaning projects, but in the end, very few of them result in viable products. Even the technical solutions that make the cut struggle to produce an impact. For example, 72 percent of respondents to the 2022 Gender Pay Equity and Transparency Survey say that pay equity is a high or very high priority for their senior leaders, although only 14 percent of companies use technology for pay equity.[81] In other words, good ideas do not always find customers.

A dispiriting trend is the quiet disappearance of a technical solution not long after the fanfare with which it was announced. For example, two search-tool extensions that revealed and rectified bias in gender representations, namely UNESCO's Her Headline (2018) and Pantene's Search.Human.Equalizer (2019), had all but disappeared from the face of the internet by 2023. Sheboard, a mobile keyboard application that aimed to boost girls' self-confidence by nudging them to use affirming language, has not been updated since August 2020. Of course, not all closures are bad: Individuals and organizations move on, arguably, to other important and useful projects. However, it is also obvious that researchers and journalists should wait to assess the viability and usefulness of technical solutions before celebrating their success.

The findings in this chapter suggest that technical solutions can be a valuable toolkit for addressing the risks and harms of AI. Managing expectations is key, though. AI researchers and developers, and the people assessing their achievements, should avoid the techno-solutionism trap. Many good projects just do not make it past the early stages. Media hype only makes things worse: Technology journalists announced the 2017 launch of DeepXplore, an automated testing framework for deep learning models, with headlines like "Science may have cured biased AI"[82] – an assertion not supported by the developers of the framework themselves,[83] and which, of course, did not come true. Some techniques to fix AI or improve life on the planet will be immensely successful in their area of application, while most are likely to produce modest or no change. Insisting on the usefulness of some techniques at the expense of other, non-technical solutions, may even be harmful, as

[81] Nicole Lewis, "Technology Can Be Used to Achieve Pay Equity," *Society for Human Resource Management* (www.shrm.org/resourcesandtools/hr-topics/technology/pages/technology-can-be-used-achieve-pay-equity.aspx).

[82] Tristan Greene, "Science May Have Cured Biased AI," *The Next Web*, October 26, 2017 (www.thenextweb.com/news/scientists-may-have-just-created-the-cure-for-biased-ai).

[83] Pei et al., "DeepXplore."

overzealous enforcers of academic integrity using AI plagiarism detection software have found to their embarrassment.

When asked about whether watermarking can address the problem of false information in a year of elections worldwide (2024), Irene Solaiman, the director of global policy at Hugging Face and former AI researcher at OpenAI, says, "… these types of technical tools aren't going to be a panacea and definitely not this year," and instead asks news media and social media platforms to invest in capacity to identify fake content in collaboration with election officials around the world.[84] This raises an important point: Attentiveness to context is crucial for any project that wants to fix the world. *Humans* in the plural should be not only in the loop but also around the loop, designing and assessing the loop, and ultimately, deciding what it is that humans want, and can get, from the loop.

[84] Julia Angwin, "AI Watermarking Is Not Going to Save Us," *Proof*, April 23, 2024 (www.proofnews.org/ai-watermarking-is-not-going-to-save-us/).

5

AI Ethics as Business Self-Regulation

Corporate Principles, Boards, Councils, and Teams

The idea that the private sector can and should incorporate the principles of accessible, accountable, accurate, fair, robust, safe, transparent, and trustworthy AI into its practice has gained traction from the mid-2010s onwards. In accordance with decades of corporate social responsibility practices, proponents of business self-regulation argue that ethical behavior is good for business, and even if not, doing the right thing should be prioritized over the conventional indicators of business success, such as profit, market share, and stock price. Accordingly, ethics may have to go above and beyond legal compliance because existing laws tend to set a low threshold for doing the right thing or worse, relevant legislation simply does not exist. For skeptics, however, ethical conduct is at best a side concern for businesses, and at worst, a cynical attempt at ethics-washing to fool consumers.

This chapter documents and assesses business self-regulation in AI. A growing trend in the technology industry is the incorporation of principles, standards, and guidelines into practice through internal or external bodies tasked with compliance oversight and guidance, and ethical conduct.[1] These bodies typically take the form of ethical and responsible technology advisory boards and councils or specialized ethical and responsible technology teams. In addition, the inclusion of ethical and responsible technology specialists in product teams has become an increasingly more common practice. Ideally, these boards, councils, and teams should exercise a soft-law compliance approach – one that relies on voluntary self-regulation rather than legal obligations – by nudging companies to put responsible technology principles into practice.

Internal and external boards in charge of ensuring compliance and providing guidance play a positive yet limited role in influencing company conduct. Meta's Oversight Board has seen a relatively high degree of compliance with content moderation decisions, and Axon complied with the advice of its AI Ethics Board between 2019 and 2022. In addition, in-house responsible technology teams have

[1] Gary Drenik, "Who Guards AI Ethics? Ending The Blame Game," *Forbes*, July 30, 2024 (www.forbes.com/sites/garydrenik/2024/07/30/who-guards-ai-ethics-ending-the-blame-game/).

pushed successfully for ethical conduct in a few product decisions – Microsoft has publicized two such cases in 2022.

The likelihood of compliance falls dramatically when advisory opinions threaten the core money-making business, however. Some advisory opinions of the Oversight Board, which lacks power to influence Meta's recommendation algorithms, have been ignored openly, and Axon's AI Ethics Board imploded when the company ignored advice not to develop taser-equipped drones in June 2022. A more troubling finding is that some companies have failed to establish boards, councils, or teams, or disbanded them soon after their establishment. Google's multiple failures at setting up an AI ethics board are a case in point.

Corporate AI ethics boards, councils, and teams should be seen beyond the binary of successful ethics compliance versus ethics-washing. Their members make potentially useful efforts to push their colleagues and supervisors toward ethical conduct within the hierarchical structure of modern corporations. Even if they fail more often than not, their agency sometimes influences corporate decision-making in ways that would not have been possible in their absence. Even the increasing number of bills and laws regulating AI will not override these responsible technology specialists, as legal regulation itself relies on a mixture of external pressure and internal buy-in from businesses to do the right thing.

Caveats are in order. First, assessing business self-regulation poses a methodological challenge because companies do not share the details of their internal workings, much less the details of negotiations resulting in rejected proposals. That is why the cases of reported ethical conduct may be a small sample of successful self-regulation. Second, some of the boards, councils, and teams listed in this chapter were disbanded a few years or mere months after their creation. This may be taken as proof of failure, but company spokespersons often insist that most employees of the disbanded bodies continue ethics-related work in their new teams.[2] Keeping these methodological difficulties in mind, this chapter assesses self-regulation on the basis of available evidence. A third caveat concerns the universe of cases: Responsible AI teams have proliferated in the technology sector, as have oversight bodies,[3] but most of them are

[2] Brandon Vigliarolo, "Meta Disbands Responsible Innovation Team, Spreads It Out Over Facebook and Co," *The Register*, September 9, 2022 (www.theregister.com/2022/09/09/meta_disbands_responsible_innovation_team/).

[3] The examples include the Ethics Research Initiative, Boston Dynamics (an American robotics company); the Data and AI Ethics Council, Orange (a French multinational telecommunications corporation); the AI Ethics Advisory Board, MeditSimple (a healthcare platform); the internal AI ethics steering committee, the AI ethics advisory panel, and the trustworthy AI working group, Team Opportunity Prediction (a French AI firm); the AI Ethics Advisory Board, Hitachi (a Japanese engineering and electronics firm); AI Advisory Board, AdventHealth (a US-based non-profit healthcare system); the AI Advisory Council, Augmedix (an American health technology company); the Generative AI Advisory Board, portal26 (an American AI company); the AI Ethics Advisory Board, Arena Analytics (an American analytics platform); AI Ethics Advisory Board, Hewlett Packard Enterprise (an American information technology company); Ethics Board, Lucid.AI (American AI

too new to allow empirical analysis.[4] Therefore, this chapter covers only the boards, councils, and teams about which publicly available information exists.

The following boards and councils are discussed in this chapter: Axon AI Ethics Board, Axon Ethics & Equity Advisory Council, Meta (formerly Facebook) Oversight Board, Microsoft Aether Committee, Microsoft Ethics & Society team, Microsoft Responsible AI Council, Google Ethics and Society research group, the Partnership on AI to Benefit People and Society, and Twitter (currently X) Trust & Safety Council. In addition, a few boards, councils, and teams are mentioned briefly without further analysis, either because they were disbanded shortly after their creation or because very little is known about their operation: Meta Responsible Innovation Team, Meta Responsible AI (RAI) Team, Microsoft's Fairness, Accountability, Transparency & Ethics in AI (FATE), Microsoft Office of Responsible AI, Google / DeepMind AI Ethics Board, Google Advanced Technology External Advisory Council, Google Responsible Innovation Team, and Google Institutional Review Committee. The scant data on all but a few exceptionally well-studied self-regulatory schemes corroborates the central message of this chapter: Bodies tasked to ensure ethical business conduct have produced limited impact at best.

BUSINESS INTEREST ALIGNMENT WITH ETHICAL AI PRINCIPLES

The rapid development of AI systems grounded in machine learning techniques has brought with it concerns around bias and discrimination, surveillance, disinformation, manipulation, data privacy violations, lack of accountability, and environmental degradation, among others, since the early 2010s. As legislatures were slow to react to these disruptions, ensuring ethical business conduct through rules not enforced by the law – sometimes what is called the *soft-law* approach to AI

company); Academia AI Advisory Council, Clarivate; AI Ethics Steering Committee, SAP (a German software company).

4 For example, Intel created, as part of its Responsible AI Charter, the Responsible AI Advisory Council to conduct ethical impact assessments in human rights, human oversight, explainable use of AI, security, safety and reliability, personal privacy, and equity and inclusion in October 2022. In May 2023, the International Association of Privacy Professionals (IAPP) announced an AI Governance Center, which would be supported by Transcend, a technology governance company, and OneTrust, a trust intelligence company. OpenAI created an Oversight Board in late May 2024, soon after dissolving its safety team. Mark Bergen, "OpenAI Creates Oversight Board Featuring Sam Altman After Dissolving Safety Team," *Bloomberg*, May 28, 2024 (www.bloomberg.com/news/articles/2024-05-28/openai-forms-board-safety-committee-after-criticism-ilya-sutskever-departure); Lama Nachman, "Responsibly Harnessing the Power of AI," *Intel Newsroom*, September 12, 2022 (www.intel.com/content/www/us/en/newsroom/opinion/responsibly-harnessing-the-power-of-ai.html); Transcend team, "IAPP AI Governance Supporter: Transcend's Commitment to Ethical AI," Transcend blog, June 24, 2023 (https://transcend.io/blog/iapp-ai-governance-supporter); "OneTrust Joins the IAPP AI Governance Center to Accelerate Responsible AI Innovation," OneTrust press release, November 2, 2023 (www.onetrust.com/news/onetrust-joins-iapp-ai-governance-center/).

regulation – rose to prominence. AI principles, codes of conduct, guidelines, and so on constitute the tools associated with self-imposed compliance.[5] Soft law may come from international organizations (e.g., the United Nations Guiding Principles on Business and Human Rights), national administrative bodies (e.g., United States Federal Trade Commission rules), professional organizations (e.g., the Institute of Electrical and Electronics Engineers standards), non-profit organizations (e.g., the Asilomar Principles promoted by the Future of Life Institute), internal company rules and regulations (e.g., Microsoft AI Principles), academic institutions (e.g., the Framework for Ethical Decision Making developed by the Markkula Center for Applied Ethics at Santa Clara University), and organizations of AI developers themselves.[6]

Justifications for ethical business practices mirror the perceived deficiencies of legal regulation. It may be challenging to catch up with the pace of technological change using traditional regulatory approaches.[7] Beyond speed, the sheer complexity of AI developments may go above and beyond the capacity of government agencies to understand, direct, or constrain technological change.[8] For its proponents, the contributions of the soft-law approach are not second best to law; instead, input from research institutions and professional societies may connect what appear to be narrow private- or public-sector pursuits with broader social, political, economic, cultural, and philosophical considerations, and with the communities potentially affected by AI.[9]

Why should an AI business conduct itself ethically above and beyond what is strictly required by the law? There exist cases when the core business goals of an AI company align with the values expressed in responsible technology principles.[10] In simple terms, good choices improve sales and profits, and bad choices hurt them.[11] For starters, algorithmic inaccuracy may derail business success. For example, Zillow closed down Zillow Offers in part because its house-buying algorithm failed

5 Jobin, Ienca, and Vayena, "Artificial Intelligence: The Global Landscape of Ethics Guidelines"; Attard-Frost, De los Ríos, and Walters, "The Ethics of AI Business Practices"; Schiff et al., "AI Ethics in the Public, Private, and NGO Sectors"; Heilinger, "The Ethics of AI Ethics. A Constructive Critique"; Kieslich, Keller, and Starke, "Artificial Intelligence Ethics by Design. Evaluating Public Perception on the Importance of Ethical Design Principles of Artificial Intelligence"; De Almeida, Dos Santos, and Farias, "Artificial Intelligence Regulation."

6 Belfield, "Activism by the AI Community."

7 Marchant, "'Soft Law' Governance of Artificial Intelligence."

8 Villasenor, "Soft Law as a Complement to AI Regulation."

9 Marchant, "Professional Societies as Adopters and Enforcers of AI Soft Law."

10 Gutierrez and Marchant, "Soft Law 2.0: Incorporating Incentives and Implementation Mechanisms into the Governance of Artificial Intelligence"; Gutierrez, "Transitioning From Ideas to Action."

11 Christopher Mims, "The AI Boom That Could Make Google and Microsoft Even More Powerful," *The Wall Street Journal*, February 11, 2023 (www.wsj.com/articles/the-ai-boom-that-could-make-google-and-microsoft-even-more-powerful-9c5dd2a6).

to value houses correctly.[12] In a clear case of business alignment with accuracy in AI, a California car dealership discovered chatbots' ability to generate falsehoods the hard way when pranksters tricked its chatbot into agreeing to sell cars for $1.[13]

In addition to accuracy, product safety is closely aligned with business interest. For example, failure to filter out violent or hateful content on an online platform may scare away its users, thereby disincentivizing advertisers and investors. This likely explains major social media companies' investment in content moderation as much as, and perhaps more than, their moral commitment to safe online spaces. Algorithms that reproduce or amplify bias and discrimination may lose not only those customers on the receiving end of bias but also intermediary business and public-sector customers who value products for both their usefulness and public-relations benefits. For example, several cities in the United States banned police use of facial recognition after 2020.[14] Thus, businesses may have a vested interest in designing, developing, and deploying accurate, safe, and unbiased AI tools. In fact, the users and consumers of AI-powered software and online platforms are more likely to share data, engage with the tools, and spend money on them if they trust the underlying AI.[15]

Alignment between business interests and values tells only part of the story, however. The notion that nonbinding principles can transform business practice has drawn criticism for ignoring the downsides of the soft-law approach.[16] AI companies may be indifferent to the values they claim to endorse or worse yet, may benefit from violating them.[17] To give an example: There is good reason to believe that inaccurate, violent, or hateful content may hurt a social media platform's bottom line by scaring away users, advertisers, and investors, but it is also well-known that incendiary content drives up engagement.[18] Thus, the rational course of action for a social media company may be to retain as much of the engagement-maximizing content as possible without triggering a public scandal that would push away users, advertisers and investors in droves. This is hardly a case of clear business value alignment.

12 Will Parker and Konrad Putzier, "What Went Wrong with Zillow? A Real-Estate Algorithm Derailed Its Big Bet," *The Wall Street Journal*, November 17, 2021 (www.wsj.com/articles/zillow-offers-real-estate-algorithm-homes-ibuyer-11637159261).

13 Kate Notopoulos, "A Car Dealership Added an AI Chatbot to Its Site. Then All Hell Broke Loose," *Business Insider*, December 18, 2023 (www.businessinsider.com/car-dealership-chevrolet-chatbot-chatgpt-pranks-chevy-2023-12).

14 It should be noted that the rate at which law enforcement agencies abandon these tools slowed down in later years. Tate Ryan-Mosley, "The Movement to Limit Face Recognition Tech Might Finally Get a Win," *MIT Technology Review*, July 20, 2023 (www.technologyreview.com/2023/07/20/1076539/face-recognition-massachusetts-test-police/).

15 Aguirre et al., "AI Loyalty."

16 Calo, "Artificial Intelligence and the Carousel of Soft Law."

17 Vaidhyanathan, *Antisocial Media: How Facebook Disconnects and Undermines Democracy*; Metcalf, "Owning Ethics: Corporate Logics, Silicon Valley, and the Institutionalization of Ethics."

18 Ghosh, "It's All in the Business Model."

Even if deploying a high-quality product is a business advantage, the cost of doing so may lead to misalignment between a company's practices and socially desirable outcomes. Businesses are under pressure to beat their competitors. The AI sector is one where the hype around innovation and quick launch of products is particularly strong.[19] What is more, the training datasets in fields like image recognition and natural language processing typically come from whatever information AI companies can get their hands on. Since high-quality data tend to be expensive, businesses likely weigh the advantages of launching the best product by ensuring data quality and output accuracy while avoiding technical machine learning problems like overfitting and underfitting against the costs of doing so. The cost-benefit analysis may conclude in favor of using low-quality data.[20] All in all, it is plausible that businesses incentivize in-house and outside researchers to find potential risks arising from AI components early on to avoid future headaches, but it is also plausible that they would hope to avoid costly safety and responsibility measures.

While the case of misalignment between ethical conduct and business interest cannot be overstated, it is worth acknowledging that businesses are not uniform actors and that internal conflict over interests and values is to be expected. The marketing team may not see eye-to-eye with the compliance team; the board and the management may not always agree on strategic priorities; and workers in a business may not feel comfortable with what the board and management ask them to do. Even if the resolution of such conflict is unlikely to be democratic in the hierarchical format of the modern corporation, there have been noteworthy instances of worker discontent forcing businesses to change course of action (e.g., Google abandoning the Maven project in 2018) or risk unwanted public attention (e.g., Meta after whistleblower allegations in 2021). Protest over unethical conduct depends largely on tech workers' leverage vis-à-vis their employers.

Opening the black box of a business is important for another reason. Most corporations have officers and teams in charge of legal compliance as well as teams dedicated to ethical conduct. Ideally, employees tasked with compliance and ethics should persuade company owners, boards of directors, executives, and team leaders that legal and ethical considerations should guide business practice. This raises the likelihood that they are at constant risk of being instrumentalized for public relations campaigns, sidelined, or outright dismissed. Nonetheless, these employees occupy a place in today's business landscape. Highly publicized examples of employee discontent, such as the one that resulted in Google's dismissal of AI ethics team co-lead Timnit Gebru in late 2020, suggest that individuals and teams in charge of the safe and responsible development of AI systems take professional risks by pushing back against the unequal power dynamic inside businesses. Even if they lose more often than not, their agency should not be ignored.

19 Kerr, Barry, and Kelleher, "Expectations of Artificial Intelligence and the Performativity of Ethics."
20 Barocas and Selbst, "Big Data's Disparate Impact."

IMPLEMENTING ETHICAL BUSINESS PRINCIPLES: ADVISORY BODIES AND RESPONSIBLE TECHNOLOGY TEAMS

The proliferation of products using AI technology, coupled with the extremely slow development of legal responses, has led to growing interest in soft-law approaches to AI ethics. Gutierrez and Marchant list 634 soft-law programs relevant to AI concerns in 2021. They find that almost all of these programs have originated after 2015, mostly in the United States and other industrialized countries. Governmental entities account for over one-third of all programs, followed by the private sector, non-profits, and joint efforts. About 79 percent of the programs are strategy or principles documents, while slightly over 9 percent are standards, 3 percent professional guidelines or codes of conduct, and under 2 percent voluntary moratoria or bans.[21]

A 2023 survey of 75 businesses finds that responsible AI management is generally seen as an important practice driving product quality, competitiveness, trustworthiness, risk regulation, corporate value, and employee relations.[22] Risk and harm assessment appears to be the most popular management mechanism among respondents, followed by the designation of persons and units tasked with responsible AI management and the adoption of AI ethics principles, internal committees, and internal policies. Delegating power to an external board is, perhaps not surprisingly, much less common. Despite growing business attention to responsible AI, however, the same survey also finds that most companies are slow at the implementation stage, and have adopted a sporadic, rather than systematic, approach to responsible AI management.[23]

Since 2017, leading technology companies have established *internal* or *external* panels, called *boards* or *councils*, in charge of ensuring adherence to ethical and responsible technology principles.[24] A few of the boards and councils are *AI-specific* (e.g., Axon's AI Ethics Board), whereas others deal with broader concerns, such as content moderation, that often intersect with AI (e.g., Meta's Oversight Board). In addition, various companies count on responsible or safe AI *teams* that work internally to advise the leadership and workers.

The institutional design and powers of these bodies have been a source of debate. Leaders of companies have often given assurances that such bodies, internal or external, would enjoy operational autonomy. It is worth noting, however, that none of these boards can veto projects or require major changes in a company's practices or

[21] Gutierrez and Marchant, "Soft Law 2.0: Incorporating Incentives and Implementation Mechanisms into the Governance of Artificial Intelligence."

[22] Hirsch, Ott, and Westover-Munoz, "Responsible AI Management: Evolving Practice, Growing Value."

[23] Hirsch, Ott, and Westover-Munoz.

[24] Veale, Matus, and Gorwa, "AI and Global Governance: Modalities, Rationales, Tensions."

TABLE 5.1 *AI Ethics Boards and Councils*

Name	Company	Type	AI-specific	Active
AI Ethics Board	Axon	External advisor	Yes	2018–2022
Ethics & Equity Advisory Council	Axon	Hybrid advisor	No	2022–
Advanced Technology External Advisory Council	Google	External advisor	No	2019–2019
AI Ethics Board	Google/DeepMind	Internal advisor	Yes	Unknown
Ethics and Society research group	Google/DeepMind	Internal team	No	2017–
Responsible Innovation Team (RESIN)	Google	Internal team	No	2018–2024
Institutional Review Committee	Google/DeepMind	Internal advisor	No	2022–
Oversight Board	Meta	External advisor and adjudicator	No	2020–
Responsible Innovation Team	Meta	Internal team	No	2018–2022
Responsible AI (RAI) Team	Meta	Internal team	Yes	2019–2023
Aether Committee	Microsoft	Internal team	Yes	2017–
The Fairness, Accountability, Transparency & Ethics (FATE) in AI	Microsoft	Internal team	Yes	2017–
Office of Responsible AI	Microsoft	Internal team	Yes	2019–
Ethics & Society Team	Microsoft	Internal team	No	2020–2023
Responsible AI Council	Microsoft	Internal advisor	Yes	2023–
Partnership on AI to Benefit People and Society	Multiple businesses	Inter-institutional advisor	Yes	2016–
Trust & Safety Council	Twitter (now X)	External advisor	No	2016–2022

business model.[25] Likewise, none of them can coerce a non-compliant company to change its course. Meta's Oversight Board, intentionally designed as a quasi-judicial body, comes closest to issuing binding decisions and its content moderation decisions have usually been heeded. However, even that body relies on Meta's voluntary compliance (and funding) for its efficacy. In fact, even if not in name, these bodies tend to be advisory in character, as they make non-binding recommendations for case-by-case or comprehensive change. Thus, this chapter codes them as either *advisors* or *teams*, with the exception of Meta's Oversight Board, which serves as both *adjudicator* and *advisor* (see Table 5.1).

Much has been said about these bodies' ability to effect change. Ideally, they can force companies to act more ethically by exposing the gaps between stated ethics principles and practice. They can be said to fill the regulatory gap, albeit

[25] Green, "The Contestation of Tech Ethics"; Seah and Findlay, "Communicating Ethics across the AI Ecosystem."

imperfectly, at a time when binding legislation is non-existent or too slow to adapt to technological change. A much more common view is that at best, these boards fail to change company behavior and, at worst, serve as a façade for companies to look ethical while avoiding binding legal regulation.[26]

Axon's AI Ethics Board and Ethics and Equity Advisory Council

Axon's (formerly TASER International) eight-member AI Ethics Board, created in April 2018, was the first of its kind. The substantive issues at the Board's semiannual meetings were the impact of AI-assisted policing on communities, given the company's focus on technology for law enforcement.[27] New York University School of Law's Policing Project played a key role in facilitating the Board's research and publications, and the Project's Founder and Faculty Director Barry Friedman served on the Board.[28]

The Policing Project's website documents the Board's impact on company behavior between 2019 and 2022.[29] Axon decided not to pursue pattern-matching products following the concerns and recommendations about the underlying technology voiced in the Board's 2019 report. In 2020, the Board published a report on the risks of automated license plate readers soon after Axon declared its intention to produce these policing tools.[30]

Axon's decision to produce taser-equipped drones to be installed in public spaces to allegedly deter mass shootings (a decision that was announced less than a week after the Robb Elementary School shooting in Uvalde, Texas, on May 24, 2022) broke the relationship between the company and the Board. On June 6, 2022, nine members resigned, citing an eight-to-four decision of the Board recommending that Axon not proceed with a pilot study (also known as "Project ION") of taser-equipped drones. The last sentence of their statement reads, "We have lost faith in Axon's ability to be a responsible partner."[31] Axon suspended the production of taser-equipped drones at the time, but a report from September 2023 suggests that the company leadership wanted to revisit the project of producing armed drones.[32]

26 Fabbri, "Social Influence for Societal Interest"; Conti and Seele, "The Contested Role of AI Ethics Boards in Smart Societies"; Marietje Schaake, "Big Tech calls for 'regulation' but is fuzzy on the details," *Financial Times*, July 26, 2021 (www.ft.com/content/a0a7f8de-f365-4e4e-a755-284df91c6e3a).

27 James Vincent and Russell Brandom, "Axon Launches AI Ethics Board to Study the Dangers of Facial Recognition," *The Verge*, April 26, 2018 (www.theverge.com/2018/4/26/17285034/axon-ai-ethics-board-facial-recognition-racial-bias).

28 Policing Project, "Axon AI Ethics Board" (www.policingproject.org/axon-ethics-board).

29 Cihon, Schuett, and Baum, "Corporate Governance of Artificial Intelligence in the Public Interest."

30 www.policingproject.org/axon-ethics-board

31 "Statement of Resigning Axon AI Ethics Board Members," June 6, 2022 (www.policingproject.org/statement-of-resigning-axon-ai-ethics-board-members).

32 Ese Olumhense, "Axon's Ethics Board Resigned Over Taser-Armed Drones. Then the Company Bought a Military Drone Maker," *Wired*, September 8, 2023 (www.wired.com/story/axon-taser-drones-ethics-board).

Soon after the resignation of nine Board members, Axon announced the formation of two new bodies, one in the United States and one in the United Kingdom, both called the Ethics & Equity Advisory Council (EEAC). Like the former Board, the Councils are designed as external bodies, but unlike the fully externally staffed Board, the US version of EEAC is led by Axon's Vice President of Community Impact. The two Councils are tasked to provide "feedback and recommendations on a limited number of products per year, and not Axon's complete product line."[33] Axon's website claims that the EEAC meets once a month and works with product teams to provide routine feedback at the product design stage.[34] One piece of publicly available information about the EEAC is its role in improving Draft One, a new software tool that drafts police report narratives based on auto-transcribed body-worn camera audio. Reportedly, the EEAC assessed the tool for "word choice selection, draft quality and potential racial bias," and provided feedback to establish default settings.[35] According to its Year End Report, the EEAC reviewed six products in 2023 and assisted product teams.[36] The report does not provide details on the conclusions of product reviews.

Google and DeepMind: Ethics and Society Research Group, and Institutional Review Board

The most famous AI ethics board that Google had was the one that it didn't. The Advanced Technology External Advisory Council (ATEAC), which would have served as an external advisory panel, was cancelled within days of its inauguration in April 2019.[37] The reason appears to be the public outcry over the inclusion of Kay Coles James, then president of the Heritage Foundation, on the Council as a way to reach out to right-wing constituencies. A group called Googlers Against Transphobia and Hate initiated a petition campaign, signed by 2,556 Google employees, to remove her.[38] Instead, Google shut the entire Council down.[39] AI and data privacy

33 www.axon.com/eeac

34 "Axon's New Ethics and Equity Advisory Council to Deliver Input from Community Voices on the Development of Public Safety Technologies," *Press releases* (Axon), September 1, 2022 (https://investor.axon.com/2022-09-01-Axons-New-Ethics-and-Equity-Advisory-Council-to-Deliver-Input-from-Community-Voices-on-the-Development-of-Public-Safety-Technologies); "The future of public safety technology: innovating through robotic security," *Resources* (Axon website), April 6, 2023 (www.axon.com/resources/the-future-of-public-safety-technology-innovating-through-robotic-security).

35 "Axon reports Q1 2024 revenue of $461 million, up 34% year over year, raises outlook," May 6, 2024 (https://investor.axon.com/2024-05-06-Axon-reports-Q1-2024-revenue-of-461-million,-up-34-year-over-year,-raises-outlook).

36 Ethics and Equity Advisory Council, *2023 Year End Report* (https://a.storyblok.com/f/198504/x/2461abae95/eeac_2023-ye-report.pdf).

37 https://blog.google/technology/ai/external-advisory-council-help-advance-responsible-development-ai/

38 https://medium.com/@against.transphobia/googlers-against-transphobia-and-hate-b1b0a5dbf76

39 Richard Waters, "Google Scraps Ethics Council for Artificial Intelligence," *Financial Times*, April 4, 2019 (www.ft.com/content/6e2912f8-573e-11e9-91f9-b6515a54c5b1).

experts trusted by academic and activist communities, like Alessandro Acquisti (who had already resigned before Google's decision to disband the Council), Joanna Bryson,[40] and Luciano Floridi found themselves explaining why they had joined, knowing that James would be their colleague.[41] The inclusion of Dyan Gibbens, CEO of military and energy company Trumbull Unmanned, also raised questions at the time, though the outrage over James appears to have dominated the media cycle. Google did not attempt to revive the ATEAC.

In 2014, Google acquired DeepMind, a company whose stated mission is to build Artificial General Intelligence (AGI). DeepMind executives agreed to the acquisition after signing an "Ethics and Safety Review Agreement."[42] Accordingly, an ethics board would have been set up to make sure DeepMind had effective control over the development of AI. At the time of the acquisition, Google had agreed to the creation of an AI Ethics Board inside DeepMind, whose spokespersons kept confirming the existence of such an internal board without publicizing the names of board members.[43] Little else is known about how the board functioned, however.[44] What is publicly known about DeepMind's AI ethics approach is that it has devoted resources to AI safety research since 2017. The definition of safety appears to prioritize future AGI scenarios at the expense of current AI risks and harms.[45]

DeepMind also established the Ethics and Society research group in October 2017 to explore the impact of AI on society.[46] The group's tasks are to "help technologists put ethics into practice, and to help society anticipate and direct the impact of AI so

[40] For Bryson's reflection on her decision to join the Council and the events that followed, see Joanna Bryson, "What We Lost When We Lost Google ATEAC," *Adventures in NI* (blog), April 7, 2019 (https://joanna-bryson.blogspot.com/2019/04/what-we-lost-when-we-lost-google-ateac.html).

[41] Kelsey Piper, "Exclusive: Google Cancels AI Ethics Board in Response to Outcry," *Vox*, April 4, 2019 (www.vox.com/future-perfect/2019/4/4/18295933/google-cancels-ai-ethics-board).

[42] Sam Shead, "DeepMind's Mysterious Ethics Board Will Reportedly 'Control' AGI If It's Ever Created," *Forbes*, March 14, 2019 (www.forbes.com/sites/samshead/2019/03/14/deepminds-mysterious-ethics-board-will-reportedly-control-agi-if-its-ever-created).

[43] Alex Hern, "Whatever Happened to the DeepMind AI Ethics Board Google Promised?" *The Guardian*, January 26, 2017 (www.theguardian.com/technology/2017/jan/26/google-deepmind-ai-ethics-board).

[44] DeepMind's broader ethics landscape is just as secretive: DeepMind Health, established in 2016, initially had a Panel of Independent Reviewers, which was disbanded in April 2019. Tang, "Independent AI Ethics Committees and ESG Corporate Reporting on AI as Emerging Corporate and AI Governance Trends."; Parmy Olson, "Google Quietly Disbanded Another AI Review Board Following Disagreements," *The Wall Street Journal*, April 16, 2019 (www.wsj.com/articles/google-quietly-disbanded-another-ai-review-board-following-disagreements-11555250401). Hal Hodson, "DeepMind and Google: The Battle to Control Artificial Intelligence," *1843 Magazine (The Economist)*, March 1, 2019 (www.economist.com/1843/2019/03/01/deepmind-and-google-the-battle-to-control-artificial-intelligence); Sam Shead, "The Biggest Mystery in AI Right Now is the Ethics board that Google Set Up after Buying DeepMind," *Business Insider*, March 26, 2016 (www.businessinsider.com/google-ai-ethics-board-remains-a-mystery-2016-3); Asaro, "Politicizing Data."

[45] https://deepai.org/profile/shane-legg

[46] DeepMind's website does not have specific information on the Ethics and Society research group, but information on its safety and ethics teams can be found at www.deepmind.com/safety-and-ethics.

that it works for the benefit of all"[47] by conducting open-access AI ethics research.[48] The researchers working at Ethics and Society have contributed to scholarship on various facets of AI. However, the Ethics and Society group is not an advisory board and is not designed to work with product teams. It has been suggested that the group was designed as a weaker version of what an AI ethics board would have been.[49] It is also worth noting that information about the research group cannot be found on DeepMind's website. CEO Demis Hassabis once stated that DeepMind's ethics structures have "evolved" since the acquisition by Google, but beyond this generic acknowledgment, little is known about the company's self-regulatory bodies.[50]

The Institutional Review Committee (IRC) is DeepMind's internal ethics board, chaired by Chief Operating Officer Lila Ibrahim. It meets once every two weeks to evaluate DeepMind projects, papers, and collaborations.[51] Dorothy Chou, head of public affairs at Google DeepMind, notes that the publication of a 2021 paper on language modeling at scale was delayed due to feedback from the IRC to assess the taxonomy of risks.[52] Likewise, AlphaFold was released after IRC endorsement.[53] Thus, the IRC appears to have exerted some influence on the company's conduct.

Google's own AI ethics principles came on the heels of public criticism and employee discontent over the leadership's plans to collaborate with the US military.[54] CEO Sundar Pichai released AI principles on June 7, 2018, which, among other things, promised not to develop or deploy AI for harmful technologies, weapons, surveillance tools, and technologies that contravene international law and human rights.[55] Despite the assurances, however, 2018 and 2019 were tumultuous years, marked by employee

47 Verity Harding and Sean Legassick, "Why We Launched DeepMind Ethics & Society," Oct. 3, 2017 (www.deepmind.com/blog/why-we-launched-deepmind-ethics-society).

48 James Temperton, "DeepMind's new AI ethics unit is the company's next big move," *Wired*, October 4, 2017 (www.wired.co.uk/article/deepmind-ethics-and-society-artificial-intelligence).

49 Alex Hern, "DeepMind Announces Ethics Group to Focus on Problems of AI," *The Guardian*, October 4, 2017 (www.theguardian.com/technology/2017/oct/04/google-deepmind-ai-artificial-intelligence-ethics-group-problems).

50 Billy Perrigo, "DeepMind's CEO Helped Take AI Mainstream. Now He's Urging Caution," *Time*, January 12, 2023 (https://time.com/6246119/demis-hassabis-deepmind-interview/).

51 Koray Kavukcuoglu, Pushmeet Kohli, Lila Ibrahim, Dawn Bloxwich, Sasha Brown, "How our principles helped define AlphaFold's release," *Blog* (DeepMind), September 14, 2022 (https://deepmind.google/discover/blog/how-our-principles-helped-define-alphafolds-release/).

52 Dorothy Chou, "AI Companies Aren't Afraid of Regulation – We Want it to be International and Inclusive," *The Guardian*, August 4, 2023 (www.theguardian.com/commentisfree/2023/aug/04/ai-companies-regulation-international-inclusive).

53 Koray Kavukcuoglu, Pushmeet Kohli, Lila Ibrahim, Dawn Bloxwich, Sasha Brown, "How Our Principles Helped Define AlphaFold's Release," *Blog* (DeepMind), September 14, 2022 (https://deepmind.google/discover/blog/how-our-principles-helped-define-alphafolds-release/).

54 Editorial, "The Guardian View on the Ethics of AI: It's about Dr Frankenstein, Not His Monster," *The Guardian*, June 12, 2018 (www.theguardian.com/commentisfree/2018/jun/12/the-guardian-view-on-the-ethics-of-ai-its-about-dr-frankenstein-not-his-monster).

55 Sundar Pichai, "AI at Google: Our Principles," *Google blog*, June 7, 2018 (https://blog.google/technology/ai/ai-principles/).

protests over sexual misconduct within the company and the Pentagon deal and accusations of retaliation against protest organizers.[56] One of the longer lasting products of the AI principles was the creation of the Responsible Innovation team (RESIN),[57] which reviewed internal projects' compliance with the principles from 2018 until its dissolution, alongside the machine learning privacy team, in 2024.[58]

Google is also home to the most storied fallout in the history of AI ethics. On December 2, 2020, Timnit Gebru, a co-lead of the AI ethics team, announced that her employment had been terminated because she and her co-authors refused to withdraw a research paper called "On the Dangers of Stochastic Parrots: Can Language Models Be Too Big?" that described the risks of LLMs. Gebru's announcement drew quick reactions from AI researchers and Google workers. A total of 2,695 Google employees and 4,302 "academic, industry, and civil society supporters" joined a letter supporting Gebru.[59] As the explanation offered by Jeff Dean, Google's head of AI research, failed to convince critics, on December 9, Google CEO Sundar Pichai apologized for the way Gebru's employment had been terminated and promised that he would investigate the incident.[60] Two months later, Google dismissed Margaret Mitchell, a co-author of "Stochastic Parrots" for allegedly moving files outside the company in her effort to document email incidents of discriminatory behavior toward Gebru.[61] Meanwhile, Google assigned AI ethics research to its vice president.[62]

All in all, Google and DeepMind have failed to set up durable and transparent internal or external business self-regulation bodies and adopted a punitive approach to internal dissent. The only exception to this trend is DeepMind's Institutional Review Committee, which has reportedly exerted some degree of efficacy. In more recent times, Google's quiet removal of AI principles in February 2025 has left commentators wondering about the future of self-regulation at the company.[63]

56 Kate Cox, "Google Fires Four Employees at Center of Worker Organization Efforts," *Ars Technica*, November 26, 2019 (https://arstechnica.com/tech-policy/2019/11/firing-of-four-google-employees-is-retaliatory-activists-say/).

57 Alfred NG, "Google Makes Changes to Privacy Oversight, Worrying Policymakers," *Politico*, July 11, 2024 (www.politico.com/news/2024/07/11/google-privacy-oversight-changes-worry-congress-00167427).

58 "Google Restructures Its Responsible AI Innovation Team," *DigWatch*, February 2, 2024 (https://dig.watch/updates/google-restructures-its-responsible-ai-innovation-team).

59 Google Walkout for Real Change, "Standing with Dr. Timnit Gebru – #ISupportTimnit #BelieveBlackWomen," *Medium*, December 3, 2020 (https://googlewalkout.medium.com/standing-with-dr-timnit-gebru-isupporttimnit-believeblackwomen-6dadc300d382).

60 Ina Fried, "Scoop: Google CEO Pledges to Investigate Exit of Top AI Ethicist," *Axios*, December 9, 2020 (www.axios.com/2020/12/09/sundar-pichai-memo-timnit-gebru-exit).

61 "Margaret Mitchell: Google Fires AI Ethics Founder," *BBC*, February 20, 2021 (www.bbc.com/news/technology-56135817).

62 Khari Johnson, "Google's New AI Ethics Lead Calls for More 'Diplomatic' Conversation," *VentureBeat*, February 18, 2021 (https://venturebeat.com/business/googles-new-ai-ethics-lead-calls-for-more-diplomatic-conversation/).

63 "Google Lifts a Ban on Using Its AI for Weapons and Surveillance," *Wired*, February 24, 2025 (www.wired.com/story/google-responsible-ai-principles).

Meta: Oversight Board, Responsible Innovation Team, and Responsible AI Team

Facebook was among the pioneers of business self-regulation: It had established a Safety Advisory Board as early as 2009. Yet, multiple scandals that rocked Facebook in the 2010s must have generated the push for an external board. The Oversight Board, approved by co-founder and CEO Mark Zuckerberg in November 2018, is funded through a $130 million trust by Meta. It has twenty-one members, consisting of an international group of legal professionals, journalists, and former politicians. Although little is known about compensation, board membership is reportedly a well-paid position.[64] The Board has published 118 case decisions and four policy advisory opinions about Facebook and Instagram between January 28, 2021, and April 15, 2025.[65] As an "independent adjudicatory body,"[66] its main goal is to serve as an appellate institution for the public to contest content removal decisions, and its design reflects an intentional imitation of high courts. Commentators compare it to the US Supreme Court to describe its structure and goals.[67]

The Board takes cases referred to it by the company or the public. Meta's community standards and human rights norms constitute its normative parameters. The procedure for decision-making involves a first-round deliberation by a five-person panel, followed by a plenary vote; however, the popularity of content moderation appeals led the Board to announce an expedited, small-panel decision-making procedure in February 2023.[68]

The Board has often countered Meta's internal content moderation decisions: 81 of the 100 single-issue cases decided by the Board between January 2021 and April 2025 overturned Meta and 19 upheld it. Meta has in principle agreed to comply with the Board's content moderation rulings, while the company interprets the Board's advisory opinions as non-binding.[69] Nonetheless, the Board's website claims that 60 percent of the recommendations have been "implemented or in progress." Upholding the ban on Donald J. Trump, imposed right after the January 6 riots to overturn the 2020 presidential election, is arguably the Board's most debated decision in the United States. That ruling, delivered on May 19, 2021, asks Meta to reconsider Trump's indefinite suspension and calls for a permanent standard for

64 Schuett, Reuel, and Carlier, "How to Design an AI Ethics Board."

65 https://oversightboard.com

66 Klonick, "The Facebook Oversight Board: Creating an Independent Institution to Adjudicate Online Free Expression."

67 Veale, Matus, and Gorwa, "AI and Global Governance: Modalities, Rationales, Tensions."

68 Sheila Dang, "Meta Oversight Board to Begin Reviewing Cases More Quickly," *Reuters*, February 14, 2023.

69 Cecilia Kang, "What is the Facebook Oversight Board?" *The New York Times*, May 5, 2021 (www.nytimes.com/2021/05/05/technology/What-Is-the-Facebook-Oversight-Board.html). The FAQ section of Facebook's Transparency Center refers to content decisions as binding and recommendations as non-binding (https://transparency.fb.com/oversight/further-asked-questions/).

suspensions. That latter is interpreted as a rejection of Meta's undue delegation of rule-making responsibility to the Board.[70]

Other notable decisions include the recommendation in December 2022 that Meta overhaul its "cross-check" system that offers users with a high number of followers preferential treatment in content moderation,[71] the recommendation in January 2023 that it revise its standards on adult nude photos,[72] a recommendation to take down the Cambodian prime minister's Facebook and Instagram accounts for inciting violence,[73] and another recommendation in late 2023 to reinstate two videos, one featuring hostages taken by Hamas and another one showing Palestinian civilians murdered in an Israeli airstrike.[74] In October 2023, the Board began a probe into a manipulated video of then US President Joe Biden, which Facebook's content moderation had chosen not to take down.

The Oversight Board is focused more on substantive content than on the algorithms recommending content or friends. Its work nonetheless intersects with AI. It hears appeals of content moderation decisions, some of which were made by algorithms. In addition, content moderation has become a major concern for Facebook and Instagram because their recommender algorithms amplify inaccurate or violent content. Meta released new guidelines on labeling AI-generated fake speech and imagery in May 2024.[75] Despite the intersections between its mandate and AI-driven content generation and amplification, however, the Board does not have the authority to audit the algorithms. In fact, Ronaldo Lemos, one of the Board members, has raised concern about the separation of content moderation decisions and the algorithms.[76] Similarly, the Board cannot issue decisions about another key component of the company's algorithmic curation, namely Facebook groups.

Meta's Oversight Board is arguably the most serious attempt by a major social media company to set content moderation standards. Its quasi-judicial structure

70 Kevin Roose, "Facebook's 'Supreme Court' Tells Zuckerberg He's the Decider," *The New York Times*, May 6, 2021 (www.nytimes.com/2021/05/06/technology/facebook-oversight-board-trump.html).

71 Adam Satariano and Sheera Frankel, "Oversight Board Criticizes Meta for Preferential Treatment," *The New York Times*, December 6, 2022 (www.nytimes.com/2022/12/06/technology/meta-preferential-treatment.html).

72 Maya King, "Instagram and Facebook Should Update Nude Photo Rules, Meta Board Says," *The New York Times*, January 20, 2023 (www.nytimes.com/2023/01/20/technology/meta-nudity-standards-overhaul.html).

73 Regine Cabato and Rebecca Tan, "Meta Oversight Board calls for Cambodian leader's accounts to be suspended," *The Washington Post*, June 29, 2023 (www.washingtonpost.com/world/2023/06/29/meta-hun-sen-cambodia-suspended-accounts/).

74 Blake Montgomery and agencies, "Meta Wrong to Remove Graphic Israel-Gaza Videos, Oversight Board Says," *The Guardian*, December 19, 2023 (www.theguardian.com/technology/2023/dec/19/facebook-moderation-israel-hamas-videos).

75 Megan Morrone, "How Big Tech labels AI," *Axios*, May 6, 2024 (www.axios.com/2024/05/06/how-big-tech-labels-ai).

76 Katya Maruri, "Facebook Oversight Board Upholds Decision to "Deplatform" Trump," *Government Technology*, May 6, 2021 (www.govtech.com/policy/facebook-oversight-board-upholds-decision-to-deplatform-trump).

and high-profile membership give it the gravitas that Meta needed to project after the scandal-ridden 2010s. The Board has not convinced many critics, however.[77] Reporters Without Borders notes that Facebook's community standards, which provide the parameters for the Board, may not be aligned with international standards for the freedom of expression.[78] A number of journalists, academics, and activists established their own board, called the Real Facebook Oversight Board, a month before the 2020 US presidential election. The alternative board has criticized Facebook for not tackling "disinformation super-spreaders" regarding the COVID-19 pandemic, US elections, or climate change, offering temporary fixes during emergency situations while refusing to alter the algorithms that promote incendiary and hateful content every day, and ultimately, maintaining the business model that encourages algorithmic amplification for profit.[79]

According to an in-depth analysis of its institutional design, the Board's ability to enhance the transparency of content moderation decisions and processes, efficacy in influencing policy reform through policy recommendations, and assertiveness in overruling Meta in content moderation decisions should be noted. However, its limited jurisdiction, limited impact, and lack of geographic, gender, and disability status diversity stand out as weaknesses.[80] The Achilles' heel from an AI governance standpoint is the lack of authority to rule on ads, algorithms or groups.[81] Recommendations serve as targeted interventions for specific content rather than as

77 Caroline Crystal, "Facebook, Telegram, and the Ongoing Struggle Against Online Hate Speech," *Carnegie Endowment for International Peace*, September 7, 2023 (https://carnegieendowment.org/research/2023/09/facebook-telegram-and-the-ongoing-struggle-against-online-hate-speech).

78 Reporters Without Borders, "Facebook's Oversight Board Is an Important First Step, but Questions Abound" (https://rsf.org/en/facebooks-oversight-board-important-first-step-questions-abound).

79 Heidi Beirich and Jessica J. González, "Repeating Facebook History, Meta Is Courting an Election 2022 Disaster," *USA Today*, October 28, 2022 (www.usatoday.com/story/opinion/2022/10/28/facebook-courts-misinformation-disaster-election-2022/10546288002/); Kari Paul, "Climate Misinformation on Facebook 'Increasing Substantially,' Study Says," The Guardian, November 4, 2021 (www.theguardian.com/technology/2021/nov/04/climate-misinformation-on-facebook-increasing-substantially-study-says); Nora Benavidez and Kate Coyer, "Facebook Ought to be Protecting Democracy Worldwide Every Day," The Boston Globe, April 14, 2022 (www.bostonglobe.com/2022/04/12/opinion/facebook-ought-be-protecting-democracy-worldwide-every-day/); Marietje Schaake, "Looming Trump Ban Ruling Is a Distraction from Facebook's Real Oversight Crisis," USA Today, March 4, 2021 (www.usatoday.com/story/opinion/2021/03/04/facebook-ban-trump-oversight-board-responsibility-column/6820842002/-disaster-election-2022/10546288002/); Kari Paul, "Climate Misinformation on Facebook 'Increasing Substantially,' Study Says," The Guardian, November 4, 2021 (www.theguardian.com/technology/2021/nov/04/climate-misinformation-on-facebook-increasing-substantially-study-says); Nora Benavidez and Kate Coyer, "Facebook Ought to be Protecting Democracy Worldwide Every Day," The Boston Globe, April 14, 2022 (www.bostonglobe.com/2022/04/12/opinion/facebook-ought-be-protecting-democracy-worldwide-every-day/); Marietje Schaake, "Looming Trump Ban Ruling Is a Distraction from Facebook's Real Oversight Crisis," USA Today, March 4, 2021 (www.usatoday.com/story/opinion/2021/03/04/facebook-ban-trump-oversight-board-responsibility-column/6820842002/).

80 Wong and Floridi, "Meta's Oversight Board."

81 Steven Levy, "Inside Meta's Oversight Board: 2 Years of Pushing Limits," *Wired*, November 8, 2022 (www.wired.com/story/inside-metas-oversight-board-two-years-of-pushing-limits/).

an impetus for behavior change.[82] Further limiting the Board's authority is the non-binding nature of its recommendations. To give examples: Meta simply ignored the Board's recommendation to conduct an audit of inconsistently enforced policies against the marketing and sale of illegal or recreational drugs,[83] and Facebook decided not to suspend Cambodia's former Prime Minister Hun Sen's account despite the Board's recommendation to do so.[84]

During a US Senate Committee on Commerce, Science and Transportation hearing in October 2021, Facebook whistleblower Frances Haugen had this to say about Big Tech companies: "They have 100 percent control over their algorithms and Facebook should not get a free pass on choices it makes to prioritize growth and virality and reactiveness over public safety. They shouldn't get a free pass on that because they're paying for their profits right now with our safety."[85] Vocal complaints about content have made social media companies, especially Meta, somewhat responsive to takedown requests, but the underlying algorithms remain beyond the pale.[86] Thus, the Board's impact on Meta's decision-making remains limited at best.[87]

The Board was not Meta's only body in charge of technology ethics. The Responsible Innovation Team was established in 2018. According to Margaret Stewart, the Vice President of Product Design at Meta, the team acted like a "general practitioner," preventing issues from arising in the first place and referring arising issues to specialists.[88] The team of about twenty engineers and ethicists was disbanded in September 2022.[89] Meta also converted its Society and AI Lab into the Responsible AI (RAI) team, only to disband it in November 2023.[90] Journalistic reporting suggests a tendency to ignore that team's research on misinformation,

82 Bietti, "From Ethics Washing to Ethics Bashing"; Alpsancar, "What Is AI Ethics? Ethics as Means of Self-Regulation and the Need for Critical Reflection."

83 Tiffany Kary and Aisha Counts, "Meta to Ignore Ethics Board's Advice on Drug-Post Oversight," *The Boston Globe*, October 26, 2023 (www.bostonglobe.com/2023/10/26/business/meta-ignore-ethics-boards-advice-drug-post-oversight/).

84 Regine Cabato, "Meta Rejects Own Board's Request to Suspend Account of Cambodian Strongman," *The Washington Post*, August 30, 2023 (www.washingtonpost.com/world/2023/08/30/meta-cambodia-facebook-hun-sen/).

85 Shannon Bond, "Facebook Whistleblower Testifies before a Senate Panel," *NPR*, October 5, 2021 (www.npr.org/2021/10/05/1043458047/facebook-whistleblower-testifies-before-a-senate-panel).

86 Elizabeth Culliford, "Analysis: If Facebook Is the Problem, Is a Social Media Regulator the Fix?" *Reuters*, October 6, 2021 (www.reuters.com/technology/if-facebook-is-problem-is-social-media-regulator-fix-2021-10-06/).

87 An April 2024 plan to lay off staffers may limit the Board's capacity even further. Naomi Nix, "Meta's Oversight Body Prepares to Lay Off Workers," *The Washington Post*, April 29, 2024 (www.washingtonpost.com/technology/2024/04/29/meta-oversight-board-layoffs/).

88 Margaret Stewart, "Breadth & Depth: Why I'm Optimistic about Facebook's Responsible Innovation Efforts," *Tech at Meta*, June 17, 2021 (https://tech.facebook.com/ideas/2021/06/responsible-innovation/).

89 Cristina Criddle and Madhumita Murgia, "Big Tech Companies Cut AI Ethics Staff, Raising Safety Concerns," *Financial Times*, March 28, 2023 (www.ft.com/content/26372287-6fb3-457b-9e9c-f722027f36b3).

90 Wes Davis, "Meta Disbanded Its Responsible AI team," *The Verge*, November 18, 2023 (www.theverge.com/2023/11/18/23966980/meta-disbanded-responsible-ai-team-artificial-intelligence).

extremism, and political polarization.[91] Thus, available evidence suggests that for all its limitations, the Oversight Board remains Meta's most serious effort to uphold ethical standards, while other efforts have produced little or no impact.

Microsoft: AI, Ethics and Effects in Engineering and Research (Aether) Committee, Fairness, Accountability, Transparency & Ethics in AI (FATE), Office of Responsible AI Ethics & Society Team

Microsoft's push for the institutionalization of responsible technology standards came on the heels of a scandal in March 2016, when a chatbot began to produce hate speech mere hours after its launch on Twitter.[92] Chief Executive Officer Satya Nadella's following address in June of the same year was a high-profile acknowledgment of responsible AI practices.[93] Since then, Microsoft has published guidelines, including its internal playbook called the Responsible AI Standard in 2021 (updated to version two a year later)[94] and supported a plethora of internal groups, interconnected through what one analysis calls a "hub-and-spoke" model.[95] The most notable of these groups are the AI, Ethics and Effects in Engineering and Research Committee (Aether), the Fairness, Accountability, Transparency & Ethics in AI (FATE), the Office of Responsible AI, and the Ethics & Society team, which operates under the Responsible AI Strategy in Engineering (RAISE). In addition, Microsoft has embedded domain experts in engineering and sales teams with its Responsible AI Champs program.

The Aether Committee was established in 2017 as an internal policymaking support body to conduct research and provide guidance to senior leadership on AI-related concerns.[96] A Microsoft publication says the Committee is set to "respond to specific issues as they arise."[97] Eric Horvitz, director of Microsoft Research Labs, once claimed that the Committee's reviews led the company to cut off "significant sales" and set rules on other transactions – without specifying which sales

91 Karen Hao, "How Facebook Got Addicted to Spreading Misinformation," *MIT Technology Review*, March 11, 2021 (www.technologyreview.com/2021/03/11/1020600/facebook-responsible-ai-misinformation).

92 Asha Barbaschow, "Microsoft and the Learnings from its Failed Tay Artificial Intelligence Bot," *ZDNet*, July 23, 2019 (www.zdnet.com/article/microsoft-and-the-learnings-from-its-failed-tay-artificial-intelligence-bot/).

93 Satya Nadella, "The Partnership of the Future," *Slate*, June 28, 2016. (https://slate.com/technology/2016/06/microsoft-ceo-satya-nadella-humans-and-a-i-can-work-together-to-solve-societys-challenges.html).

94 Microsoft, Responsible AI Standard, v2 (https://blogs.microsoft.com/wp-content/uploads/prod/sites/5/2022/06/Microsoft-Responsible-AI-Standard-v2-General-Requirements-3.pdf).

95 World Economic Forum, "Responsible Use of Technology: The Microsoft Case Study."

96 www.microsoft.com/en-us/ai/our-approach

97 Microsoft, *The Future Computed: Artificial Intelligence and Its Role in Society*, Microsoft Corporation, Redmond, Washington, USA. 2018 (https://blogs.microsoft.com/blog/2018/01/17/future-computed-artificial-intelligence-role-society/).

or transactions.[98] Another publicly acknowledged accomplishment of Aether was collaboration with Microsoft Research and the Responsible AI Team to develop Microsoft Video Authenticator, a deepfake detector.[99]

Findings of racial bias in facial recognition software, which led Microsoft to turn down a contract with a police department, is reportedly the reason for the creation of the Fairness, Accountability, Transparency & Ethics in AI (FATE), a research and development lab, in 2017.[100] Its website states that the aim is to "facilitate computational techniques that are both innovative and responsible, while prioritizing issues of fairness, accountability, transparency, and ethics as they relate to AI, ML, and NLP by drawing on fields with a sociotechnical orientation …"[101] FATE's website lists sixty-six publications between 2018 and 2024. In addition, three projects, namely Human-Centered Transparency & Intelligibility in AI, AI Fairness Checklist, and Data Documentation, appear on the website, but there is no information on how much those projects have been incorporated into Microsoft's operation.

Functioning as part of the Responsible AI Strategy in Engineering (RAISE) team, the Ethics & Society team was expected to bring a "design thinking approach" to ethics.[102] Its most visible product was the Responsible Innovation Practices Toolkit, launched in May 2020. The decision to discontinue the team raised eyebrows in March 2023, in part because it coincided with the company's ambitious approach to reinvigorating its products with the latest AI tools in partnership with OpenAI. The closure of the Ethics & Society team is justified by Microsoft on the grounds that they had already incorporated many of that team's members into user research and design teams and that the reorganization affected only seven employees.[103] Journalistic reporting suggests an alternative explanation: Even though Microsoft has not been lacking for responsible technology teams, the Ethics & Society team was uniquely well-placed to promote concrete changes in a way that, say the Office of Responsible AI, with its emphasis on developing rules and principles, was not.[104]

98 Alan Boyle, "Microsoft Is Turning Down Some Sales over AI Ethics, Top Researcher Eric Horvitz Says," *GeekWire*, April 9, 2018 (www.geekwire.com/2018/microsoft-cutting-off-sales-ai-ethics-top-researcher-eric-horvitz-says/).

99 Tom Burt, "New Steps to Combat Disinformation," *Microsoft On the Issues* (blog), September 1, 2020 (https://blogs.microsoft.com/on-the-issues/2020/09/01/disinformation-deepfakes-newsguard-video-authenticator/).

100 Anil Ananthaswamy, "How to Fight Hate Online," *MIT Technology Review*, October 27, 2021 (www.technologyreview.com/2021/10/27/1037109/data-science-fighting-hate-online/).

101 www.microsoft.com/en-us/research/theme/fate/

102 World Economic Forum, "Responsible Use of Technology: The Microsoft Case Study."

103 Natasha Crompton, "Reflecting on Our Responsible AI Program: Three Critical Elements for Progress," *Microsoft On the Issues* (blog), May 1, 2023 (https://blogs.microsoft.com/on-the-issues/2023/05/01/responsible-ai-standards-principles-governance-progress/).

104 Esther Ajao, "Reasons for and Effects of Microsoft Cutting AI Ethics Unit," *TechTarget*, March 14, 2023.

According to reports, as the business strategy required close collaboration with OpenAI, the team was let go.[105]

Soon after the OpenAI breakthrough, Microsoft announced the formation of the Responsible AI Council under the leadership of President Brad Smith and Chief Technology Officer Kevin Scott. According to Microsoft's Chief Responsible AI Officer Natasha Crampton, the Council brings together "representatives of our core research, policy, and engineering teams dedicated to responsible AI, including the Aether Committee and the Office of Responsible AI, as well as senior business partners who are accountable for implementation."[106] Reporting on the Council is scant; therefore, the results of its efforts are yet to be assessed.

Microsoft publicized evidence of ethically motivated conduct. In June 2022, the company announced that it would not use age, gender, and emotion recognition in the Azure Cognitive Service for Vision in line with its Responsible AI Standard. Furthermore, in an effort to stop the abusive deployment of its products, Microsoft began to require users to explain how they were going to use the company's facial recognition and voice recognition tools.[107] A year later, the launch of the Copilot 365 workplace productivity tool came with the assurance that Microsoft's AI Principles and Responsible AI Standard were adhered to in the development of the tool, meaning that the LLMs powering Copilot were not trained on customer content, including individual prompts.[108] More recently, Microsoft's launch of Recall, a Copilot feature that would store all of a user's information and actions on a computer for AI integration, was delayed due to enormous criticism. While Microsoft agreed to allow users to opt in to Recall, there is no indication that the decision came from its AI ethics councils or teams.[109]

In conclusion, Microsoft appears to have opted for relative transparency in how its ethics principles were operationalized at the product development, design, and deployment stages. It remains the only major corporation that has maintained internal councils and teams to ensure safe and responsible development of AI. Nonetheless, the impact of these bodies remains questioned at times: Current and former employees questioned whether the principles laid out by the Office of

105 Zoë Schiffer and Casey Newton, "Microsoft Just Laid Off One of Its Responsible AI Teams," *Platformer*, March 13, 2023 (www.platformer.news/p/microsoft-just-laid-off-one-of-its).

106 Natasha Crampton, "Reflecting on Our Responsible AI Program: Three Critical Elements for Progress," *Microsoft On the Issues* (blog), May 1, 2023 (https://blogs.microsoft.com/on-the-issues/2023/05/01/responsible-ai-standards-principles-governance-progress/).

107 Kashmir Hill, "Microsoft Plans to Eliminate Face Analysis Tools in Push for 'Responsible A.I.,'" *The New York Times*, June 21, 2022 (www.nytimes.com/2022/06/21/technology/microsoft-facial-recognition.html).

108 Microsoft News Center, "Introducing Microsoft 365 Copilot: Your Copilot for Work," March 16, 2023 (https://news.microsoft.com/2023/03/16/introducing-microsoft-365-copilot-your-copilot-for-work/).

109 Steven Levy, "Relevance! Relevance! Relevance! Microsoft at 50 Is an AI Giant – and Still Hellbent on Domination," *Wired*, November 21, 2024 (www.wired.com/story/at-age-50-microsoft-is-an-ai-giant-an-open-source-lover-and-bad-as-it-ever-was/).

Responsible AI, created in 2019 under the Corporate, External, and Legal Affairs division, were consistently enforced or followed.[110] Thus, the integration of responsible AI commitments at a time of rapid LLM adoption will be a test of Microsoft's commitment in the future.

The Partnership on AI to Benefit People and Society (Partnership on AI, PAI)

The Partnership on AI (not to be confused with the intergovernmental Global Partnership on AI summit) is a non-profit organization co-founded by Google, DeepMind, Facebook, Amazon, and Microsoft in 2016 and joined by Apple a year later, to bring the AI industry together with academics and media organizations. The PAI is not a pure advisory board; rather, it seeks to combine pilot projects and international events with advisory functions. Recommending best practices, educating the public about AI and encouraging industry conversations on responsible AI are the goals set by its founders.[111]

Perhaps one of the distinguishing features of the PAI is the inclusion of industry-wide concerns in its ambit. Its website lists thirty-six "Research and Publications" entries between 2020 and mid-2025 on a wide-ranging array of topics, including emotional intelligence, synthetic media, labor, algorithmic risk assessment, and data enrichment.[112] In February 2023, it released its guidelines on Responsible Practices for Synthetic Media,[113] supported by a total of eighteen companies and media organizations. The guidelines are in the process of being operationalized through eleven case studies.[114]

The PAI is sometimes praised as a voluntary initiative enjoying the backing of industry leaders who want to avoid destructive competition dynamics. Yet, an early analysis from 2019 finds that its design lacks enforcement mechanisms. In fact, it has remained silent when members announced business initiatives with reportedly troubling ethical implications, and none of the other members issued a condemnation.[115] In 2020, Access Now resigned, arguing that the structure of the Partnership

[110] Nico Grant and Karen Weise, "In A.I. Race, Microsoft and Google Choose Speed Over Caution," *The New York Times*, April 7, 2023 (www.nytimes.com/2023/04/07/technology/ai-chatbots-google-microsoft.html).

[111] Gijs Leenders, "The Regulation of Artificial Intelligence – A Case Study of the Partnership on AI," *Becoming Human: Artificial Intelligence Magazine* (Medium blog), April 13, 2019 (https://becominghuman.ai/the-regulation-of-artificial-intelligence-a-case-study-of-the-partnership-on-ai-c1c22526c19f).

[112] https://partnershiponai.org/resources/

[113] Partnership on AI, "Responsible Practices for Synthetic Media: A Framework for Collective Action," February 27, 2023 (https://partnershiponai.org/wp-content/uploads/2023/02/PAI_synthetic_media_framework.pdf).

[114] Leibowicz and Cardona, "From Principles to Practices: Lessons Learned from Applying Partnership on AI's (PAI) Synthetic Media Framework to 11 Use Cases."

[115] Leenders, "The Regulation of Artificial Intelligence – A Case Study of the Partnership on AI."

did not allow non-profit partners to make an impact.[116] All in all, the PAI seems to work well as a community-building exercise among corporations and as a functional research unit but is not designed for adversarial decision-making vis-à-vis corporate conduct.

Twitter: Trust and Safety Council

Twitter had a Trust and Safety Council, established in 2016 to counter online abuse by collaborating with advocacy groups. In addition to the Council, Twitter entrusted issue-specific advisory groups working on content-related self-regulation specifically around online safety and harassment, human and digital rights, child sexual exploitation, suicide prevention and mental health, and dehumanization.[117] It seems that the relationship between the Council and Twitter's leadership was rocky in the best of times. A letter addressed to the leadership by Council members in 2019 reads: "There have been no advance heads-up of Twitter's policy or product changes to the council, leaving many of us to have no prior warning or let alone knowledge when answering press and media inquiries."[118]

Before his acquisition of Twitter, Elon Musk even circulated the idea of starting a council similar to Meta's Oversight Board, but he reneged on that promise later. Yoel Roth, the chair of the Trust & Safety Council, resigned on November 10, 2022. Three of its members resigned on December 8, 2022, protesting Musk's approach to safety. The Council was disbanded four days later. Musk did not create a new council for content moderation or algorithmic risk mitigation.

CONCLUSION

Perhaps the best summary of business self-regulation through ethics guidelines, and compliance and guidance boards, councils, and teams is what law professor Evelyn Douek wrote about Meta's Oversight Board at the time of its creation: "It may be a Supreme Court yet – or a local court, Potemkin court, or ad hoc consultant."[119] Internal and external bodies are often staffed by reputable experts interested in effecting change from within or, in the case of external boards, at arm's length. Even if the cynical motivations of ethics-washing in the absence of compliance cannot be ignored, company executives may find it in their best interest to comply with ethical principles, if for nothing else, to avoid negative attention. The modern corporation,

[116] Veale, Matus, and Gorwa, "AI and Global Governance: Modalities, Rationales, Tensions": 258.

[117] "Twitter 2020 Global Impact Report" (https://about.twitter.com/content/dam/about-twitter/en/company/global-impact-2020.pdf).

[118] Louise Matsakis, "Twitter Trust and Safety Advisers Say They're Being Ignored," *Wired*, August 23, 2019 (www.wired.com/story/twitter-trust-and-safety-council-letter/).

[119] Douek, "What Kind of Oversight Board Have You Given Us?": 11.

for all its hierarchical structure and single-minded focus on conventional success metrics, has been forced to allow dissidents and reformers in its midst. Yet, agents of change push for corporate social responsibility and ethical conduct under extreme constraints. Companies may partially obey or simply ignore ethics advice or disband the boards and teams issuing that advice. Worse yet, companies may not even bother to set up any self-regulation scheme, as some of the examples in this chapter suggest. What aggravates the situation is that periods of austerity, such as the one that reshaped the tech industry in early 2023, mean substantial layoffs for responsible AI teams.[120]

The evidence presented in this chapter suggests limited corporate behavioral change. The best-documented cases of board-guided change are the Meta Oversight Board's content moderation decisions, and Microsoft's ongoing support for internal AI ethics councils and teams. Axon's external AI Ethics Board persuaded the company not to pursue some projects between 2019 and 2022; Google's DeepMind has reported adherence to feedback from its internal Institutional Review Committee; and Microsoft has publicized compliance with its own principles in the development of Azure and Copilot products. What is more, research teams operating within technology companies or collaborating with them have published invaluable scholarship on the safe and responsible design, development, and deployment of AI, and may have quietly influenced their colleagues on other teams to adopt AI ethics measures in their business pursuits.

Yet, business self-regulation is much more a story of ignoring advice for good conduct than compliance with it. Meta has at times ignored its Oversight Board's advisory opinions. Axon's decision not to heed its AI Ethics Board's advice led to the Board's implosion. Even if Google created an AI ethics body after its acquisition of DeepMind, the secrecy around its powers and members makes one wonder about its efficacy. Elon Musk's hostile takeover of Twitter resulted not only in the dismissal of Trust & Safety but also in the disappearance of ethics and compliance from the company's public statements altogether. And even when internal and external boards, councils and teams exist, their powers may be too limited to effect substantial change. A case in point is Meta's Oversight Board, which has no authority to question Facebook's and Instagram's algorithmic curation. Thus, we are left with a global picture in which some companies have no internal or external panel in charge of ensuring tech ethics in general and AI ethics in particular, while others have designed such panels with minimal or no power to influence product decisions, let alone business models.

Ultimately, an analysis of business self-regulation should take into account the contradictions embedded in business ethics. AI ethics can at best uphold a minimal

[120] Cristina Criddle and Madhumita Murgia, "Big Tech Companies Cut AI Ethics Staff, Raising Safety Concerns," *Financial Times*, March 28, 2023 (www.ft.com/content/26372287-6fb3-457b-9e9c-f722027f36b3).

notion of business ethics, which allows reform at isolated instances, rather than advance social justice or freedom.[121] Thus, those who advocate broader transformations for a more just, equitable, and sustainable society should think above and beyond the limitations of business self-regulation. Nonetheless, even if self-regulation alone cannot nudge the AI industry toward ethical conduct, future AI governance will have to incorporate business self-regulation, not as its main component but rather as a complementary element. The rise of legal regulation may have raised hopes that AI risks and harms can be addressed without relying on voluntary acts by businesses, but even proposed bills leave leeway for business self-regulation. The European Union's Digital Services Act, for example, requires independent oversight of social media user appeals, thereby breathing new life into Meta's embattled Oversight Board and similar bodies (see the section on business incentives and technical solutions in Chapter 6).[122] Thus, even though business self-regulation began in the absence of legal technology regulation, it is becoming clear that the combination of law and self-regulation may shape future AI governance.

[121] Greene, Hoffmann, and Stark, "Better, Nicer, Clearer, Fairer: A Critical Assessment of the Movement for Ethical Artificial Intelligence and Machine Learning."

[122] Naomi Nix, "Meta created a 'Supreme Court' for Content. Then It Threatened Its Funds." *The Washington Post*, June 30, 2024 (www.washingtonpost.com/technology/2024/06/30/meta-facebook-content-moderation-oversight-board/).

6

Governing AI with Laws and Policies

For a long time, an enduring trope about contemporary technologies was that they have developed in a regulatory vacuum. Cheerleaders and skeptics alike painted a picture of lawlessness to describe the current state of affairs in the technology industry. Cheerleaders rejoiced at the absence of perceived impediments to endless innovation that has given us the internet, social media, AI, and more, while skeptics said that the absence of democratic control over these innovations is precisely why we endured their harms.

That landscape is beginning to change, even if slowly. Legislative proposals to regulate AI have proliferated since 2019 around the world.[1] The European Union's (EU) AI Act (2024) and South Korea's AI Basic Law (2025) are the only regional or national statutes ratified by respective legislatures, but politicians have voiced their willingness to put in place guardrails to direct the future development of AI through law in Brazil, where an AI law cleared the Senate in late 2024, as well as Canada, Chile, China, Colombia, India, Japan, Mexico, the United Kingdom (UK), the United States (US), and Venezuela. However, as of mid-2025, none of these bills are in effect. Even if the adoption of *AI-centric* laws (i.e., laws that take AI as their only or main subject matter) is slow, *AI-relevant* laws are already shaping the landscape of AI. The right to privacy is recognized as a constitutional norm in many countries. Laws regulating digital privacy, consumer rights, content moderation, and market competition can be reinterpreted to protect citizens from certain categories of AI risks and harms. What is more, inaction by the national legislation in the US has pushed states and cities to enact laws regulating AI risks and harms in their jurisdictions.

This chapter documents AI-centric and AI-relevant laws and bills around the world. In addition to AI-centric statutes in the EU and South Korea, it offers examples from AI bills that have not been legislated into law to offer a global picture of where regulation is likely to head. It also provides an overview of AI-related provisions of privacy, content moderation, antitrust, and consumer protection laws around the globe. A

[1] A number of projects led by academics and legal professionals track AI-related legislation, policies, and court cases. For the Emerging Technology Observatory's AI Governance and Regulatory Archive, see: www.cset.georgetown.edu/publication/eto-agora/. For OECD's legislation tracker, see: www.oecd.ai/en/

core finding of this chapter is that the relevant laws and bills typically avoid regulating entire areas of AI research and development. Instead, they identify risks and harms once AI-powered products are developed and deployed. In European Union parlance, they are "technology-neutral." Classifying AI-powered computer systems and products by risk (i.e., the "risk-based model"), exemplified by the EU's AI Act, is the most common approach to AI regulation. This model sets obligations primarily for high-risk AI developers and deployers, while opting for a light-touch approach to AI systems posing lower risk. An alternative approach is to focus legislation on specific industries (i.e., banking or healthcare) or deployers (i.e., public-sector procurers).[2]

Caveats are in order. First, laws and bills exclusively promoting AI development and use in the absence of guardrails are not listed, as this chapter's goal is to take stock of legislative developments around responsible, safe, and ethical uses of AI. Also, this chapter makes brief references to relevant directives, administrative decisions, and court rulings but does not describe them separately – with the exception of former President Joe Biden's 2023 Executive Order on AI, which was the most consequential law-like text in its national context until it was revoked by President Donald Trump in early 2025. Finally, it is worth acknowledging that while some laws, like the EU's AI Act, and bills, like Canada's AI and Data Act, have received enormous academic and newspaper attention, others, like the legislative deliberation session in Venezuela, have received no attention at all, so the descriptions and analyses in this chapter reflect available information.

There are still few AI laws in place. Lawmakers around the world, especially in the countries that produce most AI software and platforms, have not done their homework. Yet, some patterns are beginning to emerge in the global regulation of AI. The EU's AI Act, with its technology-neutral and future-proof risk-based model, will set a global example. China's model of sector-by-sector administrative rulemaking can be another model. The future of legal AI governance is likely to look multilevel, as international organizations, like the Council of Europe, and subnational entities, like the US state of Colorado, have indicated their willingness to step up to the challenge. No matter how AI legislation evolves, however, it can remain relevant only if it addresses pressing challenges like environmental degradation, the loss of human jobs, and the development of lethal autonomous weapons systems.

REGULATING AI THROUGH LAW: WHAT IS AT STAKE?

Governing technology through the law has a long history.[3] From cars to airplanes, mail communication to phone communication, and household appliances to

[2] For example, Canada's Directive on Automated Decision-Making (2019) sets standards for the use of automated decision systems by the federal government.

[3] Throughout this chapter, "the law" without qualifiers refers to the combination of constitutional norms, statutes, administrative regulations, and court decisions.

bridges, there is hardly any product of modern science and technology whose design, development, and use is not regulated through legal means. Yet, opposition to legal regulation as an impediment to boundless technological progress was vocal throughout the 2010s, especially in the US. The notion that lawmakers are too uninformed and slow to direct technology remained a popular trope in academia and public debates.[4] Nonetheless, scandals that put technology firms' data collection, storage, and analysis practices under the spotlight began to draw increasing attention from lawmakers, as troubling revelations showed that companies developing or using emerging technologies, AI included, could not be trusted to regulate themselves for attendant risks and harms. Rejection of the characterization of regulation and innovation in zero-sum terms had always been strong among academics and activist circles critical of technology companies' certain practices, but it was not until the early 2020s that the call for regulation caught up with an increasing number of lawmakers who began to sponsor subnational, national, and international laws. The desire for AI law became so overwhelming that Sam Altman, OpenAI's CEO, began to position himself as an advocate for legal regulation from 2023 onwards. In fact, one commentator predicts what he – somewhat disapprovingly – calls a "regulatory tsunami" that will wash away the societal gains of generative AI.[5]

The characterization of today's technology landscape as devoid of legal regulation is misleading. The law permeates every sphere of modern life, technology being no exception. A more accurate description of law's role in regulating technology since the early 1990s is that the specific content of laws, directives, court decisions, and policies has been exceptionally permissive toward the technology sector, especially in the US, where much of the pioneering technology research and development has taken place.[6] The law has enabled and directed technological developments, though not in ways that protect vulnerable persons and populations from risks and harms. The development of contemporary AI has thus begun not in the absence of law, but rather in the presence of business-friendly and rights-indifferent law.

Today, the debate on using legal instruments to regulate AI focuses less on *whether* than *how* and *what for*. The deficiencies of business self-regulation in curbing risks and harms (Chapter 5) serve as a leading justification for binding laws to regulate AI.[7] The *how* question concerns the tools. On the one hand, most countries already have consumer protection, privacy, children's safety, and antitrust laws that can be repurposed to regulate AI. For example, US Federal Trade Commission (FTC) Chair

4 Marchant, Allenby, and Herkert, *The Growing Gap Between Emerging Technologies and Legal-Ethical Oversight: The Pacing Problem*; Downey, "Emerging Legal Concepts at the Nexus of Law, Technology and Society: A Case Study in Identity"; Hadfield and Clark, "Regulatory Markets: The Future of AI Governance."

5 Eric Goldman, "Generative AI is Doomed," Santa Clara University Legal Studies Research Paper (2025), available on *SSRN*, posted on April 25, 2024 (www.ssrn.com/abstract=4802313).

6 Schaake, *The Tech Coup: How to Save Democracy from Silicon Valley*.

7 Vöneky, "Key Elements of Responsible Artificial Intelligence – Disruptive Technologies, Dynamic Law."

Lina Khan once argued that her agency was "well equipped with legal jurisdiction to handle the issues brought to the fore by the rapidly developing A.I. sector, including collusion, monopolization, mergers, price discrimination and unfair methods of competition."[8] On the other hand, AI challenges existing legal frameworks as a novel and at times unpredictable technology.[9] As this chapter shows, the emerging practices of legal regulation use a combination of both approaches: Existing laws are used to address AI risks and harms in numerous countries, *and* AI-centric laws and bills are becoming increasingly more common around the world.

The *what for* question concerns the goals of AI law. Metaphors tend to connote constraint: Law imposes "guardrails" to rein in runaway technology. However, as legal scholar Frank Pasquale argues, law directs (instead of merely constraining) the development of technologies like AI,[10] including in ways that shape development and use decisions. In fact, lawmakers in the EU have taken pains to justify the AI Act as an innovation booster, reasoning that providing businesses with a predictable legal environment will make them more productive. Likewise, the Basic AI Law is intended to promote AI in South Korea as much as mitigate its problems. Thus, AI law can be understood as a potential force multiplier for a particular kind of innovation – one that respects constitutional rights – in addition to serving as a constraint against rights violations.

THE STATE OF LEGAL AI REGULATION

Human-Centered AI's AI Index Report 2025 lists an increasing number of laws that mention AI around the world, but most of those laws tend to focus on fostering AI capacity rather than limiting negative impact.[11] This is an indication of policy priorities: Lawmakers around the world want to promote economic development through AI, and the potential risks and harms are usually considered an afterthought. Nonetheless, bills that take issue with negative impact have emerged since the late 2010s. So far, only the EU's AI Act and South Korea's Basic AI Law have been signed into law.[12] Legislative debates elsewhere have not yielded concrete results. In the absence of federal legislation in the US, states have taken the initiative to propose a record number of AI bills.

AI-relevant legislation that addresses AI-exclusive as well as non-AI considerations is much more common. Since the legislation of the EU's General Data Protection Regulation in 2016, data privacy and protection measures have advanced in public

[8] Lina Khan, "We Must Regulate A.I. Here's How," *The New York Times*, May 3, 2023 (www.nytimes.com/2023/05/03/opinion/ai-lina-khan-ftc-technology.html).

[9] Guihot, "Coherence in Technology Law."

[10] Pasquale, "Data-Informed Duties in AI Development."

[11] Maslej et al., "Artificial Intelligence Index Report 2025": Chapter 6.

[12] Reinforcing the relative success of region-wide legislation, EU member states have developed their own strategies and laws as well (for the example of Germany, see Jobin et al. 2021).

and legislative debates considerably in various countries. Lawmakers in Canada, India, and the UK have taken the initiative to overhaul data and privacy laws to bring data protections up to date with contemporary technological developments. In addition, the protection of children from online harms has been on the legislative agenda in the US, Canada, and the UK – and more recently, Australia. The removal of illegal and harmful content from digital platforms – a challenge with AI and non-AI components – is also on lawmakers' minds around the world.

Needless to say, laws do not make AI risks and harms disappear. First of all, conflicts over contending rights claims complicate the picture (see Chapter 2). To give an example, AI companies invoke trade secrets to guard their data and algorithms from external scrutiny, which conflicts with emerging algorithmic transparency and audit requirements. Second, laws in effect tend to leave considerable leeway to regulators for future implementation and interpretation. Framework legislation that puts administrative agencies and courts in charge of spelling out details in the future is typical in the context of fast-moving technologies. In fact, the open-endedness of definitions and flexibility of interpretations stand out as a key feature of EU law – and a source of business frustration. Third, neither the drafting of the bills nor their interpretation happens in a vacuum; the power relations shaping contemporary politics and society are found at every step of legislation as well. For example, observers of EU legislative procedure have noticed unusual levels of overt and covert lobbying by American Big Tech companies in technology legislation.[13] Therefore, the laws and bills described in this chapter should be seen as the outcome of the multiple interests and values reflecting power relations rather than objective rules of the game. Finally, most legal documents discussed in this chapter are either bills or new laws awaiting full implementation; therefore, governing AI through the law is still more aspiration than fact.

AI LAWS AND BILLS AROUND THE WORLD

Lawmakers in Brazil, Canada, China, Colombia, Japan, Mexico, South Korea, the UK, the US, and Venezuela have followed their European counterparts' lead to draft AI-centric bills between 2021 and 2024. The variation in the length and sophistication of AI-centric legal documents is wide: The EU's AI Act, at around 90,000 words, is the size of a short novel, while the UK's Artificial Intelligence (Regulation) Bill barely fills five pages.

As of mid-2025, only the EU and South Korea have AI-centric laws. Brazil's AI bill passed a senate vote in late 2024. Meanwhile, former President Biden published the Executive Order on the Safe, Secure, and Trustworthy Development and Use

[13] Jillian Deutsch, "US Tech Firms Hid Lobbying Efforts, European Parliament Says," *The Washington Post*, October 14, 2022; Jennifer Rankin, "MEPs Launch Site for EU Officials to Report 'Shady Lobbying' by Big Tech," *The Guardian*, February 2, 2023.

of Artificial Intelligence ("Biden's Executive Order") in October 2023, followed by the Artificial Intelligence Risk Management Framework published by the National Institute of Standards and Technology (NIST), and a presidential memorandum in 2024[14] – documents that collectively served as the closest approximation to a federal statute in the US until January 2025, when incoming President Trump revoked the Executive Order. The absence of federal legislation prompted numerous US states to pursue AI-centric legislation. In 2024, Colorado's An Act Concerning Consumer Protections in Interactions with Artificial Intelligence Systems (SB 205) became the first AI-centric state law, while California's Safe and Secure Innovation for Frontier Artificial Intelligence Models Act, which received considerable media coverage, was vetoed by Governor Gavin Newsom.

The EU puts forward a risk-based and technology-neutral approach to AI legislation. While other countries tend to follow the European model, China stands out as an exception with its industry-specific design, development, and regulation model.[15] China's regulations have so far taken the form of government directives and guidelines rather than statutory law.[16]

Laws and bills tend to define AI as a computer system offering estimation, inference, classification, and prediction through applications of machine learning. Few texts go much deeper into conceptual elaboration. In fact, the only legal document that includes logic- or knowledge-based models (see Chapter 1) as a type of AI is the EU's AI Act.[17] A noteworthy detail is that Mexico's proposed Law for the Ethical Regulation of Artificial Intelligence is the only bill with an ambition to regulate *robotics* alongside AI.

The final version of the EU's AI Act adds specific provisions for *general-purpose AI*, including standards of technical documentation and criteria for the designation of AI models as general-purpose.[18] The popularity of applications using large language models, like OpenAI's ChatGPT, appears to have pushed lawmakers to put more thought into general-purpose AI between 2021 and 2024. The Brazilian bill, which requires all AI providers to conduct a preliminary risk assessment, obliges the providers of general-purpose AI systems to state the intended purposes

[14] The memorandum is called "Advancing the United States' Leadership in Artificial Intelligence; Harnessing Artificial Intelligence to Fulfill National Security Objectives; and Fostering the Safety, Security, and Trustworthiness of Artificial Intelligence."

[15] Reportedly, the Japanese government intends to adopt a similar approach by using existing sector-specific laws rather than promoting new AI legislation. Hiroki Habuka, "New Government Policy Shows Japan Favors a Light Touch for AI Regulation," *Center for Strategic & International Studies*, February 25, 2025 (www.csis.org/analysis/new-government-policy-shows-japan-favors-light-touch-ai-regulation).

[16] Na Na, Sophia Wenrui Gu, Freda Hua Tong, Bella Wenjing Xu, and Ya Yu, "Blueprint to Action: China's Path to AI-Powered Industry Transformation," World Economic Forum (in collaboration with Accenture) White Paper, January 2025 (www.reports.weforum.org/docs/WEF_Blueprint_to_Action_Chinas_Path_to_AI-Powered_Industry_Transformation_2025.pdf).

[17] EU AI Act, Recital 12.

[18] EU AI Act, Section 5, Annex XI and Annex XII.

or applications of those systems.[19] China's bill designates the "special requirements" for general-purpose AI to ensure safety, trustworthiness, transparency, and explainability.[20] California's vetoed bill would regulate frontier AI models – a term often used interchangeably with general-purpose AI models.[21]

The EU's AI Act is the most complex regulatory document on AI systems to date. It envisions a combination of prior assessments, human oversight, post-market monitoring, and technical documentation requirements to oblige AI providers and deployers to comply with the law – and penalties as a last resort to keep them in line. The Act envisions a multilevel and multistakeholder governance scheme: The supranational European AI Office will supervise, implement, and enforce the Act alongside national market surveillance authorities. Advisory bodies representing the EU member states (the European Artificial Intelligence Board), independent AI experts (the Scientific Panel), and external stakeholders (the Advisory Forum) will provide guidance.[22]

The European Commission announced the draft bill for an EU-wide law enforceable simultaneously in all member states on April 21, 2021.[23] According to the final draft, the Act aims to regulate uses of AI rather than the underlying technology itself. Also, keeping in mind that AI tools are usually embedded in more complex technical systems, the Act regulates AI systems rather than AI tools or technologies.[24] It

19 Provision for the Use of Artificial Intelligence (Brazil), Article 13(1).

20 Artificial Intelligence Law draft bill (China), Article 76.

21 Instead of defining what a frontier model is, however, the bill leaves the definition of a "covered model" to the Government Operations Agency. www.leginfo.legislature.ca.gov/faces/billNavClient.xhtml

22 www.digital-strategy.ec.europa.eu/en/policies/ai-act-governance-and-enforcement

23 Council of the EU, Interinstitutional File 2021/0106(COD). The relevant documents can be accessed at www.oeil.secure.europarl.europa.eu/oeil/popups/ficheprocedure.do?lang=en&reference=2021/0106(COD). The European Commission built upon the work of the High-Level Expert Group, a 52-member panel of experts from all the member states, to prepare the draft. The Group's task was to convert ethical or responsible AI principles into actionable items. See Smuha, "The EU Approach to Ethics Guidelines for Trustworthy Artificial Intelligence." The Group published the Ethics Guidelines for Trustworthy AI in 2019 (www.digital-strategy.ec.europa.eu/en/library/ethics-guidelines-trustworthy-ai) and the White Paper on Artificial Intelligence in 2020 (www.commission.europa.eu/publications/white-chapter-artificial-intelligence-european-approach-excellence-and-trust_en). The documents' approach to AI regulation, embodied in their aspiration to create "an ecosystem of excellence and trust," ended up shaping the bill's goal to protect rights and facilitate innovation. It took the European Parliament another two years to deliberate and vote on the draft bill. Some sticking points toward the end of negotiations included introducing a compensation scheme for creators of copyrighted content used to trained AI models, setting the contours of the ban on biometric identification, and ensuring the safety of systems using generative AI models. On June 14, 2023, 499 members of the European Parliament voted in favor and 28 voted against the bill, while 93 abstained. The troika of EU institutions, namely the Commission, the Parliament, and the Council of the EU, negotiated the final version in deliberations known as the "trilogue," and finally, the EP took the final vote to approve the Act with an overwhelming majority on March 13, 2024.

24 An AI system is defined as a "machine-based system designed to operate with varying levels of autonomy and that may exhibit adaptiveness after deployment and that, for explicit or implicit objectives, infers, from the input it receives, how to generate outputs such as predictions, content, recommendations,

lists two sets of parameters: Fundamental rights as defined under the EU Charter of Fundamental Rights and the promotion of innovation. Arguably, the amalgamation of a rights-affirming discourse with a business-friendly one seeks to reassure EU citizens that the act will protect their basic rights in the face of fast-paced development and deployment, while assuaging fears that regulation would stifle innovation. In fact, the Act mentions the economic gains to be reaped from legal certainty and market unification to justify its *raison d'être*.

The AI Act proposes a fourfold risk-based scheme whereby the producers of AI systems are expected to assume legal obligations based on the degree of risk those systems pose to EU citizens rather than the type of industry they operate in or on the kind of technology they develop. Applications posing minimal or no risk will be allowed to develop with no restrictions; limited-risk applications will be subject to information and transparency requirements; high-risk applications will be permitted only if reporting and conformity requirements are met;[25] and applications posing unacceptable risk will not be permitted.[26] The high-risk applications include real-time public biometric surveillance, predictive policing, and algorithmic decision systems used in banking, schools, and critical infrastructure. The Act, which requires high-risk systems to be managed with a risk management system in place, has set the global standard on AI regulation.[27]

South Korea's Basic AI Law sets a general framework for combining national competitiveness in AI development with the protection of fundamental rights. Although its approach to regulation is closely aligned with the European model, nuances deserve mention: The South Korean law is concerned primarily with "high-impact," rather than "high-risk" AI systems, and the objective of shoring up national AI capabilities is more pronounced than in the AI Act.[28] Finally, it is worth emphasizing that the South Korean law, just like the EU AI Act, requires foreign companies operating

or decisions that can influence physical or virtual environments." www.artificialintelligenceact.eu/assessment/eu-ai-act-compliance-checker/

25 The draft bill did not list applications by risk category, but it does state that unacceptable applications will include purposefully manipulative uses of AI, uses that exploit vulnerabilities, and social credit systems. See: Veale and Borgesius, "Demystifying the Draft EU Artificial Intelligence Act – Analysing the Good, the Bad, and the Unclear Elements of the Proposed Approach"; Smuha, "From a 'Race to AI' to a 'Race to AI Regulation'"; MacCarthy and Propp, "Machines Learn That Brussels Writes the Rules: The EU's New AI Regulation."

26 Church and Cumbley, "Data and Data Protection."

27 Bills elsewhere diverge from the EU's approach in small but significant ways. Canada's AI and Data Act refers to a "high-impact system," rather than the "high-risk system" used in the EU's AI Act. China's bill uses "critical AI." The US Algorithmic Accountability Act uses concepts like "critical decision" or "augmented critical decision process," which include education, employment, essential utilities, family planning, financial services, healthcare, housing, legal services, and other services affecting consumers' lives (Algorithmic Accountability Act, Section 2. Definitions #8). Biden's executive order addresses "critical and emerging technologies."

28 Kyoungsic Min, "The United Korean AI Act Bill: Contents in Comparison with the EU AI Act (with English Translation of the Bill)," *LinkedIn* (blog), December 11, 2024 (www.linkedin.com/pulse/united-korean-ai-act-bill-contents-comparison-eu-english-min-h98kc/).

in the domestic market to designate representatives to fulfill their AI-related obligations. Thus, the impact of these AI-centric laws will be global in scope.

At the subnational level, Colorado's Act Concerning Consumer Protections in Interactions with Artificial Intelligence Systems, expected to go into effect on February 1, 2026, is the first US state law to regulate AI. Substantively, it seeks to protect consumers and eliminate discrimination in areas like employment and housing. The law assigns obligations to developers and deployers of "high-risk" AI systems. Documentation and impact assessments are the two measures envisioned by the law.[29]

In addition to successful legislation, it is worth mentioning AI bills that have not advanced in the legislative journey – at least not yet. In the US, the first Congressional efforts to legislate on AI began in 2017. Soon after, Rep. John K. Delaney founded the House AI Caucus in early 2018. The Senate kicked off its AI Caucus in March 2019, led by Rob Portman (R-Ohio) and Martin Heinrich (D-N.M.). Yet, regulating AI through a comprehensive federal law looks unlikely. It has been suggested that even if no AI-centric law comes into being, the use of AI in consumer products, financial services, healthcare, and fields covered under civil rights and employment laws may result in liability claims as an alternative legal mechanism.[30] China's AI governance scheme, which incorporated a number of government principle papers and draft bills since 2017, may include a draft bill, called the Artificial Intelligence Law (popularly known as the "Scholars' Suggestion Draft" because it was developed by university scholars), that one commentator finds unlikely to come into effect quickly.[31] Canada's efforts to legislate the Artificial Intelligence and Data Act as part of its Digital Charter Implementation Act came to an abrupt end with the prorogation of Parliament in early 2025. India's political leadership has made it clear that legal and policy interventions will prioritize AI competitiveness rather than regulate potential negative impact. Electronics & Information Technology Minister Ashwini Vaishnaw announced that the government had no plan to draft a law to

[29] Tyler Thompson and Abigail Walker, "What You Need to Know About Colorado's New Comprehensive AI Law," *Data Privacy Dish* (blog), May 16, 2024 (www.gtlaw-dataprivacydish.com/2024/05/what-you-need-to-know-about-colorados-new-comprehensive-ai-law/). The law has been criticized by business groups, most notably the Colorado Technology Association, for its vague definitions and requirements. Consumer protection groups, meanwhile, find its enforcement scheme weak and its small-business exception rather broad. Interestingly, Governor Jared Polis urged lawmakers to make improvements before the law went into effect while signing it into law.

[30] Sean Christy and Chuck Hollis, "AI, Machine Learning & Big Data Laws and Regulations 2023 | USA," *Global Legal Insights* (www.globallegalinsights.com/practice-areas/ai-machine-learning-and-big-data-laws-and-regulations/usa).

[31] Zeyi Yang, "Four Things to Know about China's New AI Rules in 2024," *MIT Technology Review*, January 17, 2024 (www.technologyreview.com/2024/01/17/1086704/china-ai-regulation-changes-2024/); Liu Caiyu, "Draft AI Law to be Reviewed by China's Top Legislature," *Global Times*, June 8, 2023 (www.globaltimes.cn/page/202306/1292241.shtml); Johanna Costigan, "China's New Draft AI Law Prioritizes Industry Development," *Forbes*, March 22, 2024 (www.forbes.com/sites/johannacostigan/2024/03/22/chinas-new-draft-ai-law-prioritizes-industry-development).

regulate AI.[32] The UK's Artificial Intelligence (Regulation) Bill, introduced by Lord Holmes, is the one that has advanced the most in the legislative process among various AI regulation proposals, as it received a second reading in the House of Lords in April 2025. The bill envisions the creation of an AI Authority, and encourages regulatory sandboxes as another measure to ensure the safe development of AI.[33] Mexico's multiple AI regulation efforts, one of which would have introduced a threefold risk scheme (unacceptable, high, and low), whereby providers of high-risk systems would be under data registry, reporting and assessment obligations,[34] have thus far not been successful. Likewise, Chile's bills would have established an EU-style risk model to AI regulation,[35] with more stringent limits on biometric identification and reportedly, a ban on emotional recognition.[36] Finally, the executive and legislative branches have taken an active interest in the regulation of AI in Colombia, where President Gustavo Petro recently announced his intention to turn the country into a global AI hub, but none of the four bills reportedly under consideration in the Senate, including one that places disclosure requirements for the use of generative AI for economic or academic purposes, has been legislated yet.[37]

32 "Not Planning Any Law to Regulate AI Growth in India: IT Minister Ashwini Vaishnaw," *The Economic Times*, April 5, 2023 (www.economictimes.indiatimes.com/tech/technology/not-considering-any-laws-to-regulate-ai-growth-in-india-it-minister-ashwini-vaishnaw/articleshow/99275493.cms?utm_source=contentofinterest&utm_medium=text&utm_campaign=cppst).

33 Jedidiah Bracy, "Proposed UK AI Regulation Bill Receives Second Reading in House of Lords," *IAPP* (news), March 25, 2024 (www.iapp.org/news/a/proposed-uk-ai-regulation-bill-receives-second-reading-in-house-of-lords/). The similarly named Artificial Intelligence (Regulation and Workers' Rights) Bill aims to protect people working alongside AI. The stated goals are to protect workers from discrimination, introduce the right to disconnect outside of work hours, and require transparency about how data is being used at work. www.bills.parliament.uk/bills/3464

34 Rodrigo Riquelme, "Ricardo Monreal presenta por segunda vez la iniciativa para regular la inteligencia artificial," *El Economista*, April 3, 2024 (www.eleconomista.com.mx/tecnologia/Ricardo-Monreal-presenta-por-segunda-vez-la-iniciativa-para-regular-la-inteligencia-artificial-20240403-0062.html); Rodrigo Riquelme, "Ricardo Monreal presenta iniciativa para regular la inteligencia artificial," *El Economista*, February 27, 2024 (www.eleconomista.com.mx/tecnologia/Ricardo-Monreal-presenta-iniciativa-para-regular-la-inteligencia-artificial-20240227-0055.html).

35 www.camara.cl/legislacion/proyectosdeley/tramitacion.aspx?prmID=16416&prmBOLETIN=15869-19; "Chile Launches National AI Policy and Introduces AI Bill Following UNESCO's Recommendations," *UNESCO* (blog), May 4, 2024 (www.unesco.org/en/articles/chile-launches-national-ai-policy-and-introduces-ai-bill-following-unescos-recommendations).

36 "Chile Submits AI Regulation Bill to Congress," *bnamericas*, May 9, 2024 (www.bnamericas.com/en/news/chile-submits-ai-regulation-bill-to-congress); "Chile Proposes Legislation to Regulate Artificial Intelligence," *Competition Policy International* (blog), May 14, 2024 (www.pymnts.com/cpi-posts/chile-proposes-legislation-to-regulate-artificial-intelligence/).

37 Juan Pablo Vásquez, "Colombia debate su futuro frente a la inteligencia artificial," *El País*, January 18, 2024 (www.elpais.com/america-colombia/2024-01-18/colombia-debate-su-futuro-frente-a-la-inteligencia-artificial.html); www.forogpp.files.wordpress.com/2023/08/pl-091-23-inteligencia-artificial.pdf; Juan David Gutiérrez R., "Nuevo proyecto de ley sobre inteligencia artificial radicado en el Congreso de la República de Colombia (PL 091 / 2023 S)," *Blog Foro Administración, Gestión y Política Pública* (www.forogpp.com/2023/08/16/nuevo-proyecto-de-ley-sobre-inteligencia-artificial-radicado-en-el-congreso-de-la-republica-de-colombia-pl-091-2023-s/); www.leyes.senado.gov.co/proyectos/index.php/textos-radicados-senado/p-ley-2023-2024/2964-proyecto-de-ley-059-de-2023; Paula Sánchez, "Fue

ADDRESSING AI RISKS AND HARMS THROUGH LAWS AND BILLS

Bias and Discrimination

The words *bias* and *discrimination* stand out as leading concerns in AI legislation, echoing extensive academic research on AI risks and harms. South Korea's Basic AI Law is the only bill or law that does not address the issue at all. Racism, sexism, and ableism receive mention in multiple legal documents around the world. The EU's AI Act warns against "biased results and discriminatory effects"[38] with regard to age, ethnicity, race, sex, or disabilities. It pays particular attention to three potentially high-risk uses: Social credit systems, public assistance in the form of "healthcare services, social security benefits, social services providing protection in cases such as maternity, illness, industrial accidents, dependency or old age and loss of employment and social and housing assistance,"[39] and the private provision of public services, such as "education, healthcare, social services, housing, administration of justice."[40] Concerning the last category, the Act requires a human rights impact assessment.

Brazil's bill requires data management practices that uphold the right to non-discrimination on the basis of "geographic origin, race, color or ethnicity, gender, sexual orientation, socioeconomic class, age, disability, religion or political opinions" and rectify "direct, indirect, illegal or abusive discriminatory biases." The main mechanism to enforce non-discrimination is the algorithmic impact assessment to determine whether a high-risk system should be discontinued.[41] China's bill, which seeks to "avoid prejudice and discrimination based on gender, faith, region, age, ethnicity, and economic capacity,"[42] requires AI security risk assessment for bias and discrimination, security risks, public interest, scientific and technological ethics, and legality. Colombia's bill mentions data bias and discriminatory decisions without further specification. The Mexican bill reiterates a commitment to non-discrimination based on "ethnic origin, race, religion, social and economic conditions."[43] Canada's bill defines a biased AI decision as one that "adversely differentiates, directly or indirectly and without justification, in relation to an individual on one or more of the prohibited grounds of discrimination set out in section 3 of the Canadian Human Rights Act."[44]

aprobado proyecto de ley para regular la Inteligencia Artificial en Colombia," *Caracol Radio*, November 14, 2023 (www.caracol.com.co/2023/11/14/fue-aprobado-proyecto-de-ley-para-regular-la-inteligencia-artificial-en-colombia/). In addition, a government-level Task Force for the Development and Implementation of AI has been in the books since 2020.

38 EU AI Act, Recital 32.

39 EU AI Act, Recital 58.

40 EU AI Act, Recital 96.

41 Provision for the Use of Artificial Intelligence (Brazil), Articles 22 and 23.

42 Artificial Intelligence Law draft bill (China), Article 42.

43 Draft decree issuing the Law for the Ethical Regulation of Artificial Intelligence for the United Mexican States, Article 17.

44 Artificial Intelligence and Data Act (Canada), Article 5(1).

Accordingly, the risk of bias and discrimination would trigger a ministry-ordered audit. The UK's bill would require any business developing, deploying, or using AI to designate an AI officer "to ensure the safe, ethical, unbiased and non-discriminatory use of AI by the business."[45] The US Algorithmic Accountability Act – a bill whose various iterations have made no progress in Congress – mentions bias and discrimination once, while Biden's Executive Order refers to them several times and vows to use existing consumer protection laws to enact safeguards.

AI laws and bills tend to address bias and discrimination within the framework of data and algorithm problems. There is little mention of underlying socioeconomic inequalities exacerbating bias. One exception is the 2023 NIST risk management framework, which argues that algorithmic bias mitigation alone cannot solve bias resulting from access differentials: "systems in which predictions are somewhat balanced across demographic groups may still be inaccessible to individuals with disabilities or affected by the digital divide or may exacerbate existing disparities or systemic biases."[46]

Surveillance

Surveillance by corporate or government entities receives limited attention in laws and bills. The EU AI Act bans real-time public remote biometric identification, arguing that such identification may "affect the private life of a large part of the population, evoke a feeling of constant surveillance and indirectly dissuade the exercise of the freedom of assembly and other fundamental rights."[47] Law enforcement agencies, including border control, may seek exemptions from this ban, which has fueled criticism from immigrant-rights groups.[48] In addition to public remote biometric identification, the AI Act also bans social scoring with detrimental or unfavorable effects.[49] The preamble to Mexico's draft bill cites the UNESCO Global Agreement on the Ethics of Artificial Intelligence (2021) to warn against social scoring and mass surveillance but does not introduce measures to combat them. The US 2023 Executive Order mentions "undue worker surveillance,"[50] and requires the Attorney General to submit a report on the use of AI in the justice system, including for police surveillance.[51]

45 Artificial Intelligence (Regulation) Bill (UK), Article 4 (1) (a).

46 NIST AI 100-1 Artificial Intelligence Risk Management Framework, Section 3.7.

47 EU AI Act, Recital 32.

48 Mügge, "The Securitization of the EU's Digital Tech Regulation"; Center for Democracy & Technology (CDT), "The Human Rights Risks of Facial Recognition AI Tech in Policing and Immigration Must be Properly Recognised in the EU AI Act," *CDT Facial Recognition Briefing Paper*, February 2023. Accessed at: www.cdt.org/wp-content/uploads/2023/02/CDT-Europe-Facial-recognition-EU-AI-Act-issue-brief.pdfs

49 EU AI Act, Article 5 (1) (c).

50 Executive Order on the Safe, Secure, and Trustworthy Development and Use of Artificial Intelligence (US), Section 2 (c).

51 Executive Order on the Safe, Secure, and Trustworthy Development and Use of Artificial Intelligence (US), Section 7.1 (b) (i) (E).

It is worth mentioning that surveillance and harmful behavior by state security institutions remain a sensitive subject around the world. Typically, laws and bills exempt law enforcement and military agencies from obligations instead of requiring them to undergo additional scrutiny or say nothing on the subject. The EU's AI Act carves out exemptions for law enforcement, border control, immigration, and asylum authorities.[52] Military uses of AI fall outside of its scope.[53] Throughout the document, there is no acknowledgment of potential misuse of AI by state security institutions. One exception to the tendency to overlook law enforcement uses of AI is the US Memorandum of 2024 that acknowledges risks to "human rights, civil rights, civil liberties, privacy, safety, national security, and democratic values" when AI is used in a defense, intelligence, or law enforcement context.[54] In a similar vein, Biden's 2023 Executive Order instructed the Attorney General, in consultation with the Secretary of Homeland Security and the Director of OSTP, to deliver a report on the use of AI in the criminal justice system, acknowledging the risks of AI-driven bias, discrimination, and abuse.[55]

Incorrect, Inaccurate, and Unreliable Output

The EU AI Act, Brazil's bill, and two US documents (the NIST AI Risk Management Framework and the 2024 Memorandum) set obligations for accuracy in AI-generated output. Article 15 of the EU AI Act, titled "Accuracy, robustness and cybersecurity," requires high-risk AI to reach an "appropriate level" of accuracy, robustness, and cybersecurity. Deployers should publicize the metrics for those levels in the instructions of use with a list of the "characteristics, capabilities and limitations of performance"[56] accompanying the AI systems. Brazil's bill requires reliability tests to ensure robustness, accuracy, and precision.[57] The NIST AI Risk Management Framework states: "Deployment of AI systems which are inaccurate, unreliable, or poorly generalized to data and settings beyond their training creates and increases negative AI risks and reduces trustworthiness."[58] One of the core functions in the Framework seeks to ensure that deployed AI systems are valid and reliable.[59]

52 Pieter Haeck, "The EU's AI Bans Come with Big Loopholes for Police," *Politico*, February 3, 2025 (www.politico.eu/article/ai-deepseek-chatgpt-openai-eu-bans-series-of-ai-practices-but-with-loopholes/).

53 EU AI Act, Recital 24.

54 US Memorandum of 2024, 4.2(c)(i).

55 Executive Order on the Safe, Secure, and Trustworthy Development and Use of Artificial Intelligence (US), Section 7.1 (iii)(b)(i).

56 EU AI Act, Recital 70.

57 Provision for the Use of Artificial Intelligence (Brazil), Article 20.

58 NIST AI 100-1 Artificial Intelligence Risk Management Framework, Section 3.1.

59 NIST AI 100-1 Artificial Intelligence Risk Management Framework, Section 5.3, Measure 2.5.

Disinformation, Misinformation, or Manipulation

Most AI-centric laws and bills are silent about the role that AI can play in mass deception. The EU's major content moderation regulation is the Digital Services Act (DSA),[60] which came into effect in 2023 to replace the E-Commerce Directive of 2000. It addresses concerns around safety and rights protection resulting from content produced and/or hosted by digital services, such as the trade and exchange of illegal goods and services, online manipulation, content moderation and false advertisement on online marketplaces, social networks, app stores, and content-sharing platforms.[61] As is frequently repeated in EU policy circles, it aims to make illegal online what is illegal offline.[62]

The DSA has explicit provisions about algorithmic systems. It bans "dark patterns," that is, confusing or deceptive user interfaces that distort consumers' ability to make free and informed decisions[63] and targeted advertising based on "special categories of personal data"[64] as defined by the GDPR. In terms of *ex ante* obligations, online platforms that fall under the jurisdiction of the DSA are expected to conduct annual reports detailing their content-moderation activities.[65] Very large online platforms and online search engines have to make assessments of risks to society and democracy[66] – an important addition that requires companies to go beyond assessment of what is illegal to include assessment of what the Act calls "unlawful or otherwise harmful information and activities."[67] Platforms are also asked to take down illegal content promptly.[68] The DSA obliges platforms to allow data access to vetted researchers for risk assessment purposes.[69] Finally, failure to comply with the DSA may result in penalties as high as 6 percent of the company's global annual turnover, and repeat offenders may face periodic penalties.[70]

The EU's AI Act alerts to the new risks of "misinformation and manipulation at scale, fraud, impersonation and consumer deception" as a result of AI-generated

60 www.eur-lex.europa.eu/eli/reg/2022/2065/oj

61 The Act assigns conditional liability exemption to companies depending on the nature of their service provision and size. The legal scheme applies to all intermediary digital service providers, but *mere conduits* and *caching providers* are exempt from liability under certain conditions, while the exemptions for *hosting service providers* and *online platforms*, especially *very large online platforms*, and *very large online search engines*, are much more limited (Articles 3–6). Broadly speaking, large digital platforms are obliged to be transparent about their content moderation policies, and exercise due diligence (Chapter 3) to fulfill ex ante obligations and avoid penalties (Chapter 4). Also see: Asha Allen, "The EU's Opaque Policy-Making Has Never Been Clearer," *Wired*, April 29, 2022.

62 Digital Services Act, Recital 12.

63 Digital Services Act, Article 25.

64 Digital Services Act, Article 26.

65 Digital Services Act, Recital 49.

66 Digital Services Act, Recital 104.

67 Digital Services Act, Recital 5.

68 Digital Services Act, Article 9 and elsewhere.

69 Digital Services Act, Article 40.

70 Digital Services Act, Articles 52 and 74.

content.[71] Its Article 5 explicitly bans "subliminal techniques beyond a person's consciousness or purposefully manipulative or deceptive techniques, with the objective, or the effect of materially distorting the behavior of a person or a group of persons by appreciably impairing their ability to make an informed decision ..." Providers of synthetic audio, image, video, or text are obligated to mark their products in a machine-readable format, and deployers of AI systems are obligated to disclose artificially generated or manipulated content – with the exception of some artistic or law enforcement uses. The AI Office is tasked with the specifics of implementing the detection and labeling of such content.[72] These measures, combined with the provisions of the Digital Services Act, constitute the EU's approach to combating manipulation and deception.[73]

In the United States, content moderation is largely regulated by digital platforms themselves, rather than through federal law. Section 230 of the Communications Decency Act of 1996 is arguably the most famous and controversial technology-related legal provision in modern history. It consists of a single sentence: "No provider or user of an interactive computer service shall be treated as the publisher or speaker of any information provided by another information content provider." Online platforms' liability exemption has, in the words of the provision's advocates, created the internet as we know it.[74] One major exception to Section 230 exemptions is the enforcement of federal or state sex trafficking laws under the 2018 Allow States and Victims to Fight Online Sex Trafficking Act and the Stop Enabling Sex Traffickers Act (collectively abbreviated as FOSTA-SESTA). Section 230 was legislated before the advent of data-intensive AI systems, but companies using AI tools to analyze user data or recommend content are generally understood to enjoy the stipulated exemptions. The growth of generative AI has sparked the debate on Section 230 and AI because today's text, image, and sound generation technologies create novel content rather than host the content uploaded by human users. In fact, in June 2023, two senators introduced the No Section 230 Immunity for AI Act – to no avail – to set constraints on generated AI content.

The UK Online Safety Act (2023) requires online platforms to exercise a duty of care.[75] Although the law is not primarily about algorithms, it asks online providers to

[71] EU AI Act, Recital 133.

[72] EU AI Act, Article 50.

[73] Beyond the European approach, another potential model could emerge from Mexico's AI bill if it becomes law: Article 18 introduces a blanket ban on the misuse of AI and robotics for "social manipulation, discrimination or violation of the rule of law."

[74] The United States Court of Appeals for the Fourth Circuit's *Zeran v. America Online, Inc.* decision (129 F.3d 327 (4th Cir. 1997)) in 1997 has cemented the immunity of internet service providers under Section 230.

[75] Its most controversial aspect is that it may require online messaging platforms to monitor communications containing illegal activity. Media reports indicate that the lawmakers are worried about a host of crimes, ranging from child sexual abuse to investment fraud, but the monitoring requirement runs the risk of effectively ending end-to-end encrypted messaging services such as iMessage, WhatsApp,

take into account the effect of the algorithms used by the platforms on the dissemination of illegal content.[76] China's AI bill focuses on the moderation of AI-generated or AI-distributed content, but Article 47 opts for a blanket prohibition instead of offering nuanced guidelines to detect illegal or harmful content: "Providers of AI services shall take measures to prevent the generation of false and harmful information and other content prohibited by laws and regulations, and where the provider discovers illegal content, it shall promptly take measures for handling it such as stopping generation and transmission, eliminating it, and reporting it to the main oversight department for AI." India's Ministry of Electronics and Information Technology published advisories in December 2023 and March 2024 to clarify the government's position on misinformation and deepfakes. In addition, Indian lawmakers expressed willingness to replace the 2000 IT Act, which provided a "safe harbour" for online platforms, with the Digital India Act, which would hold platforms liable for illegal content – though the legislative deliberations have not advanced.[77]

Harm to Life, Livelihood, and Well-Being

Laws and bills cover serious threats to life, livelihood, and well-being indirectly, as they reference the relevant provisions of constitutions and international treaties as guiding norms. Despite the media's attention to chatbots' and recommendation algorithms' role in exacerbating political violence and self-harm, however, none of the laws and bills mentions the risks of mass murder, suicide, or self-harm explicitly.[78] It is worth mentioning that AI-centric bills' inattention to harm is only part of the story, as those who claim to have been harmed could file lawsuits under existing bodies of law such as tort law.

Privacy Violations

Almost all AI-centric laws and bills mention data privacy and data protection, but arguably, data privacy and protection safeguards are built into regional and national

and Signal. Analysis by Trisha Thadani, with research by David DiMolfetta, "US Tech Companies Say U.K. Privacy Bill Poses 'Serious Threat' to Communication," *The Washington Post*, August 1, 2023 (www.washingtonpost.com/politics/2023/08/01/us-tech-companies-say-uk-privacy-bill-poses-serious-threat-communication/).

76 UK Online Safety Act 2023, Article 9 (5) (b) (ii).

77 Romita Majumdar, and P. Suraksha, "Digital India Bill Draft to be Available in June First Week: MoS IT Rajeev Chandrasekhar," *The Economic Times*, May 23, 2023 (Digital India Bill draft to be available in June first week: MoS IT Rajeev Chandrasekhar).

78 In the US, complaints concerning self-harm due to AI center on product liability, and deceptive and unfair trade practices statutes at the national and state levels. Gabby Miller and Ben Lennett, "Breaking Down the Lawsuit Against Character.AI Over Teen's Suicide," *Tech Policy Press*, October 23, 2024 (www.techpolicy.press/breaking-down-the-lawsuit-against-characterai-over-teens-suicide/).

legal systems thanks to privacy-focused legislation. For example, the EU's main data protection law is the General Data Protection Regulation (GDPR), which has become the global trendsetter for data safeguards in the digital age after it came into effect in 2018 to replace the Data Protection Directive (1995).[79] It does not mention AI or algorithms explicitly,[80] but its provisions are closely connected to rules on the collection, storage, and use of data for AI. Principles of fairness and transparency, purpose limitation, data minimization, accuracy, and storage limitation can be said to enhance the safe and responsible practice of AI.[81] The two areas in which the GDPR intersects with AI are notification and non-discrimination, as it requires data controllers or processors using AI to notify data subjects of that use, and to avoid the use of sensitive and discriminatory data types unless there is a good reason to do so.[82] Article 22 acknowledges a data subject's right not to be subjected to a decision based solely on automated processes and the right to contest automated decisions.

The GDPR's popularity has led lawmakers in other countries to propose data privacy and protection legislation. The UK's AI-relevant data privacy issues fall under the Data Protection Act, updated in 2018 to make data standards compliant with the GDPR around the time of Brexit.[83] In addition, the Information Commissioner Office, which is tasked with data protection and freedom of information complaints and requests, announced the Age Appropriate Design Code of 2020 to protect children's rights in the digital age. Canada already has a federal data protection law, the Personal Information Protection and Electronic Documents Act (PIPEDA), as well as provisional privacy laws.[84] The Digital Charter Implementation Act,

79 The GDPR is concerned with the processing of personal data, defined as "any information relating to an identified or identifiable natural person" (Article 4(1)). It requires companies collecting, storing, and processing personal data to inform the data subjects about use and storage. Data subjects may have access to the data collected about them, and exceptions notwithstanding, ask for the data to be deleted. GDPR also sets limits on how long and why data can be stored. The law imposes on violating businesses penalties as high as 4 percent of their global annual turnover. www.data.europa.eu/eli/reg/2016/679/oj

80 The Scientific Foresight Unit of the European Parliament published a report in 2020 to argue that while the GDPR can regulate AI-related data concerns, tensions between the principles laid out by the law and AI practice should be acknowledged Scientific Foresight Unit, "The Impact of the General Data Protection Regulation on Artificial Intelligence."

81 AI developers have pushed back against constraints on the amount, content, and publicness of the data they are allowed to collect, store, and analyze. See: *Artificial Intelligence: GDPR and Beyond*. One of the recommendations of the European Parliament report is to specify which AI applications pose high or unacceptable risks – something that is found in the AI Act, drafted soon after the report. Scientific Foresight Unit, "The Impact of the General Data Protection Regulation on Artificial Intelligence."

82 Church and Cumbley, "Data and Data Protection."

83 The Data Protection and Digital Information Bill (2024), if adopted, will amend the Data Protection Act.

84 In 2023, the federal Office of the Privacy Commissioner (OPC), joined by privacy commissioners in Quebec, British Columbia, and Alberta, opened an investigation into OpenAI's collection and use of data for possible violations of PIPEDA. For the OPC's statement, see www.priv.gc.ca/en/opc-news/news-and-announcements/2023/an_230525-2/

proposed in July 2022,[85] would have consisted of the Consumer Privacy Protection Act (CPPA) in addition to the Personal Information and Data Protection Tribunal Act, and the Artificial Intelligence and Data Act. Yet, the prorogation of Parliament in early 2025 halted legislative progress.

India's Digital Personal Data Protection Act (2023)[86] requires companies to ask users' consent before collecting their personal data and using the data for the stated uses.[87] It entrusts "data fiduciaries" with the authority to handle personal data.[88] The Act stipulates the creation of a Data Protection Board – its authorities and membership are yet to be announced in mid-2025. It seeks parental consent for age verification for children – a requirement that has raised security concerns around the sharing of children's ID card information[89] and protects children from targeted advertising, tracking, and behavioral monitoring. It is important to note that the Act does not have AI-centric provisions.[90] The specifics of the law will be decided by another set of rules, to be drafted by the government.[91]

The US does not have a federal data privacy law, but laws enacted for specific industries offer specialized protections. For example, the Gramm-Leach-Bliley Act addresses how financial institutions use personal information, and the Health

85 Marie-Danielle Smith and Jim Bronskill, "Privacy Bill Sets Out Rules on Use of Personal Data, Artificial Intelligence," *The Globe and Mail*, July 4, 2022 (www.cbc.ca/news/politics/privacy-bill-artificial-intelligence-1.6490665).

86 Arjun Adrian D'Souza, "India's Foray into Regulating AI," *IAPP* (news), April 24, 2024 (www.iapp.org/news/a/indias-foray-into-regulating-ai/); Amrit Dhillon, "Indian Opposition Walks Out as Narendra Modi Refuses to Discuss Manipur Conflict," *The Guardian*, August 10, 2023 (www.theguardian.com/world/2023/aug/10/indian-opposition-walks-out-as-narendra-modi-refuses-to-discuss-manipur-conflict).

87 Newley Purnell, Tripti Lahiri, "Meta, Alphabet and Other Tech Firms Face New Data Rules in India," *The Wall Street Journal*, August 9, 2023 (www.wsj.com/articles/meta-alphabet-and-other-tech-firms-face-new-data-rules-in-india-90a68e7f); for an overview of the law, see Aditi Agrawal, Kamesh Shekar, and Prateek Waghre, "Assessing India's Digital Personal Data Protection Bill," *Tech Policy Press* (podcast, hosted by Justin Hendrix), August 13, 2023 (www.techpolicy.press/assessing-indias-digital-personal-data-protection-bill/).

88 Jatin Grover, "Data Protection Bill: New Version Eases Norms on Info Transfer," *Financial Express*, July 11, 2023 (www.financialexpress.com/tech-trends/data-protection-bill-new-version-eases-norms-on-info-transfer/3164067). It is worth noting that an earlier version of the bill had restricted the transfer of data to allowed countries through data fiduciaries, but the final version allows free transfer of data abroad except to a list of disallowed countries and territories.

89 Suraksha P, "Verifying ID for Social Media Use Could Pose Security Risk: Experts," *The Economic Times*, August 10, 2023 (www.economictimes.indiatimes.com/tech/technology/verifying-id-for-social-media-use-could-pose-security-risk-experts/articleshow/102583346.cms).

90 The Act has been criticized for providing the government with exemptions to process personal data, potentially amount to the risk of state surveillance of citizens. Guest contributor, "Auguring Well for Data Privacy: The Digital Personal Data Protection Bill 2023 Shows an Evolution in Legislative Reasoning," *Financial Express*, August 12, 2023 (www.financialexpress.com/opinion/auguring-well-for-data-privacy-the-digital-personal-data-protection-bill-2023-shows-an-evolution-in-legislative-reasoning/3208245/).

91 Newley Purnell, Tripti Lahiri, "Meta, Alphabet and Other Tech Firms Face New Data Rules in India," *The Wall Street Journal*, August 9, 2023 (www.wsj.com/articles/meta-alphabet-and-other-tech-firms-face-new-data-rules-in-india-90a68e7f).

Insurance Portability and Accountability Act protects certain types of health information. In effect since 2000, the Children's Online Privacy Protection Act[92] aims to protect children from online harms and privacy violations. Its text does not mention algorithms or AI, but provisions on data privacy have implications for businesses' data collection practices. Perhaps the most famous state data privacy law is California's Consumer Privacy Act (2020), which was introduced soon after the passage of the GDPR in the EU. The Act requires employers to disclose information about how applicants' data is used by algorithms and recognizes applicants' right to access the data collected about them and right to ask for that data to be deleted.[93] In addition, Colorado, Connecticut, Iowa, and Virginia, and more recently Montana, Indiana, Tennessee, and Texas, have passed data privacy and/or consumer protection laws. A report from 2021 lists Illinois,[94] California, Washington, New York, Arkansas, Louisiana, Oregon, and Colorado as states with protections for biometric data.[95]

Decline in Product and Service Quality

A few legal documents require private- or public-sector deployers of AI systems to maintain or improve the quality of their products and services. The EU's AI Act goes furthest to require providers of high-risk AI systems to establish a quality management system.[96] Brazil's bill includes "frequent quality control tests" as part of its monitoring regime.[97] While a full-fledged quality management system is a rarity, several laws and bills mention "high-quality data" for training, testing and validation (EU's AI Act),[98] "a mechanism for assessing data quality" (US Memorandum of 2024),[99] and an evaluation of data quality (US Algorithmic Accountability Act).[100] Finally, the Council of Europe Framework Convention requires member states to ensure "adequate quality and security throughout the lifecycle of artificial intelligence systems."[101]

[92] www.uscode.house.gov/view.xhtml?path=&req=granuleid%3AUSC-prelim-title15-section6501&f=&fq=&num=0&hl=false&edition=prelim

[93] Lobel, *The Equality Machine: Harnessing Digital Technology for a Brighter, More Inclusive Future*: 70.

[94] In fact, the Illinois Biometric Information Privacy Act of 2008 is the earliest of its kind, and inspired a federal bill.

[95] Kathleen Wills, "Privacy Law Considerations of AI and Big Data – In the U.S. & Abroad," *Center for Intellectual Property x Innovation Policy* (blog), July 27, 2021 (www.cip2.gmu.edu/2021/07/27/privacy-law-considerations-of-ai-and-big-data-in-the-u-s-abroad/).

[96] EU AI Act, Recital 81, Article 17, Annex VI and VII.

[97] Provision for the Use of Artificial Intelligence (Brazil), Article 24 (IV)(§1)(h).

[98] EU AI Act, Recitals 67 and 68.

[99] Advancing the United States' Leadership in Artificial Intelligence; Harnessing Artificial Intelligence to Fulfill National Security Objectives; and Fostering the Safety, Security, and Trustworthiness of Artificial Intelligence.

[100] Algorithmic Accountability Act, Section 4, Article 7 (C) (ii).

[101] Council of Europe Framework Convention on Artificial Intelligence and Human Rights, Democracy and the Rule of Law, Article 12.

Political Polarization, Online Radicalization, and Algorithmic Censorship

Election manipulation in the form of AI-generated deepfakes amplified through algorithms came into sharp focus in 2024, when billions of people in more than 70 countries cast their votes in national and local elections around the world. Yet, the risk of political polarization and online radicalization through algorithmic amplification is not mentioned in any of the AI laws and bills, even though most of them emphasize the importance of defending democracy, elections, the rule of law, and fundamental rights in the age of AI. The EU's AI Act mentions disinformation in the context of AI's risk to "democratic processes, civic discourse and electoral processes" but does not elaborate further on the subject. Biden's executive order mentions disinformation once without setting up clear guardrails. The Cyberspace Administration of China put together 24 provisional measures in 2023 to establish safety guardrails that combine the prevention of discrimination and disinformation with a national security focus on technology development without mention of political polarization or radicalization.[102] All in all, AI laws and bills are surprisingly silent about combating explicitly political disinformation and misinformation.

Likewise, none of the domestic AI laws and bills mentions censorship and shadowbanning as potential problems. The Council of Europe Framework Convention includes, in its list of repressive uses of AI, "arbitrary or unlawful surveillance and censorship practices that erode privacy and individual autonomy" without elaboration.[103]

Job Replacement

Fears of losing human employment to machines have thus far received close to no legislative attention. Biden's Executive Order required the Secretary of Labor to submit a report in order to "support workers displaced by the adoption of AI and other technological advancements."[104] Bills in Mexico and Colombia refer to "the replacement of humans by machines" and "job displacement," respectively, without elaborating further.

Environmental Degradation

Interestingly, the EU's AI Act mentions AI and other emerging technologies as a potential contributor, rather than a threat, to environmental protection. There is

[102] Matt Sheehan, "China's AI Regulations and How They Get Made," *Carnegie Endowment for International Peace* (blog), July 10, 2023 (www.carnegieendowment.org/research/2023/07/chinas-ai-regulations-and-how-they-get-made); Jing Xuan Teng, "China's New Rules On AI-generated Content," *Agence France-Presse* via *Barron's*, August 18, 2023 (www.barrons.com/news/china-s-new-rules-on-ai-generated-content-b035363b).

[103] Council of Europe Framework Convention on Artificial Intelligence and Human Rights, Democracy and the Rule of Law, Preamble.

[104] Executive Order on the Safe, Secure, and Trustworthy Development and Use of Artificial Intelligence (US), Section 6 (ii).

no mention of the carbon footprint or water usage to power AI infrastructure. In a similar vein, Biden's Executive Order envisioned AI foundational models as potentially improving "community preparedness for climate-related risks," "clean-energy deployment" and "grid reliability and resilience."[105] Article 15 of China's bill "promotes the green and low-carbon development of compute infrastructure."

Exploitation of Labor

Biden's Executive Order stood alone for its workplace provision: "In the workplace itself, AI should not be deployed in ways that undermine rights, worsen job quality, encourage undue worker surveillance, lessen market competition, introduce new health and safety risks, or cause harmful labor-force disruptions."[106] Other than that, none of the AI-related bills or laws mentions precarious or exploitative labor conditions.

Market Concentration

AI-centric laws and bills say little about the increasing market power of AI pioneers. Laws and bills in the EU, China, Colombia, and Brazil mention free and competitive markets in connection to AI, but none of them develops provisions to ensure it. The 2025 AI Action Summit's Statement on Inclusive and Sustainable Artificial Intelligence for People and the Planet, a nonbinding resolution at the international level, makes a single mention of the commitment to "avoiding market concentration."[107]

The Digital Markets Act (DMA)[108] is the EU's legal intervention to ensure competitiveness in the digital markets.[109] Even though its primary target is unfair

[105] Executive Order on the Safe, Secure, and Trustworthy Development and Use of Artificial Intelligence (US), Section 5.2 (g)(4).

[106] Executive Order on the Safe, Secure, and Trustworthy Development and Use of Artificial Intelligence (US), Section 2(c).

[107] "Statement on Inclusive and Sustainable Artificial Intelligence for People and the Planet," AI Action Summit, Co-chaired by France and India, February 10–11, 2025, Paris (www.onu.delegfrance.org/statement-on-inclusive-and-sustainable-artificial-intelligence-for-people-and).

[108] www.data.europa.eu/eli/reg/2022/1925/oj

[109] The DMA addresses two types of business actors: *core platform services* that have a €7.5bn in annual revenue or €75bn market capitalization, and *gatekeepers*, which, in addition to being core platform services, have at least 45 million monthly end users in the EU and 10,000 annual business users (Article 3). It uses the standard tools of competition policy, including assessment of market power and design of *ex ante* and *ex post facto* remedies and sanctions European Commission Joint Research Centre, *The EU Digital Markets Act*. Its main pillars are contestability, a common term in EU competition law, and fairness between business users and big companies. In a nutshell, the legislation prevents gatekeepers from preferencing their own products and platforms (Recital 52), expects gatekeepers to enhance the interoperability of their services and platforms (found in multiple recitals and articles), and grants the Commission power to review new acquisitions referred to by national authorities (Recital 71). Finally, its *ex post facto* sanction regime prescribes potentially hefty fines that carry a maximum fine of 10 percent of the total annual global turnover (Article 30).

competition and not AI regulation, it covers a broader range of technological change than competition law. For example, considering the prominent use of AI and ML algorithms by digital platforms, it has been suggested that the DMA could be a more influential regulation of AI than the AI Act.[110] In April 2025, the European Commission announced hefty fines for Apple and Meta (roughly $570 million and $230 million, respectively) for violations of the DMA.[111]

The US counts on established antitrust jurisprudence, but it has not been used for AI governance. Signals from the Biden administration suggested a more proactive approach: Biden's Executive Order stated that AI should not "lessen market competition,"[112] without further elaboration. Former Justice Department antitrust chief Jonathan Kanter made several remarks linking AI with his agency's work, including making a connection between the scale requirements in AI development and the tendency toward monopolization.[113] Former FTC chair Lina Khan's *New York Times* op-ed on AI regulation gives the example of IBM's unbundling of software and hardware in the 1960s to argue that antitrust work can promote innovation.[114]

REGULATORY TOOLS TO ADDRESS AI RISKS AND HARMS

Penalties and Fines

A penalty or fine appears to be the globally acknowledged instrument to enforce laws. All the analyzed legal documents except Biden's Executive Order have punitive provisions. The EU vows "proportionate and dissuasive penalties," which translate to administrative fines that amount to a percentage of the offending company's annual turnover or seven- or eight-digit figures in Euros.[115] South Korea's law likewise imposes administrative fees for failing to fulfill transparency requirements or rectify violations, and for non-Korean businesses, not registering a domestic agent.[116] Brazil's bill has sanctions ranging from warnings and fines to the suspension of business activity for violators of any part of the law.[117] China's bill likewise contains

110 Hacker, Cordes, and Rochon, "Regulating Gatekeeper AI and Data."

111 Adam Satariano, "Apple and Meta Are First to Be Hit by E.U. Digital Competition Law," *The New York Times*, April 23, 2025 (www.nytimes.com/2025/04/23/technology/apple-meta-eu-fines-competition-law.html).

112 Executive Order on the Safe, Secure, and Trustworthy Development and Use of Artificial Intelligence (US), Section 2 (a).

113 Adi Robertson, "The US government Is Gearing Up for an AI Antitrust Fight," *The Verge*, March 28, 2023 (www.theverge.com/2023/3/28/23660101/ai-competition-ftc-doj-lina-khan-jonathan-kanter-antitrust-summit).

114 Lina Khan, "We Must Regulate A.I. Here's How," *The New York Times*, May 3, 2023 (www.nytimes.com/2023/05/03/opinion/ai-lina-khan-ftc-technology.html).

115 EU AI Act, Recital 168 and Articles 99–101.

116 South Korea Basic AI Law, Article 43.

117 Provision for the Use of Artificial Intelligence (Brazil), Article 36.

a monetary fine provision alongside the threat of getting the offender's business license revoked in the case of serious violations – interestingly, the bill also envisions exemptions from administrative penalties for developers and providers that establish effective AI risk compliance systems.[118] Finally, Canada's bill would have gone farthest in characterizing some violations as criminal offenses, and thereby imposing punishments in addition to administrative fines.[119]

Impact and Conformity Assessment

The assessment of AI systems, especially risky ones, for their potential impact on the well-being of consumers is the most common legal tool to identify problems. Impact assessments, generally speaking, are prior studies that identify (1) the potential harms of an action or product on people or the environment and (2) remedies to eliminate or mitigate the harms. Ideally, impact assessments enable communication between regulators, businesses, and other stakeholders about future problems.[120]

Prior to the regulation of AI, the EU had already incorporated such assessments in the form of a "data protection impact assessment" into the GDPR. The terminology of AI ethics, safety, and responsibility has found its way into some assessment proposals as well. According to the EU's AI Act, high-risk AI products should undergo a conformity assessment to be carried out by third-party assessment bodies authorized to issue accreditation certificates.[121] Throughout the text, there are references to conformity to safety, human rights norms, and cybersecurity. In addition, the Act requires fundamental rights impact assessment for public-sector deployers of high-risk AI systems and private deployers that provide certain public services.[122]

Likewise, South Korea's Basic AI Law requires businesses using high-impact AI to conduct impact assessments for conformity with fundamental human rights but leaves implementation details to a future presidential decree.[123] Colorado's AI Consumer Protection Law requires impact assessment for high-risk AI systems but does not specify the normative standards the assessment is expected to uphold. Brazil's bill requires a preliminary assessment to determine the risk of an AI system before market deployment. High-risk systems should undergo algorithmic impact assessment, carried out by an expert team functionally independent from the AI provider.[124] The assessment will include an in-depth analysis of potential risks and

[118] Artificial Intelligence Law draft bill (China), Articles 82 and 93.
[119] AI and Data Act, Articles 29–30.
[120] Wernick, "Impact Assessment as a Legal Design Pattern – A 'Timeless Way' of Managing Future Risks?"
[121] EU AI Act, Article 6(1)(b), 43 and 44.
[122] EU AI Act, Article 27.
[123] South Korea Basic AI Law, Article 35.
[124] Provision for the Use of Artificial Intelligence (Brazil), Articles 13 and 22–26.

harms, as well as mitigation and transparency measures. If the assessment determines that the risks cannot be eliminated or substantially mitigated, the use of the AI system in question "shall be discontinued."[125]

The proposed assessment mechanism in China's bill relies as much on the AI developers and providers, which are expected to assess the safety risks of AI products and services either by themselves or through third parties,[126] as on the state, which "coordinates the establishment of an AI assessment and evaluation platform, establishes a unified, authoritative, and dynamically updated AI assessment framework, assessment dataset, and assessment standards, and opens up the technical interface of the platform for enterprise assessment."[127]

In the United States, the main objective of the Algorithmic Accountability Act was to "direct the Federal Trade Commission to require impact assessments of automated decision systems and augmented critical decision processes" for performance, fairness, bias and discrimination, transparency, contestability, privacy, safety, efficiency, and cost.[128] The 2023 NIST Guidelines probably go furthest to explain what AI impact assessments are meant to achieve: "accountability, combating harmful bias, examining impacts of AI systems, product safety, liability, and security, among others." The document adds, "AI actors such as impact assessors and evaluators provide technical, human factor, socio-cultural, and legal expertise."[129]

Transparency Requirements

AI transparency requirements date back to the GDPR in the EU: Article 22 of the GDPR recognizes a data subject's right not to be subjected to solely automated decisions. The AI Act requires the design and deployment of high-risk AI systems to be "sufficiently transparent,"[130] and introduces notice requirements for certain AI systems, especially those interacting with natural persons.[131] In addition, high-risk AI systems are expected to come with detailed "instructions of use"[132] and technical documentation (see section below). Article 78 balances out the transparency requirements with the confidentiality of information and data.

[125] Provision for the Use of Artificial Intelligence (Brazil), Article 21 (6) (§2).
[126] Artificial Intelligence Law draft bill (China), Articles 9 and 42.
[127] Artificial Intelligence Law draft bill (China), Article 64.
[128] Algorithmic Accountability Act, Section 4(a)(11).
[129] NIST AI 100-1 Artificial Intelligence Risk Management Framework, Appendix A.
[130] EU AI Act, Article 13.
[131] Article 50 requires notification of natural persons when they are interacting with an AI system, with two caveats: a law enforcement exemption is added, as well as the proviso that the transparency obligation holds unless this is obvious from the point of view of a "natural person who is reasonably well-informed, observant, and circumspect, taking into account the circumstances and the context of use." EU AI Act, Article 50.
[132] EU AI Act, Article 13.

In the United States, the failure to legislate the Algorithmic Accountability Act, which listed appealability and contestability among its normative principles,[133] has meant that transparency requirements did not advance at the federal level. Nonetheless, Colorado's AI Consumer Protection Act requires the deployers of high-risk AI systems making consequential decisions to disclose such use and deployment, describe in plain language the nature of the AI system, and provide consumers with the option to appeal adverse decisions. Appealability finds legislative support elsewhere: The Brazilian bill, which lists "transparency, explainability, intelligibility, and auditability" among core principles for AI development and use,[134] and recognizes the right to prior information and the right to an explanation for persons affected by AI systems,[135] states, "A person affected by an artificial intelligence system shall have the right to contest and to request the review of decisions, recommendations, or predictions generated by such a system that produce relevant legal effects or that significantly impact their interests."[136] Canada's AI and Data Act would have required those who deploy and manage a high-impact AI system to disclose how the system is used, the types of content, decisions, recommendations, and predictions it makes, and what mitigation measures are available.[137]

Post-deployment Monitoring, Documentation, and Reporting

Laws and bills do not devote much space to ensure AI systems' conformity to legal and ethical principles prior to their deployment. Nonetheless, the importance of continuous monitoring throughout the lifecycle of AI-powered products is recognized in the EU AI Act, Colorado's AI law, the Brazilian bill[138] and Biden's Executive Order.[139] The EU AI Act stipulates a post-market monitoring system, built into the technical documentation, to ensure compliance beyond deployment.[140] It also requires technical documentation for high-risk AI systems (Annex IV), which includes a description of the AI system, its processes, risk management system, relevant changes made by the provider through its lifecycle, a copy of the EU declaration of conformity, and a post-market monitoring plan. The Colorado law also mentions "post-deployment monitoring" without further elaboration.[141]

133 Algorithmic Accountability Act, Section 4 (a) (11) (C).
134 Provision for the Use of Artificial Intelligence (Brazil), Article 3.
135 Provision for the Use of Artificial Intelligence (Brazil), Article 5.
136 Provision for the Use of Artificial Intelligence (Brazil), Article 9.
137 AI and Data Act (Canada), Article 11 (2).
138 Provision for the Use of Artificial Intelligence (Brazil), Article 30 (f).
139 Executive Order on the Safe, Secure, and Trustworthy Development and Use of Artificial Intelligence (US), Section 10.1 (b) (4).
140 EU AI Act, Article 72.
141 An Act Concerning Consumer Protections in Interactions with Artificial Intelligence Systems (Colorado), 6-1-1703.

Stakeholder Engagement

Various laws and bills include stakeholder engagement as part of their governance model, yet only one sets binding obligations on AI providers or deployers to decide together with stakeholders. That one exception is the EU AI Act, which requires the formation of an advisory forum representing "industry, start-ups, [small and medium enterprises], civil society and academia" to provide technical expertise and advice to the European Artificial Intelligence Board and the European Commission.[142] In addition, the Act envisions stakeholder participation in setting up codes of practice and standards.[143] Brazil's bill asks for "public participation, through a consultation procedure with interested parties, even if in a simplified manner" for updating algorithmic impact assessments.[144]

Biden's Executive Order tasked various government agencies to consult with relevant stakeholders to identify AI risks and harms and disseminate informal guidance. The NIST document indicates willingness to include all stakeholders in the development of the AI Risk Management Framework. The vetoed California bill would have asked the Government Operations Agency to include input from stakeholders, "including academics, industry, the open-source community, and government entities," to develop definitions.[145] Finally, the Council of Europe Framework Convention encourages stakeholder engagement, where appropriate, as a general principle to identify and address AI-driven problems.

Regulatory Agencies

Most AI laws and bills designate novel administrative bodies or add novel responsibilities to existing ones to carry out the implementation of regulatory provisions. The EU's AI Act envisions a European Artificial Intelligence Office ("AI Office") as a specific function of the European Commission to enforce the Act.[146] More specifically, the AI Office will collaborate with member states and experts to enforce rules governing general-purpose AI systems. South Korea's Basic AI Law creates a National AI Committee, an AI Policy Center, and an AI Safety Research Institute.[147] The UK's bill would establish an AI Authority, and the Chinese bill mentions a "main oversight department for AI" to coordinate the development and regulation of

142 EU AI Act, Article 67.

143 EU AI Act, Articles 57, 62, and 95.

144 Provision for the Use of Artificial Intelligence (Brazil), Article 25 (2).

145 An act to add Chapter 22.6 (commencing with Section 22602) to Division 8 of the Business and Professions Code, and to add Sections 11547.6 and 11547.6.1 to the Government Code, relating to artificial intelligence (California), Section 4 (d) (3) (C).

146 EU AI Act, Article 3 (47) and Article 64.

147 Basic AI Law (South Korea), Articles 7, 11, and 12.

AI at the provincial level and above. Biden's Executive Order stands out for resorting to numerous existing agencies in the executive branch to regulate AI.

Business Incentives and Technical Solutions

AI laws and bills do not only generate obligations; they provide opportunities for the safe development of AI as well. Every single bill and law discussed in this chapter is framed as an effort to promote AI development. More specifically, the EU AI Act seeks to foster innovation through regulatory sandboxes and testing in real-world conditions, especially for small-and-medium enterprises and startups. Following the EU's lead, Brazil and the UK also propose regulatory sandboxes. Legal documents vow to facilitate the pre-deployment safety testing of frontier AI models (US Memorandum of 2024)[148] and develop public infrastructure to support the private sector in testing, verification, and certification (South Korea's Basic AI Law).[149]

As argued elsewhere in this book, the different government models are complementary, rather than mutually exclusive. The technical solutions covered in Chapter 4 are routinely recommended by laws and bills. Biden's Executive Order in particular would have granted businesses leeway to regulate AI through their own tools, as it required multiple federal agencies to set standards in watermarking and red-teaming. In fact, the Executive Order followed a public red-teaming exercise promoted by the White House at the DEF CON in August 2023. The EU's AI Act mentions voluntary best practices and codes of conduct that businesses may adopt in addition to mandatory requirements. South Korea's Basic AI Law vows public support for voluntary verification and certification of AI safety and reliability.[150] Brazil's bill states, "Voluntary adherence to a code of good practices and governance may be considered indicative of good faith on the part of the agent and shall be taken into account by the competent authority for the purposes of applying administrative sanctions,"[151] thereby acknowledging the lawmakers' willingness to incorporate business self-regulation into the law.

CONCLUSION

As personal computers and the internet began to revolutionize modern life in the 1990s, technology legislation around the world, especially in the United States, was permissive toward technology companies, whose actions met little or no resistance from lawmakers and the general public.[152] The development of the internet, and later

[148] US Memorandum of 2024, 3.3 (c).
[149] Basic AI Law (South Korea), Article 24.
[150] Basic AI Law (South Korea), Article 30.
[151] Provision for the Use of Artificial Intelligence (Brazil), Article 30 (§3).
[152] Tarnoff, *Internet for the People: The Fight for Our Digital Future.*

social media, took place in the absence of meaningful government regulation of all but the most egregious violations of fundamental rights. It was only in the mid-2010s, with scandals like Cambridge Analytica, that calls to regulate technology companies grew louder. Even then, however, advocates for a more permissive approach kept pushing back against the legal regulation of technologies like AI, arguing that regulation would stifle innovation or that technology would develop solutions to its own problems. What complicated the picture for the legal regulation of AI was the perception that AI was too complicated for lawmakers to understand, let alone set rules on. In fact, the notion that lawmakers lack a basic understanding of today's technologies remains a popular trope. Mark Zuckerberg's Congressional hearing on April 10, 2018, during which some senators were asking blatantly misinformed questions, has served to strengthen this view. Thus, overcoming the widely held perceptions that the legal regulation of AI is undesirable and unfeasible took a while, but today, regulating AI risks and harms through the law finds more support globally.

Not surprisingly, the laws and bills covered in this chapter are addressed primarily to the businesses that develop or use AI systems. Public-sector users are under the same set of obligations as private-sector ones, broadly speaking, but law enforcement exemptions exist in laws like the EU's AI Act. In terms of problem definitions, AI-centric laws and bills tend to identify bias and discrimination on the basis of gender or race (and sometimes disability) as risks. Likewise, assuring data quality appears to be a cross-cutting concern. Beyond these two areas, however, they share little by way of problem definitions. Even though AI-centric laws and bills say little about data privacy and protection or harms resulting from AI-generated or AI-amplified content, multiple data privacy, content moderation, consumer protection, and children's online safety laws around the world broach these issues. AI-centric laws and bills are silent on structural problems, such as labor considerations and environmental degradation. Antitrust laws in the EU and the US, while certainly not AI-specific, may be used to address another structural problem, namely market concentration in the AI industry. Finally, military uses of AI have thus far remained out of scope for AI laws and bills.

AI-centric laws and bills combine fines and penalties with less punitive tools, such as pre-deployment impact and conformity assessments and post-deployment transparency, monitoring, and documentation requirements, to keep businesses in check. The EU's AI Act is the only one to lay out these legal obligations in clear and detailed fashion; vague definitions and obligations in all the other laws and bills mean that the nuances will be worked out at the implementation phase. The repurposing of existing agencies to implement AI-related provisions is common practice, but in addition, the EU and South Korea envision new regulatory agencies to enforce the new AI laws. The laws and bills do more than set limits on business conduct: Incentivizing businesses to develop AI safely through regulatory sandboxes, self-regulation, and voluntary codes of conduct are found in the laws and bills of several countries. Finally, the EU's AI Act envisions a structured approach to stakeholder engagement in the future, and a few other legal documents make somewhat vague allusions to public participation.

Addressing AI risks and harms should not be imagined through false binaries, such as government vs. business, law vs. technology, or regulation vs. innovation. Rather, legal regulation forms one component of governance. In fact, several laws and bills covered in this chapter contain provisions to facilitate technical solutions and promote business self-regulation. Laws create a secondary market as well. Especially the complex legal requirements associated with the EU's AI Act are likely to encourage a cottage industry of data protection, assessment readiness, technical documentation, and auditing support professionals.

AI governance without laws is unimaginable. Yet it is not a panacea. Lawmakers are torn between promoting their country's or region's AI companies, no matter what the cost, and setting meaningful guardrails against them. Many of them do not understand or care about the potential risks and harms. Some of them are simply starstruck by technology leaders. AI governance is unlikely to rise so high on voters' agenda as to prompt lawmakers to do better. Thus, those who are concerned about the future of AI should, individually and collectively, push lawmakers to address the multiple potential and real harms.

7

Another Way to Govern AI

A Radical-Democratic Vision

The quintessential AI doom narrative is that machines will eventually learn to disable their kill-switch to subjugate, even exterminate, humanity. Even though most of the people who develop or seriously reflect on AI do not spend much time or energy worrying about the Terminator scenario, out-of-control machines remain a popular trope. Some commentators note that our fear of machines may be a projection of our controlling and abusive attitude toward those machines, which is an extension of how we treat living beings, including fellow humans.[1] After all, playwright Karel Čapek came up with the word *robot* after the Czech word for serf labor, *robota*.[2] The fear of out-of-control machines may be a projection of powerful technology leaders' anxiety: *What if a higher intelligence treats us the way we treat everything and everyone around us?*

This chapter's premise is that the widespread anxiety around AI stems from concrete human experiences that predate, but are amplified by, the advent of modern AI. Technology is embedded in political, economic, social, cultural, and military structures that are experienced as disempowering and alienating to most people today. Existing structures interact with the latest technologies to reshape the distribution of power in societies – and perhaps not surprisingly, people in positions of economic and political power seek to retain and expand their power through technology, while others are left to fear for their lives and well-being. It is not humans vs. machines; it is humans vs. humans.

This chapter aims to answer the question: *Does it have to be this way?* Commentators disagree on just how narrow humanity's options are once AI is unleashed and what those options are like. Perhaps the future of AI is open-ended – whether this is cause for hope or dread is another question: Optimists assert that an emerging technology like AI will let a thousand flowers bloom, as more innovators build on existing

[1] Vallor, *The AI Mirror: How to Reclaim Our Humanity in an Age of Machine Thinking*.

[2] The association between technology and forced labor is not uniquely modern: mythical automata were likened to slaves in antiquity. Adrienne Mayor, *Gods and Robots: Myths, Machines, and Ancient Dreams of Technology* (Princeton & Oxford: Princeton University Press, 2018), p. 93.

know-how to come up with new products, jobs, and ways of being in completely unpredictable ways, while pessimists see in open-ended technological development the potential for planetary catastrophe. The other end of the intellectual spectrum is technological determinism: The goals, methods, and logics associated with AI narrow down the options to such an extent that humans face inevitability. Again, technological determinism comes with optimistic and pessimistic flavors, the latter being a lot more common: Optimistic determinists believe that what is inevitable is happiness and prosperity,[3] while pessimists expect tyranny and widespread misery.[4]

I believe that the future of AI is not overdetermined: There exists no single path to bliss or misery. The AI governance decisions we make today will shape the AI of tomorrow. Yet, it would be wrong to portray technology as a field of endless possibilities – either exhilarating or terrifying. Social structures interact with technology in ways that limit the direction of technological change. AI was born into a world of socioeconomic inequality, corporate economic control, democratic backsliding, environmental degradation, and military competition. It has so far aggravated these structural conditions,[5] which no technological breakthrough or technology governance scheme can reverse magically. Thus, a technology like AI can bring about meaningful positive change if the societies in which it is embedded are reorganized along with the technology.

Thus, this chapter diagnoses the social–structural conditions that underlie the AI-related problems described throughout this book and calls for citizens' constant vigilance and participation in the development, design, use, and regulation of AI – in two words, *radical democracy*. The premise of this chapter is that contemporary technologies, AI included, do not effect change in a vacuum; instead, they are "sociotechnical entities"[6] embedded in the social structures that powerfully shape, and in turn are shaped, by them. We are not the first generation to experience and reflect on technology's negative impact in the form of disempowerment, alienation, labor exploitation, bias and discrimination, disinformation, privacy violations, environmental degradation, and more. We have the luxury of thinking together with intellectuals of earlier generations, especially those who lived through some of the worst excesses of technology-enabled inequality and violence in the twentieth century, to diagnose problems and imagine solutions in a different context. AI is often marketed as a novel and unprecedented phenomenon, but many of its attendant features (such as the datafication and quantification of human experience, and the reduction of complex social issues to estimation and classification problems)

3 Kelly, *The Inevitable: Understanding the 12 Technological Forces That Will Shape Our Future*.

4 Harari, "Why Technology Favors Tyranny."

5 Atoosa Kasirzadeh, "Algorithmic Fairness and Structural Injustice: Insights from Feminist Political Philosophy," in *Proceedings of the 2022 AAAI/ACM Conference on AI, Ethics, and Society* (Oxford, UK; New York, NY, 2022), pp. 349–56; Zhiyuan "Jerry" Lin and others, "The Limits of Human Predictions of Recidivism," *Science Advances*, 6.7 (2020), pp. 1–8.

6 Kasirzadeh, "Algorithmic Fairness and Structural Injustice," p. 354.

worried thinkers like Herbert Marcuse and Hannah Arendt, who kept questioning what it means to be human in the age of industrialization, authoritarianism, mass-produced death, and nuclear warfare. In their minds, economic and technological change could not be disentangled from the political. Having left their homeland during the Nazi regime and experienced the destruction of the world they grew up in, they kept asking all their lives: How were these horrors possible at a time of breathtaking technological change?

This chapter invites readers to a dialogue with past and present social theory to diagnose the underlying causes of disempowerment and alienation at a time of rapid technological transformation and proposes radical democracy as a collective solution. Three intellectual traditions are the source of inspiration: Critical Theory, Science and Technology Studies, and Democratic Theory. The section called "Technology, Domination, and the Loss of Purpose" rereads Herbert Marcuse's work alongside Andrew Feenberg and Langdon Winner to explore the ways technological change perpetuates unequal social relations. "Disempowerment and Alienation in the Face of AI" offers concrete connections between contemporary AI and disempowerment in light of contemporary social thought. Then, this chapter offers a reading of Hannah Arendt to make the case for reclaiming politics in the face of technology-induced disempowerment. The final section lays out a radical-democratic program.

TECHNOLOGY, DOMINATION, AND THE LOSS OF PURPOSE

Ordinary people are disempowered and alienated in the face of emerging technologies, AI included. Despite media assurances that anyone with a little bit of training can be a competent user, if not a developer, of the latest gadget on the shelves, most people have no control over the design, development, and use of high-tech products. It is true that billions of people have interacted with chatbots, and used AI indirectly through recommender systems, but worldwide fascination with AI should not be mistaken for universal AI access, literacy, or satisfaction. Most people still do not understand or use, much less design or develop, AI tools. In fact, national and global discrepancies in AI access and literacy threaten to deepen the digital divide.[7] Furthermore, AI-driven bias, discrimination, and privacy violations do not target voluntary users only: Individuals and communities are adversely affected as a result of governments' or corporations' use of AI tools without their consent. In other words, many people are cut off from the benefits of AI while bearing its risks.

There is no doubt that today's technologies present unprecedented opportunities and challenges. Yet, it would be a mistake to conclude that the problems they bring are entirely novel. As Ruha Benjamin notes with respect to digital labor

[7] Turner Lee, *Digitally Invisible: How the Internet Is Creating the New Underclass.*

platforms, these technologies are "embedded in and reinforce long-standing forms of racial, gender, and class inequity."[8] The two-way relationship between oppressive social structures and technology was modeled by Herbert Marcuse, a member of the Institute for Social Research (popularly known as the "Frankfurt School") at the time he was forced to leave Germany in the 1930s. His essay "Some Social Implications of Modern Technology," published in 1941 in the Institute's journal, fears for the loss of freedom in the age of mechanization. Working through themes Marcuse would explore further in *One-Dimensional Man* two decades later, the 1941 essay explains how modern technology, far from supporting the kind of *individualistic rationality* that the liberal spirit of early modernity had promised, has destroyed independent thinking and spontaneity for the individual worker. That is because the mechanization and rationalization that come with technology serve the interests of giant enterprises. Put simply, the motive for invention has become "power over other men" rather than "technical efficiency."[9]

Portending the age of AI, Marcuse starts his 1958–1959 lecture "From Ontology to Technology: Fundamental Tendencies of Industrial Society" with a description of the parallels between scientific developments and social ones: The search for efficiency, quantification, and the reduction of all relations to exchange value connect them as a unifying principle, to the point that every advancement in society, technological ones included, ends up accompanying repression. In typical Marcusean fashion, he combines Freud and Marx to argue that civilization has subjugated people to work, and that technical progress, despite unleashing the realistic possibility of doing away with labor, has instead resulted in repressing and alienating workers.[10] All in all, we could have lived in societies with little or no need for labor, but instead, the specific kind of rationality that modern labor conditions and the accompanying technology impose on us ends up producing the irrational situation where "technology itself perpetuates misery, violence, and destruction."[11]

Marcuse stands out among his peers in and around the Frankfurt School for his willingness to engage the burgeoning field of Science and Technology Studies (STS). The very first citation in the 1941 essay is Lewis Mumford's 1936 *Technics and Civilization* – one of the pioneering texts in STS. The 1958–1959 lecture takes up a theme that would later become a favorite for the STS scholarship: The critique of technical neutrality. He argues that tools do not exist independently of "an

8 Ruha Benjamin, *Viral Justice: How We Grow the World We Want* (Princeton University Press, 2022), p. 147.

9 Herbert Marcuse, "Some Social Implications of Modern Technology," in *Technology, War and Fascism: Collected Papers of Herbert Marcuse Volume One*, ed. Douglas Kellner (London and New York: Routledge, 1998), pp. 39–41.

10 Herbert Marcuse, "From Ontology to Technology: Fundamental Tendencies of Industrial Society," in *Critical Theory and Society: A Reader*, ed. by Stephen Eric Bronner and Douglas MacKay Kellner (Routledge, 1989), pp. 119–27: 123–126.

11 Marcuse, "From Ontology to Technology," p. 124.

ensemble, a technological totality" within which they have a purpose.[12] To refer to this totality, he uses the French word *technicité*. Modern technology has destroyed all prior teleology; by losing its concrete purpose, it has abstracted itself from society, too.[13] Consequently, what remains as its purpose is pure instrumentality (an idea that he borrows from Martin Heidegger), which ultimately feeds into the domination of nature as a "hostile, destructive, and violent force," and consequently, domination over other people.[14]

He scrutinizes the role of technology in society again in his famous book *One-Dimensional Man*, to argue that technology foregrounds political, cultural, and social processes in modern times: "The technological *a priori* is a political *a priori* inasmuch as the transformation of nature involves that of man."[15] In other words, tools are not just there to be used for whatever purpose people designate for them; instead, technology "circumscribes an entire culture; it projects a historical totality – a 'world'."[16] The specific way in which modern technology shapes society is as a form of "social control and domination."[17]

These observations on technology are closely linked to his analysis of science and technology as professional endeavors. The instrumental nature of modern technology means that "pure science" has become increasingly operationalized under "applied science."[18] In relation to that, scientists and technologists no longer ask questions about the goals of science and technology; instead, they are focused on getting their work done. The 1958–1959 lecture does not mince words in describing the science and technology specialists of his day: "Contemporary positivism, semantics, symbolic logic, and linguistic analysis define and filter the universe of discourse for the use of technicians, specialists, and experts who calculate, adjust, and match without ever asking *for whom* and *for what*. The occupation of these specialists is to *make things work*, but not to give an end to this process."[19]

What do we get to learn from Marcuse's reflections on the automation technologies of the mid-twentieth century? Marcuse is sometimes mistaken for a pessimistic thinker due to his rather bleak predictions in *One-Dimensional Man*, but his contention that oppressed social groups that have been excluded from capitalist co-optation mechanisms will revolutionize society is often credited for inspiring the 1968 student protests. In his simultaneous pessimism and optimism lies a complex vision of modernity and technology. Despite his diagnosis of modern science and

[12] Marcuse, "From Ontology to Technology," p. 123.
[13] Marcuse, "From Ontology to Technology," p. 120.
[14] Marcuse, "From Ontology to Technology," p. 124.
[15] Herbert Marcuse, *One-Dimensional Man: Studies in the Ideology of Advanced Industrial Society* (Beacon Press, 1991), p. 156.
[16] Marcuse, *One-Dimensional Man*, p. 154.
[17] Marcuse, *One-Dimensional Man*, p. 158.
[18] Marcuse, *One-Dimensional Man*, p. 154.
[19] Marcuse, "From Ontology to Technology," p. 122.

technology as a potentially totalitarian endeavor and specialists as unthinking executors of know-how, Marcuse never gave up the hope that science and technology could serve as elements of collective liberation in a different society.[20] If put in the service of concrete human needs, technology could liberate humans from labor, and through that, help to construct a more egalitarian society.

Andrew Feenberg offers a Marcuse-inspired critique of recent technological developments in the age of AI. Accordingly, the functional rationality of modern technology is separated from its social meaning.[21] Technology in and of itself does not favor a specific political or social order; nonetheless, "modern forms of hegemony are based on a specific type of technical mediation of a variety of social activities."[22] Marcuse's synthesis of phenomenology and Marxism, far from falling into obsolescence in retrospect, has become newly relevant as digital technologies unfolded. People's lived experiences are shaped by technology today much more than in the 1960s, when Marcuse warned against instrumental control through technology. In turn, ordinary people are engaged with questions surrounding the impact of science and technology – something Marcuse could not have predicted in the 1960s.[23]

For all his attentiveness to early STS work, Marcuse offers rather generic insights into technology in the modern world. His works offer a broad overview of what technology can and cannot do in capitalist nation-states while leaving gaps in our understanding of how the goals, methods, and logics built into specific products or services interact with the societies in which they are embedded. This is the precise starting point for "Do Artifacts Have Politics?" – Langdon Winner's genre-defining 1980 article. It takes issue with deterministic views that see in technology either a mere reflection of social, political, economic, or cultural power relations, or an all-powerful force shaping those relations unilaterally.[24] He does acknowledge, much like Marcuse, that particular power relations may be embedded in modern technology – what he calls "technopolitics" elsewhere.[25] Nonetheless, he pays due attention to specific instances in the design, development, deployment, and use of technology to unearth embedded power relations. He offers the example of Long Island overpasses that were designed intentionally low to block public buses, and their low-income riders, convenient access to affluent neighborhoods[26] – a contention that

20 Douglas Kellner, "Schoolman on Marcuse," *New German Critique*, no. 26 (1982), pp. 185–201.

21 Andrew Feenberg, *Between Reason and Experience: Essays in Technology and Modernity* (MIT Press, 2010), p. 18.

22 Andrew Feenberg, *Between Reason and Experience: Essays in Technology and Modernity* (MIT Press, 2010), p. 6.

23 Andrew Feenberg, "Marcuse's Critique of Technology Today," *Philosophy & Social Criticism*, 49.6 (2023), pp. 672–85.

24 Winner, "Do Artifacts Have Politics?"

25 Winner, "Where Technological Determinism Went."

26 Winner, "Do Artifacts Have Politics?" pp. 123–125.

has been criticized on empirical grounds.[27] Even when technology is not designed for such narrowly instrumental goals, the combination of scientific research, technological invention and the profit motive in capitalism may reinforce one another in complex ways: He gives the example of tomato-harvesting machines, which could have benefited many of the participants in that line of work but ended up benefiting large-scale producers, not as a result of technological imperatives but rather, due to the big players' oversized power to use technological change to their advantage.[28]

Yet, Winner refutes the deterministic idea that a single dominant form of power inheres in a period's technology: "Consciously or unconsciously, deliberately or inadvertently, societies *choose* structures for technologies that influence how people are going to work, communicate, travel, consume, and so forth over a very long time."[29] He gives a few examples to make this point: He finds the notion that nuclear power necessitates a "techno-scientific-industrial-military elite" unduly deterministic.[30] Likewise, he asserts that the inaccessibility of many technologies has less to do with malicious intentions toward persons with disabilities than with the failure to build in remedies into design. The same technology could have been designed differently to ensure accessibility.[31] This is in part disconcerting: Technologies do not have to be designed maliciously to produce harmful outcomes. Yet, Winner's analysis opens the door to hope: Most technologies can be designed and redesigned in more ways than one – including through democratic means and toward socially beneficial goals.

AI has unleashed possibilities for transformation in almost every walk of life. It can potentially benefit humanity in multiple ways. Yet, narratives of disempowerment and alienation take over those of common good in future visions of AI. Why is that? The next section investigates the structural roots of disempowerment and alienation influencing the design, development, and use of AI today.

DISEMPOWERMENT AND ALIENATION IN THE FACE OF AI

The advent of AI did not create disempowerment and alienation out of the blue. To the contrary, AI was born into a world where lack of political and economic control was already the lived reality of most people. Once deployed, AI tools assist in decisions that shape individuals' and communities' access to opportunities, exposure to risks and harms, and relationships to others. School admission, hiring and promotion, arrest and parole, and mortgage are among the many decision areas in which automated tools help to determine life-transforming outcomes for people, including members of vulnerable populations that are already excluded from the governance

27 Joerges, "Do Politics Have Artefacts?"
28 Winner, "Do Artifacts Have Politics?" p. 126.
29 Winner, p. 127.
30 Winner, p. 130.
31 Winner p. 125.

of schools, businesses, financial institutions, and governments. Thus, the net effect of the interaction between AI and social realities is deepening disempowerment and alienation.

The power relations that deserve scrutiny in the age of AI are ones that we have already been living with. This is not a story of evil machines wresting control from humans; rather, AI risks deepening the domination of nature and many humans by a few humans. In Kate Crawford's words: "… AI is neither *artificial* nor *intelligent*. Rather, artificial intelligence is both embodied and material, made from natural resources, fuel, human labor, infrastructures, logistics, histories, and classifications. … In fact, artificial intelligence as we know it depends entirely on a much wider set of political and social structures. … AI systems are ultimately designed to serve existing dominant interests. In this sense, artificial intelligence is a registry of power."[32]

More specifically, there are five broad reasons why so many people feel alienated from the development and use of today's AI. Misalignment between the profit motive and human interests, the market concentration of a few major companies, the presentation of AI as an expert field, research and development gaps favoring a few companies in a few countries, and finally, the hierarchical nature of the modern capitalist workplace all contribute to AI disempowerment and alienation. Each dynamic is described in detail as follows.

Misalignment between the Profit Motive and Human Interests

In an interview, science fiction writer Ted Chiang says: "I tend to think that most fears about A.I. are best understood as fears about capitalism. … And technology and capitalism have been so closely intertwined that it's hard to distinguish the two."[33] Why should that be the case? There is no doubt that private companies' profit motive may align with consumers' interest in safe and useful products in a capitalist economy – as many of the examples in this book illustrate. However, cases in which individuals and entire social groups find themselves at risk due to the monetization of AI cannot be ignored.[34] Since their inception, data-driven AI products have privatized gains while socializing risk. Ordinary people contribute to the development of AI by sharing information about themselves, including personal details and creative output, only to be excluded from decisions concerning how the collected data will be used, and to what end. The pursuit of the common good is made conditional on the long-term profitability of AI companies. Thus, ordinary people's collective interests in AI are reduced to the dictates of profit – and it would

32 Kate Crawford, *Atlas of AI* (Yale University Press, 2021), p. 8.

33 "Transcript: Ezra Klein Interviews Ted Chiang," *The New York Times*, March 30, 2021 (www.nytimes.com/2021/03/30/podcasts/ezra-klein-podcast-ted-chiang-transcript.html).

34 Noble, *Algorithms of Oppression: How Search Engines Reinforce Racism*.

be an understatement to say that profitability and the common good, no matter how defined, are not always aligned.[35]

Most AI research and development takes place in corporate settings that treat training data, algorithms, and model weights as proprietary. Even supposedly open-source companies often conceal one or some of those elements. What that means is that outside experts, let alone laypeople, cannot assess the impact of AI tools on individuals and communities, despite the fact that some of the groundbreaking research assessing AI risks and harms has come from replication studies that reconstruct or slightly tweak existing algorithms with relevant data – think about *ProPublica* researchers' discovery of racial bias in crime-prediction algorithms in 2016. If inclusivity and auditability are significant principles to keep AI companies accountable, then the proprietary character of data and algorithms runs the risk of disempowering potential contributors and critics. Obviously, inclusivity and auditability do not mean that everyone should get access to all data and algorithms at all times, but the refusal to allow independent researchers to assess data and algorithms in the name of private gains risks further disempowerment.

Market Concentration

Deepening the alienation of most people from AI is the fact that today's technology sector, despite all the rejoicing for a startup revolution, are still deeply concentrated in the hands of a few businesses.[36] Anyone with a computer (or pen and paper, for that matter) can devise algorithms, but generating meaningful insights using them supersedes the capacity of most individuals and businesses, as that requires large-scale data collection, as well as computation infrastructure to store and analyze data. While it may be plausible to compete by developing AI systems that use smaller quantities of data more efficiently (after all, Chinese company DeepSeek[37] succeeded in shocking American tech leaders by releasing an LLM that was claimed to meet comparable levels of success at a fraction of resource use) or to encourage the sharing of resources through open-sourcing, the advantage of monopolistic or oligopolistic competition for large companies cannot be denied.

Market concentration adds yet another layer of alienation because even people who see themselves as AI researchers or entrepreneurs face the pressure of pooling their labor and investment into a small number of companies or being sidelined. AI for social good research takes place in large companies, not universities or small companies. Exceptions notwithstanding, the small-scale research projects and business initiatives that serve the common good through AI face irrelevance. All in all, AI today has favored oligopolistic competition rather than

35 Fuchs, *Digital Humanism: A Philosophy for 21st Century Digital Society*.

36 Schaake, *The Tech Coup: How to Save Democracy from Silicon Valley*.

37 https://deepseek.ai

the flourishing of a vibrant marketplace, resulting in the reduction of vast technological possibilities to the interests and visions of a few companies.

AI as an Expert Field

Everyone must have seen the typical stock image accompanying AI news: A giant brain or an android face, superimposed on a blue grid illuminated by a glowing lightbulb – or a variation on the theme. The desire to convey a message of machine intelligence and insightfulness is unmistakable, as is the uncanny inhumanness of what is supposed to represent a humanlike faculty. This is perhaps an apt metaphor for AI: The more industry leaders try to anthropomorphize AI, the more the ordinary person feels alienated from it. In fact, the trust gap between AI experts and the public could not be greater, at least in the United States: A Pew Research Center survey finds that the percentage of AI experts anticipating AI's positive effect vs. negative effect in the next 20 years is 56 percent to 15 percent. Among non-expert adults, the percentages are 17 percent to 35 percent.[38] This is in great part because AI tends to be portrayed as an expert field led by computer scientists, data scientists, and mathematicians, superseding laypeople's abilities and understanding.

Does this necessarily pose a problem? It is undeniable that knowledge of coding, machine learning, statistics, linear algebra, and social network theory is necessary for AI research and development. What is more, the layperson does not have to understand the inner workings of every tool: After all, what do most passengers know about airplanes, drivers about cars, or patients about medical diagnostic machines? The distribution of risks and benefits in AI cannot be compared to that of earlier technologies, though. Most technologies produce tangible, immediate risks and harms when they malfunction. Airplanes generally function well, and the times they don't make the headlines. Cars usually work, and when they don't, they are taken to a mechanic.

Unlike these examples, any kind of AI-related negative impact imposes complex, probabilistic risks on affected persons. There is no specific component to fix; rather, a piece of problematic input or algorithmic oversight can generate ripple effects across an entire AI system. Furthermore, a functioning airplane, when piloted with due diligence, serves its designers,' owners,' pilots,' and passengers' interests. A perfectly functional AI tool, say, an autonomous weapon, may serve its developers,' owners,' and users' interests while negatively affecting those on the receiving end, say, targeted civilians. In fact, even the engineers developing AI products do not always control the uses they are put to. Also, good policy cannot be left to specialists. Aviation policy is not single-handedly determined by airplane manufacturers

38 Colleen McClain, Brian Kennedy, Jeffrey Gottfried, Monica Anderson, and Giancarlo Pasquini, "How the U.S. Public and AI Experts View Artificial Intelligence," *Pew Research Center*, April 3, 2025 (www.pewresearch.org/internet/2025/04/03/how-the-us-public-and-ai-experts-view-artificial-intelligence/).

or pilots; healthcare policy takes more than insurance companies and health professionals; and transportation policy should not be taken over by car manufacturers. Thus, leaving the decisions about the design, development, deployment, and use of AI to experts alone comes at great risk to ordinary people.[39]

Research and Development Gaps

"The present age favors the big laboratory and the man who is sensitive to the profit motive."[40] Norbert Wiener's words from 1954, written for a different moment in technological developments, shed light on the reduction of AI research and development (R&D) to the dictates of the profit motive in the context of oligopolistic competition in the tech industry, the disparities in infrastructure investment that benefit those oligopolies, and the employment of AI researchers by businesses rather than universities and other research institutions. Today's AI development takes place in "silos, disparate laboratories, secret government facilities, elite academic institutions, and the offices of very large companies working independently throughout the world."[41]

AI R&D reinforces socioeconomic and technological hierarchies within countries and globally. Corporations have overtaken the government in R&D investment: The private sector in the United States accounts for about 72 percent of R&D,[42] reversing the trend of government-funded technology development in the post-World War II period. The profit motive dominates any other drive or consideration in the development of AI.

Even though universities still lead in research excellence, corporate recruitment of academic talent and corporation-university collaboration mean that some of the best research in AI could move away from universities in the future. Thus, modern societies' mechanisms for assessing the quality of science and technology, such as the peer review system and university tenure and promotion, are losing their ability to maintain standards of research excellence. Along with that comes an inability to shape academic and intellectual discourses around technology. Anyone who wants to design, develop, deploy, improve, or criticize a piece of technology is incentivized to work at a major technology company – or risk irrelevance.

Further deepening inequalities globally is the fact that most AI-related research still comes from the United States, Europe, and China, and to a lesser extent countries like India, South Korea, Singapore, and Canada. Africa, Latin America, and

39 Waldman, "Challenging Technology Expertise."

40 Wiener, *Invention*.

41 Flynn Coleman, *A Human Algorithm: How Artificial Intelligence Is Redefining Who We Are* (Melville House UK, 2020), p. 49.

42 Darrell M. West, "R&D for the Public Good: Ways to Strengthen Societal Innovation in the United States," *Brookings* Institute (blog), October 10, 2022 (www.brookings.edu/articles/rd-for-the-public-good-ways-to-strengthen-societal-innovation-in-the-united-states/).

the Middle East do not show up in any investment, R&D, or patent figures.[43] Most of the world's populations provide raw data while hoping to benefit from AI tools as end-users but do not participate in the development of AI in any way. Technologies like AI-assisted facial recognition and lethal autonomous weapons systems will affect the well-being of immigrants at borders and unarmed civilians in conflict zones – among the most vulnerable groups imaginable. Yet, the vast majority of the world's people do not have a voice in AI governance.

Undemocratic Workplace and Unequal Social Relations

The technical nature of AI development should not obscure the fact that AI jobs are jobs. A 2024 McKinsey survey finds that employees who identify as users and non-users of generative AI alike find cognitive and social-emotional skills to be more important than technical ones for performing their jobs. The same survey finds that AI-using employees who plan to stay in their current jobs value workplace flexibility, meaningful work, and support for employee health and well-being as the top three engagement factors. The report that came out of the survey calls for reimagining jobs to be more human-centric, redefining workplace flexibility, and incentivizing good communication.[44] Yet, AI is being developed in a hierarchical business context in which shareholder value dominates all other considerations for boards and managers. What is more, today's AI was born into a context in which conventional institutions to protect workers' rights, such as labor unions, traditional employment contracts, and social safety nets, had already been weakened.[45] Thus, people who participate in the AI economy as tech workers have little or no control over what gets produced and to what end – not to mention the "gig workers" who face even more precarious labor conditions.[46]

It is no wonder that many people's reaction to AI is fear. The discrepancy between human needs and the imperatives of capitalist competition explains the trepidation around job replacement through AI: Productivity-enhancing tools are seen as competitors to human laborers, not because of specifications intrinsic to the tools but because the power to make employment-related decisions resides with professional management and shareholders, to the exclusion of workers.

43 Maslej et al., "Artificial Intelligence Index Report 2025": Chapter 1.

44 Aaron De Smet, Sandra Durth, Bryan Hancock, Marino Mugayar-Baldocchi, and Angelika Reich "The Human Side of Generative AI: Creating a Path to Productivity," *McKinsey Quarterly*, March 18, 2024 (www.mckinsey.com/capabilities/people-and-organizational-performance/our-insights/the-human-side-of-generative-ai-creating-a-path-to-productivity).

45 Diane E. Bailey and Stephen R. Barley, "Beyond Design and Use: How Scholars Should Study Intelligent Technologies," *Information and Organization*, 30.2 (2020), p. 100286.

46 Frey, *The Technology Trap: Capital, Labor, and Power in the Age of Automation*; Pasquinelli, *The Eye of the Master: A Social History of Artificial Intelligence*; Murgia, *Code Dependent: Living in the Shadow of AI*.

MAKING THE CASE FOR POLITICS: TECHNOLOGY, ACTION, AND CREATIVITY

If the last section was about how the concatenation of social structures and technology ties our hands, this section is about how that does not have to be the case. The lore about technology is that it is a realm of innovation, imagination, and creativity. Contrast this with what many people believe is politics: A roomful of serious-looking people changing little or nothing while harping on and on about procedural minutiae. Thus, it would come as a surprise that Hannah Arendt's 1958 *The Human Condition*, arguably her most famous book, inverts these associations: Politics is how we make meaning in a world where technology provides material stability but no novel meanings.

The Human Condition starts with Sputnik and ends with reflections on why scientists – even more than politicians – have been making the headlines in the late 1950s. It is a critique of modern science and technology through and through: Modern societies have alienated themselves from their *world*, as modern science and technology displaced political action by disrupting the taken-for-granted relationship between human activities.

To understand how *The Human Condition* problematizes modern technology, it is important to situate it in the context of Arendt's threefold categorization of human activities as *labor*, *work*, and *action*. *Labor* refers to the repetitive and necessary activities that sustain life and enable social reproduction. *Work* is the molding of natural elements to create objects that form the world of artifacts. *Action* is the quintessentially political activity of bringing something genuinely new into the world collectively.[47] Arendt provides a brief overview of the history of modern technology refracted through this phenomenological lens. Technology, that is, using elements of nature and tools to create new things, fits into Arendt's category of *work*. It is a more creative endeavor than reproducing the life cycle (*labor*) but also lacking in the collective creativity and imagination Arendt associates with *action*.

Even though people always used elements of nature to create a world of artifacts, until the modern period, technology relied on a strict separation of nature and the human world, or what Arendt at times calls the "human artifice." According to Arendt, pre-modern technology imitated nature for the purpose of creating things. Humans' relationship to their tools was strictly instrumental: We had tools, no matter how sophisticated, to make beneficial things. Early breakthroughs, such as the invention of the steam engine, still relied on the imitation of nature as their principle

[47] Arendt's strict separation of human activities has drawn criticism for failing to appreciate the creative and political character of labor – domestic labor in particular – and consequently, for idealizing an abstract conception of politics as action in concert to the disparagement of concrete political struggles for equality and justice. My objective here is not to scrutinize Arendt's political philosophy as such. Instead, I hope to rethink the possibilities opened up by Arendt's critique of modern technology as well as its limitations to situate AI in contemporary society.

of operation. Even the second stage of modern inventions, exemplified by the use of electricity, retained the separation of nature and the human world.

The modern period began to blur the boundaries between nature and human artifice, and work and other human activities as a result of automation and the harnessing of nuclear energy. Modern societies have "channeled [the forces of nature], along with their elementary power, into the world itself."[48] By automation, she means the introduction of machines that not only make the creation of objects more efficient but also require the creation of even more objects to improve their operational capacity. In other words, machines disrupt the unilinear relationship between means and end, tool and product, because production in the age of machines feeds a loop in which the tool becomes an end. Living in a world of machines rather than a world of end products means that we are losing the real *world*, for the world of machines has become a substitute for it without ever being able to give the necessary permanence and stability.[49]

Channeling the forces of nature this way evokes a quintessentially Arendtian fear: The replacement of the realm of *homo faber* (the maker) with that of *homo laborans* (the laborer). Arendt believes that things should be produced to satisfy end goals. Nails are produced to fasten objects, and cars help us get around. However, the introduction of machinery as the era-defining technology of modernity has meant producing things for the sake of producing things.[50] Machines make production more efficient, which merely translates into making more production possible. Technological work is swept up in a cyclical motion, akin to the reproduction of the life cycle, in which societies are alienated from the actual goals for which making and using tools are required.

The failure of modern technology to guard the boundary between instrumentality (*work*) and cyclical reproduction (*labor*) is tied to yet another quintessentially Arendtian fear: The conflation of *work* (or *labor*) with *action*. The world of objects we produce through technology is not a substitute for human interrelatedness. This insight is presented through two activities that Arendt singles out for their political character, namely promise-making and forgiving. As action is inherently irreversible and carries with it human unpredictability, it can end up harming others. That is why we need promise-making and forgiving to undo the potential damage. Modern science and technology can do enormous damage as they act on nature instead of imitating it, yet they possess no power to undo such harm.[51] In other words, technology can create new things but cannot imbue the world with meaning or relationships in the way that future-oriented promise-making or past-oriented forgiveness can.

48 Hannah Arendt, *The Human Condition (with an Introduction by Margaret Canovan)*, 2nd ed. (University of Chicago Press, 1998), p. 149.

49 Hannah Arendt, *The Human Condition (with an Introduction by Margaret Canovan)*, 2nd ed. (University of Chicago Press, 1998), pp. 149–152.

50 Arendt, *The Human Condition*, pp. 144–151.

51 Arendt, *The Human Condition*, p. 238.

Arendt's analysis of modern technology as "acting into nature" should give us pause in the age of AI. Many deep learning systems rely on data collected about people living life – traveling, shopping, listening to music, watching shows, chatting with others, applying for jobs, taking exams, visiting the doctor's office, crossing borders, facing law enforcement, and more – to then feed models that describe or predict who they are or how they live so that businesses (and sometimes governments) make suggestions, if not binding decisions, about who they should be and how they should live. Needless to say, the suggestions and decisions based on AI output can make humans happy, prosperous, safe, and healthy, but these desirable outcomes are neither intrinsic to AI technology nor can they be arrived at through automated decisions alone. For all the talk of moral decision-making by AI, such morality is still a derivative of human conceptions of what is right, just, fair, and good, distilled through hundreds of thousands of years of human-to-human interactions. The messiness of human disagreement over what is right cannot be overcome by algorithms, no matter how sophisticated they may be.

The contention that technology, while capable of creating new objects, is not creative in the political sense should be taken seriously at a time when futurists raise the possibility of novel communities interconnected through the internet and possibly populated by human and non-human citizens. What makes political action unique is not that people are always imaginative, creative, and unpredictable, but that their interactions are. An Arendtian interpretation of contemporary AI would argue that chatbots may successfully imitate human speech, and in fact, individual bits of AI-generated text may be as creative as outstanding human speech and writing, but ultimately, their capacity to inspire the birth of new identities, institutions, promises and forms of reconciliation are limited to what humans feed into them.

It is perhaps obvious, if not trivial, to argue that we need collective decision-making – in a word, politics – to address the challenges posed by AI today. In fact, the more technology forecloses avenues for democratic politics, the more we should reclaim our political faculties and spaces.[52] Yet, what kind of politics do we need? After all, established political institutions have already been deliberating AI laws and policies around the world – as Chapter 6 describes in detail. What more politics do we need?

RADICAL DEMOCRACY IN THE AGE OF AI

What Is Radical Democracy?

At its core, radical democracy calls for the expansion of citizens' agency in making collective decisions. The limitations of aggregating citizen preferences through politicians, political parties, elections, and legislatures in representative democracy explain the appeal of direct forms of participation, but the qualifier *radical* (from

[52] Timcke, *Algorithms and the End of Politics: How Technology Shapes 21st-Century American Life.*

the Latin word for *root*) refers to more than that. The striving to democratize social, political, economic, and cultural institutions and interactions by transforming the relations of domination at their root gives meaning to the radical element. The call to question all power relations separates it from liberal, representative models of democracy that treat many hierarchies as normal or even necessary. Thus, radical democrats find inspiration and common cause with struggles for equality and justice that reject justifications for patriarchy, racism, capitalism, colonialism, ableism, and other hierarchical social orders as natural, private, technical, or outside the scope of politics.[53]

Beyond a commitment to citizens' agency, collective decision-making and the questioning of hierarchies, radical democrats have branched out to various projects driven by different priorities and methods. The demand for citizens' regular and unmediated participation in decision-making has fueled interest in direct and deliberative democracy in the 1980s and 1990s. An enduring debate from that time is whether citizen participation should be aimed at consensus-based decision-making along the lines Jürgen Habermas suggests in his theory of communicative action or whether ongoing conflict and disagreement is a better portrayal of democratic politics than the search for consensus, along the lines of Chantal Mouffe and Ernesto Laclau's agonistic democracy.[54]

The rise of online platforms in the 2000s created initial optimism around the possibility of bringing radical-democratic politics to life, whatever the definitional differences may be.[55] The internet and online platforms afford billions of people with instant and massive connectivity. For deliberative democrats, this has opened up endless possibilities for communication and decision-making among citizens who otherwise face temporal and spatial barriers to political participation. For agonists, online platforms have provided social movements with valuable tools to organize and communicate in the context of contentious protests. Although enhancing democratic participation through technology still remains a powerful idea, the capture of online platforms by repressive states, the prominence of hate speech and online trolling in what should be deliberative arenas, and the subversion of citizen preferences through algorithmic targeting in the 2010s tempered the early enthusiasm.

53 Ernesto Laclau and Chantal Mouffe, *Hegemony and Socialist Strategy: Towards a Radical Democratic Politics* (Verso, 1985); Peter Dahlgren, "Civic Identity and Net Activism: The Frame of Radical Democracy," in *Radical Democracy and the Internet*, ed. by L. Dahlberg and E. Siapera (Palgrave Macmillan, 2007); Martin Breaugh and Dean Caivano, "A Living Critique of Domination: Exemplars of Radical Democracy from Black Lives Matter to #MeToo," *Philosophy & Social Criticism*, 2022, p. 019145372210937; Bart Cammaerts and Robin Mansell, "Digital Platform Policy and Regulation: Toward a Radical Democratic Turn," *International Journal of Communication*, 14 (2020), pp. 135–54.

54 Mouffe, *The Return of the Political*.

55 Laclau and Mouffe, *Hegemony and Socialist Strategy: Towards a Radical Democratic Politics*; Dahlgren, "Civic Identity and Net Activism: The Frame of Radical Democracy"; Breaugh and Caivano, "A Living Critique of Domination"; Cammaerts and Mansell, "Digital Platform Policy and Regulation: Toward a Radical Democratic Turn."

The call for radical democracy in the age of AI should take into account the multiple forms of disempowerment and alienation most people experience today. The radical-democratic agenda does not supplant the technical, legal, and business regulation models but rather foregrounds them. It would be a net positive if experts produced ethically aligned technologies under well-meaning company guidelines and binding statutes, but these avenues have produced little positive change so far. Unless ordinary people have a seat at the table to envision a better society *and* better technology, existing governance models will remain limited in their capacity for change.

Philosopher Andrew Feenberg provides important clues to a radical-democratic program to reorient societies' relationship to technology.[56] Feenberg's democratic imagination goes beyond the mitigation of risk and harm through law and policy; taking note of technology's role in shaping nothing less than "what it means to be human," he calls for democratic control at the design level: "What human beings are and will become is decided in the shape of our tools no less than in the action of statesmen and political movements. The design of technology is thus an ontological decision fraught with political consequences. The exclusion of the vast majority from participation in this decision is the underlying cause of many of our problems."[57]

What Radical Democracy Should Look Like in the Age of AI

AI problems are not *just* AI problems. We got here because the producers of technology should not have been trusted to rectify the problems they caused. Lawmakers have done too little too late – or in some cases, absolutely nothing – to rein in growing socioeconomic inequality, anti-competitive tendencies in capitalism, environmental degradation, and technology-specific risks and harms. The societal pressure for businesses to do better has given life to corporate social responsibility initiatives for equality, diversity, sustainability, and technology ethics in the 2000s. While those initiatives have brought modest gains, they have not propelled national or global systemic change to eliminate the harms they seek to address.

What should radical-democratic politics look like in the age of AI? While the very spirit of radical democracy necessitates leaving the answer to people themselves, I would like to present broad guidelines in light of the lessons learned from a decade of global AI governance. Langdon Winner delivered a virtual talk, called "The Democratic Shaping of Technology: Its Rise, Fall and Possible Rebirth" in 2020, in which he gave a historical overview of the Office of Technology Assessment,

56 Feenberg, *Transforming Technology: A Critical Theory Revisited*; Feenberg, *Between Reason and Experience: Essays in Technology and Modernity*; Feenberg, *Technosystem: The Social Life of Reason*. Also see Neil Turnbull, "At Modernity's Limit: Technology as World and Idea," *Theory, Culture & Society*, 23.5 (2006), pp. 135–50; Darryl Cressman, *The Necessity of Critique: Andrew Feenberg and the Philosophy of Technology* (Springer Nature, 2022).

57 Andrew Feenberg, *Critical Theory of Technology* (Oxford University Press, 1991), p. 3.

established in the United States in the 1960s and abolished by Congress in 1995.[58] Winner was among those who advocated encouraging citizen participation in what was otherwise an expert-led effort to rein in the risks and harms of technology.[59] Fast-forwarding to today, when the triple movement of monopoly capitalism, rising socio-economic inequality, and what he calls the "cult of innovation" have been shaping societies' relationship to technology, he calls for a social democratic framework for civic engagement that goes beyond the weak efforts for technology regulation in the context of what he calls the "American framework of New Deal liberalism."[60]

A radical-democratic politics of AI governance should learn from the history of technology-critical movements of the past. Demanding governmental representation, which was the spirit behind the Office of Technology Assessment in the 1960s and the Biden-era AI guidelines in the early 2020s, can be seen as another radical-democratic proposal. Representation is literally a feature of representative democracy, of course, but AI governance can still benefit from movement-driven institutional reform. Lawmakers, bureaucrats, and judges do not always have clear mandates, tasks, or goals when it comes to technology regulation, so movements can play a crucial role in pushing for such reform. Without the radical imagination of social movements asking for change, the momentum for such change cannot be taken for granted. If stakeholder engagement is not to remain a hollow slogan, social movements with a critical outlook should participate in the governance of AI.

Technology that is produced in an undemocratic workplace cannot serve the interests of most people. The structure of the modern firm, which undoubtedly provides organizational benefits and efficiency gains, has produced a hierarchy of shareholders or owners, chief officers, managers, relatively secure and well-paid workers, and informal workers. The benefits are distributed top to bottom, while the risks are distributed bottom to top in the modern firm. This hierarchy needs to be upended with more direct forms of workers' participation in decision-making. If workers want any chance to make AI a contributor to their productivity and creativity rather than a competitor, they should fight for strong unions that will have a seat at the negotiation table. Workers' representatives should take part in business decision-making to shape the future of technology together with the owners of capital and the managerial class.

If workplace democracy is one component of a radical-democratic program, another is democracy across workplaces: Decisions about a technology like AI, which puts general-purpose products and services on the market, cannot be confined to one firm or even one sector. Ideally, healthcare professionals, truck drivers, lawyers, shop floor workers, educators, artists, call center workers, and more should

[58] Langdon Winner, "The Democratic Shaping of Technology: Its Rise, Fall and Possible Rebirth," *Engaging Science, Technology, and Society*, 7.1 (2021), pp. 95–103.

[59] Winner, "The Democratic Shaping of Technology," p. 97.

[60] Winner, "The Democratic Shaping of Technology," p. 99.

be at the table when AI tools are designed and developed because people outside of the AI-producing sectors benefit from useful tools and suffer the negative impact of risky and harmful ones.

It would be a mistake to assume that efforts to ensure a better technological future are confined to specialists in technology ethics or technology regulation. Human rights organizations, labor unions, environmentalists, anti-racist activists, feminists, the LGBTQ movement, the anti-war movement, and other social groups that do not self-identify exclusively as technology ethics or regulation advocates have contributed immensely to the struggle for safe, fair, and responsible technology, past and present. That is simply because we cannot have a better society without better technology, and we cannot have better technology without a better society. Existing advocacy networks have considerable experience in listening to people, gauging their interests and values, and coordinating for action. Technology ethics specialists should learn from, share their expertise with, and ultimately collaborate with these networks.

It is worth noting that citizens' direct participation is not only an entitlement; it is also a responsibility. One defining feature of radical democracy is public-mindedness: Decisions should reflect, to the extent possible, the interests of all affected parties. Given that people approach AI from various angles, as investors, researchers, designers, developers, testers, users, or affected persons, it is imperative to take the viewpoints and interests of others into account. After all, participating in society requires taking responsibility for contributing to social injustices, even those we do not cause intentionally.[61]

CONCLUSION

Philosopher of technology Don Ihde concludes his 1989 article "Technology and Prognostic Predicaments" with a rule: "If technologies embody, both structurally and historically, the possibilities of multiple uses and unintended side effects, and all instantiate these in particular fashions, then one exclusionary rule for prognosis can be advised: *avoid ideological (utopian and dystopian) conclusions*."[62] Perhaps this is where we are: AI does not have to be a source of dread, and maybe, it will be a source of hope. Future possibilities exist, but they are not completely open-ended, as the future of AI is tied to the society in which it came into existence.

This chapter invites us to think with the great philosophers of science and technology to understand AI better. For all their differences, Arendt and Marcuse share a profound preoccupation with the implications of modern technology as a whole. Even though specific tools, such as nuclear weapons, are mentioned in their corpus, they take a holistic view of technology as such. For Arendt, it is the internal transformation of technology from an instrument of human needs to a self-perpetuating

[61] Young, *Responsibility for Justice*.

[62] Don Ihde, "Technology and Prognostic Predicaments," *AI & Society*, 13.1–2 (1999), pp. 44–51: 50.

cycle that is at the root of the problem, while for Marcuse, it is the dual movement toward the domination of others and the domination of nature that culminated in the tragedies of the twentieth century. Arendt and Marcuse are spot-on in their analyses of what modern technology is capable of: It is not just the possibility of abuse by totalitarian regimes but the risk that the underlying logic of technology itself can be totalitarian under any regime type. For that reason, they share a dislike for predictability: As lived experiences are increasingly more susceptible to calculation, classification, estimation, and prediction, people become more controllable. They worry that efficiency and convenience are not powerful enough motivations to anchor modern technology to the common good. It is impossible to read passages from their works without reflecting on AI, whose *modus operandi* is collecting large amounts of data on human subjects as well as other living or non-living beings to run classification, estimation, and prediction algorithms.

Revealingly, Arendt and Marcuse both find emancipation in activities or social groups least connected to measurement, repetition, standardization, categorization, and prediction – hallmarks of AI. For Arendt, hope lies with political action, which unleashes the open-ended, pluralistic, and inherently unpredictable ability to build something genuinely new together. Marcuse argues that modern human activities, technological ones included, could carry enormous emancipatory potential if they were not so tied up with economic and political agendas of domination and control. Thus, Marcuse's thought points to the struggles of the marginalized who escaped – or were forcibly excluded from – complicity in the reproduction of capitalism, the nation-state, and militarism for society-wide liberation.

Arendt and Marcuse have so much to teach us about emerging technologies of today, AI included: Technology alone does not create new meanings or relationships; technological change devoid of a purpose drives its own creators to alienation; equating science and technology with the control of nature results in the domination of most people by a few others; and human interaction and decision-making are the only ways to give a sense of purpose and meaning to technology. Of course, Arendt and Marcuse cannot give all the answers we need. One of their limitations was that they painted a rather broad-brush portrait of modern technology. Later generations of STS scholars and philosophers, like Langdon Winner and Andrew Feenberg, have moved away from these generalizations by studying the societal and ethical implications of specific tools and services. Likewise, social movements resisting the abuses of contemporary technologies have transformed technology critique since the 1970s.

Reclaiming democratic citizenship is more important than ever. AI is presented as the engine of life-transforming innovations brought to ordinary people by brilliant experts and the companies employing them. Some of its applications, like chatbots, are praised for interactivity, but what that means is that people interact with the final product that is given to them. In spite of all the corporate talk of stakeholder engagement, people affected by AI tools have almost no say in designing, developing, or deploying them. It is argued that anyone with skills and a vision can be the next technology leader, but the truth is that the concentration of R&D severely limits competitiveness in the AI sector. It is safe to say that unless they organize to take part in the decisions that affect their lives, labor market transformations will happen *to* workers, not *with* them.

Readers of this book must have come across many conversations about AI with friends, family, and colleagues. What are some of the things people say? Do people rejoice at the possibility of working shorter hours? Enjoying themselves more at work? Or are they worried that their jobs will be taken over by AI? Do people say they have been building more meaningful and lasting connections than before? Or does the mention of AI bring up complaints about filter bubbles, deepfakes, and disinformation? Are people excited about high-quality medical care in the future? Or are they worried that their first point of contact with the healthcare system will be an AI-powered virtual assistant taking over the functions of a human doctor, nurse, or therapist? If the answer to these questions is not an unequivocal affirmation of AI as a force for good, it is worth questioning not only AI but also the society within which it is developed and deployed.

To be clear, blaming technology for society's ills is the easy way out. We have doubts and fears, not because AI is inherently bad. In fact, all those questions earlier could have been answered in the affirmative: Embedding AI in productivity software saves humans a lot of time; AI-powered recommender systems discover music, movies, and people that we could not have found on our own; and AI in medicine has been revolutionizing drug discovery and diagnostics. Technology expands the frontier of possibilities. We could have had, and perhaps still can have productive, enjoyable, safe, healthy and meaningful personal lives, and interconnected and democratic publics thanks to technology. *We could have*, because much AI has already been developed under conditions that will likely further disempower most people, and *we still can*, because it is not too late to reorder social and political life in ways that encourage a different kind of technology production and use. What we need is people's participation in the decisions affecting their lives.

Prologue

What Is to Be Done?

Writing this book has been rewarding yet challenging for many reasons. Chief among them is the speed with which the technology and technology regulation landscape has been changing. By the time I could write down a paragraph, some of the information in it would need to be updated. AI itself and AI governance will surely look very different in a few years. The AI of tomorrow will redefine healthcare, housing, education, banking, entertainment, law enforcement, relationships, and travel. Jobs will be performed differently. The pace of change will reward early adopters and punish slackers. Jobs that seem secure today may have gone extinct by the time you pick up this edition of the book. Change is inevitable.

Plus ça change? Maybe AI-driven change will make us all happy, healthy, and rich. What if not, though? AI may force most of us to train for a better job or simply fight for the one we have. Medical advances thanks to AI may eradicate many diseases and disorders ... for those who can afford healthcare. Responsibility for war crimes may be difficult to identify while wars become even more lethal. Corporate power and an eroding information ecosystem may make it impossible to hold on to electoral democracy. Entertainment may be readily available, but joy?

Two diametrically opposed tropes shape media coverage, academic discourses, and public perceptions around AI: *AI is all new* and *AI is nothing new*. The former emphasizes the unprecedented, revolutionary, and disruptive potential of AI. Give it a couple of years, perhaps decades, and AI will transform our jobs, activities, tastes, value systems, politics, and ultimately, what it means to be human. It is out there with the invention of the steam engine, writing or the wheel for pushing the frontier of innovation beyond our wildest dreams. Its reach will not spare any certainty we have about the economy, culture, society, and politics. It cannot be stopped in its tracks anymore. Naturally, AI enthusiasts make up a good number of those who view it as a one-of-a-kind novel technology, but the emphasis on novelty also fuels fears of unprecedented disruption. All in all, humanity will have to jump on the bandwagon, willingly or not. Some think that we should try hard not to fall off, while others tell us to enjoy the wild ride!

The *nothing new* viewpoint starts from the observation that today's AI was born into established economic, social, political, military, and cultural relations. At their most benign, more accurate and efficient versions of existing mathematical models will combine with big data to provide humans with better solutions to their problems. A less optimistic view of AI is that most of what it does is enrich a small number of investors, senior managers, and tech workers while offering the rest of the population the freedom of consuming novel products and the unfreedom of mass surveillance, job insecurity, and a disinformation crisis. Great powers dream of weaponizing it to gain the military upper-hand. AI obviously did not invent labor exploitation, racism, sexism, or environmental degradation, but it will likely reproduce and aggravate them. Thus, AI will bring about a different version of the bad old problems societies have been facing.

I believe AI is neither entirely novel nor a continuation of the same. I agree with the latter camp that AI is embedded in existing economic, social, political, military, and cultural relations, including relations of power and domination. These relations shape the research questions guiding theoretical researchers and AI practitioners, the form and content of data used to train algorithms, as well as their problems, and the final products. To some extent, they replicate existing problems, too. Thus, addressing the challenges arising from AI requires empowering organized actors fighting for equality, justice, and peace, rather than focusing on technical challenges alone.

However, AI systems also unleash novel opportunities and challenges that cannot be understood or addressed with the existing conceptual and practical toolkit alone. The datafication of the economy has disrupted business models that rely on little or no data analysis. The management of labor has taken a turn with the replacement of old models with data-intensive surveillance. Misinformation and disinformation probably started with the first community of *homo sapiens* capable of verbalizing their experiences, but algorithmic amplification takes these problems to a qualitatively and quantitatively novel scale. As unethical as today's wars are, the human rights and international humanitarian law norms developed sometime between the 1860s and 1950s will have to be rethought in light of the possible introduction of autonomous lethal weapons systems onto the battlefield. Authoritarianism is certainly nothing new, but the technical opportunities of mass surveillance afforded to dictators today may make the totalitarian control of populations in the 1930s and 1940s relatively benign compared to future iterations of personal, military or one-party dictatorships. Thus, we have genuinely new problems even if they are rooted in old ones.

This book is a call for dialogue between the science and technology community and social movements fighting for equality and justice. The complex nature of problems caused by today's AI requires such communication and collaboration. Nobody can fight alone, no matter how smart, connected, or experienced they may be. No proposed solution will be sufficient, no matter how well thought-out, authoritative, or sophisticated it may be. Rectifying AI's problems through technical solutions that reverse-engineer data and algorithm failures will travel some distance, but not close to where we want to be. Supporting the multiple struggles against inequality and injustice, caused by AI or otherwise, is definitely the way to go, but awareness of AI's technical affordances and limits is required of social movements that want to navigate the seemingly complicated technological landscape today. The conceptual, philosophical, and practical know-how built around human rights, democracy, business ethics, and sustainability is immense, yet the translation of these concepts to the age of AI necessitates novel and collaborative ways of thinking and acting.

BEST PRACTICES FOR AI GOVERNANCE MODELS

What does a good, workable governance model look like? There is not one correct answer, but critical literature on technical solutions, business self-regulation, and legal regulation suggests some best practices. For technical solutions to work, they should be designed with human needs in mind. The questions guiding the research, design, and development stages should be: What problem does this proposed idea solve? Whom does it help? Does it cause harm? If so, how can that harm be mitigated? Acknowledging social, political, cultural, and economic dynamics while designing a technical fix goes a long way. It is also important that technical solutions receive ongoing support and funding. What separates a helpful solution from an expensive gimmick is consistent backing by the private or public sector throughout the lifecycle of a product or platform that is born out of a solution-minded idea.

Separating genuine business self-regulation from ethics-washing is no less tricky. Ideally, boards and councils tasked with ensuring ethical conduct should enjoy operational and financial autonomy from the company they oversee. Their mandate should cover all the risks and harms arising from the development and use of AI by that company. Their binding decisions should be enforced and advisory opinions should be taken into consideration. Businesses should be transparent about their compliance with board and council decisions and opinions. Internal teams should likewise have a broad mandate and clearly defined powers.

For legal regulation to become meaningful, the first step is … to legislate laws! The disconnect between legal talk and actual legislation is truly disheartening in AI governance. Yet, not any law will do: Future legislation should take into account the whole gamut of risks and harms arising from AI, including systemic risks to labor markets, the environment, and market competition. The clearer its definitions of basic technical and legal terms, the more likely that a law will promote legal certainty and predictability. The need for clarity applies for the punishments and rewards stipulated in the laws, as well. Finally, lawmakers should take stakeholder engagement seriously by inviting business, worker, nonprofit, and academic participation at the drafting, deliberation, legislation, and post-legislation stages.

BEYOND AI GOVERNANCE MODELS

This book's premise is that a bleak future is possible, even probable, but not necessary. We can shape the future of AI collectively. It will take hard work, as there is no quick fix. The next software update will not get us there. Business leaders have no reason to align their incentives with people facing negative consequences. Laws regulating AI are on the horizon, but whether those laws will set adequate guardrails against risks and harms remains to be seen.

This is not to deny existing governance models their rightful place. I would not have written half a book on AI governance models if I didn't believe that technical solutions, business self-regulation and – especially – legal regulation would help to make the world a better place. Technologists and the businesses employing them should develop and deploy the safest and most useful products possible. Lawmakers will hopefully ignore false binaries like innovation vs. regulation and step up to direct technological change in the public's interest. These governance models are absolutely needed.

Yet, technology governance requires more than that, for various reasons. First, the empirical evidence presented in this book does not leave much room for unqualified optimism. The governance models presented here deliver positive results up to a certain point. Technical solutions should be incentivized while acknowledging that they have so far contributed little to society-wide change. When faced with the choice of maximizing profits and market share or establishing robust self-regulation mechanisms, major AI companies have usually chosen the former. Small businesses have not even brought up self-regulation as a possibility. Getting lawmakers to set up adequate guardrails has remained an aspiration rather than a reality except in a few countries. Much positive change in AI has come from social movements, journalists, legal professionals, and academics who have exposed scandalous revelations about certain AI products and forced businesses and lawmakers to do better. Keeping the pressure on the powerful is the only way to get them to act lawfully and ethically.

Second, we need a better society along with better AI. Expecting AI (or AI governance) to deliver much-needed social reform does nothing but deepen disillusionment. AI can provide humanity with necessary but insufficient solutions to pressing problems. It can enhance emergency preparedness without addressing climate change, give us effective medications without setting rules about their distribution in society, and make us more efficient without making our jobs more secure or meaningful. Likewise, targeted AI governance schemes can be part of broader structural change agendas but cannot replace such change. Imagining a just, democratic and peaceful world includes but cannot be reduced to a serious rethinking of human societies' relationship to AI.

Third, the cultivation of fundamental values in the face of rapid technological change should invite a pluralistic societal debate. Moral questions surrounding AI simply do not have a single correct answer. Letting markets decide moral questions does not work when AI tools' negative impact is difficult to pinpoint or when such negative impact falls on non-customers. Laws would ideally mediate the relationship between moral debate and binding decision-making, but the limitations of legislation in AI mean that important moral considerations around this subject are simply not represented in politics. What is more, as countless examples throughout this book illustrate, product design and development decisions matter. Of course, expanding the debate means amplifying the risk of moral disagreement and fragmentation, but this is exactly what needs to happen in a democratic society.

All in all, it falls upon each one of us to reimagine the relationship between AI and humanity, one decision at a time. How is this going to happen, though? Are people going to take time off from their jobs to attend AI companies' design team meetings? How are we going to get through security in the first place? Is everyone going to take up residence in a global hub to keep an eye on AI producers? Are we all going to become software engineers in the effort? Are we going to spend all our evenings and weekends in town halls to shape the future of AI?

Clearly, none of these scenarios need to happen for citizens' participation in shaping the future of AI. The central message of radical democracy is that any place and social relation can be a locus of power and contestation. Even if we cannot devote unlimited time and resources to learning about, assessing, questioning, and reimagining the design, development, and use of AI, we can all make individual and more importantly, collective, decisions about how we live, work, learn, and travel with AI. These decisions can be categorized under five headings: Organize, learn, participate, care, and resist.

FIVE STRATEGIES TO SHAPE THE FUTURE OF AI

Organize

Most of us have absolutely no way to influence companies or governments individually, but collectively, we have power. All concerned citizens should consider joining existing nongovernmental organizations, labor unions, and social movements, or starting new ones. Dozens of nongovernmental organizations have emerged since the 2010s, if not earlier, to draw attention to the risks and harms of AI, protect people from those negative outcomes, or promote good legislation. They focus on children's safety on online platforms, artists' intellectual property rights, digital surveillance in border areas, gig workers' compensation, and much more. Collective advocacy for rights in the face of AI risks and harms happens in conventional organizational settings, too. Human rights organizations and labor unions do not just organize around AI-related issues, but their established membership and organizational structure help to fight back for rights.

One of the greatest barriers to organizing is the fragmentation among the producers of emerging technologies, workers in other sectors, individual end-users, and the negatively affected. After all, one could argue that a gig worker and a software engineer or a migrant crossing a border and a middle-class citizen of a wealthy country do not have shared interests. While the fragmentation of interests and value systems cannot be denied, most people have a lot more in common than they first realize. When reports of bias and discrimination first hit the news, more than a few people must have thought that such misfortunes befall someone unlike them – the imprisoned, the poor, the racial or gender minorities. Fast forward a few years, and even those who enjoy markers of privilege in their society began to fear algorithmic bias, unsafe online spaces for children, and massive surveillance enabled by facial recognition. It was not that long ago that computer programmers would half-joke that theirs would remain the only secure and well-paying job when machines took over. In the age of LLMs, they are among the first group of workers feeling the pressure of automation. There is no doubt that existing patterns of power and privilege still determine who is likely to win and lose as a result of technological change, but the disruptions in the age of AI may also lead to intersectoral and cross-class alliances.

Learn

One of the messages of this book is that the development of AI tools requires expertise, but AI is not magic. The more we bring the underlying science down from the heavens to the Earth, the better-off we will be. Only an informed citizenry will have a meaningful chance of shaping the future of AI, which is why we should constantly educate ourselves about its benefits and risks. The underlying science and mathematics for AI are admittedly complex, but the intuition behind that complexity can be understood by non-experts. The more we demystify what AI is and what it does, the better we can use it for our ends and assess its risks.

Learning about AI has to be cross-disciplinary because taking stock of how AI shapes our individual and collective lives requires at least a basic understanding of mathematics, computer programming, marketing and sales, philosophy and ethics, and technology law, among other things. The knowledge coming from these fields is interrelated. For example, accuracy in AI output means that certain statistical benchmarks are met, which has implications for the ethics of AI use, and those statistical and ethical considerations are likely to determine how the law should assess the riskiness of deploying an AI system. We can only understand the implications of AI in one field of study if we know enough about other fields.

Learning is a two-way street. Expertise in AI-related fields definitely qualifies people to teach about AI, but they have much to learn from people who experience the positive and negative impact of AI in their everyday lives. Much of what we know about algorithmic bias, digital surveillance, and online disinformation comes from people whose lives were upended when they were forced to interact with AI-powered technologies. Thus, we should teach and learn *about* AI as much as we teach and learn AI.

Participate

Everyone has an interest in shaping the future of technology, AI included. Today's AI has become possible thanks to data collected from each one of us. We have also financed technological progress indirectly through taxes, some of which funded the kind of scientific research that gave birth to contemporary AI applications. If and when things go wrong with AI, many of us will end up paying the price. Thus, it is only normal that we all participate in AI-related decisions.

As argued earlier, we do not have to sit at the board of major AI producers to be able to participate. AI decision-making can happen everywhere. In what ways does AI help you learn, communicate, work, travel, and have fun? And in what ways does it not? Do you think AI adoption in your workplace will improve efficiency, augment human labor and benefit customers? What kind of chatbot access do you think is appropriate for your children? What kind of healthcare do you want from your provider in the age of AI? What should an automated decision-making system not be allowed to decide? These questions should be decided in homes, schools, workplaces, and hospitals among family members, teachers and students, co-workers, and patients and physicians.

Needless to say, participation works thanks to an organized and informed citizenry. Organized participation in the form of civil society organizations, labor unions and social movements is the surest way to get our voices heard. The more we know about AI, its uses and risks, the more likely that we can shape it. Thus, participation is at once a call to organize and educate ourselves.

Care

If we want technological change to be socially and environmentally sustainable, we need to develop an ethic of care toward others, especially the most vulnerable members of society. As Chapter 2 suggests, multiple ethical paradigms compete to foreground moral decision-making around AI. My call for an ethic of care is a desire to complement, not necessarily supplement, the pluralism of moral philosophy. It is simply an acknowledgment that the mindset of dominating other humans and nature raises the risks and harms associated with today's AI.

Technologies like AI produce too many unforeseen consequences and negative externalities (see Chapter 3) for self-interested technology development and use to benefit all of society "as if by an invisible hand," to quote Adam Smith. Every time we weigh the potential benefits and costs of technology adoption, we should ask ourselves whether our decisions could harm other humans as well as non-human nature. Sometimes the harms are not immediate or direct: My picking a quick and cheap AI-generated visual for a flyer indirectly harms visual artists, your decision to sift through resumés with an AI tool probably discriminates against a qualified worker with an unusual background, and anything we do using today's generative AI models spends enormous environmental resources.

Adhering to an ethic of care does not mean refusing technology at all times. We all face situations in which the benefits of using a technology outweigh the costs considerably or we have no choice but to use a certain tool. In fact, even having the option of not using AI can be a marker of privilege – a study shows that "essentially all 92 million low-income people in the U.S. states" have some aspect of their lives decided by AI.[1] An ethic of care is thus simply a call to assess AI from the perspective of those most likely to be adversely affected by it.

Resist

There is no doubt that technology is a force to reckon with. Every single person reading these lines uses electronic appliances, some kind of motorized vehicle, and emails, perhaps every single day. Yet, the aura of inevitability must be resisted. Frequent users of an electronic appliance like the television set "screen time" for their kids. More than a few drivers, especially in US cities, petition urban planners to make public transportation options and cycling more readily available. One cannot even begin to imagine today's world without the email, but as any office worker would know, setting time aside from one's email account is as important to workplace productivity and personal self-care as using it.

A central message of Chapter 7 was that the scientific and technical specifications of technologies shape their users and the broader societies they are embedded in forcefully, but their influence is not overdetermined – in other words, humans can make design and use decisions that shape those technologies in turn. Commercial airplanes cannot travel at five times the speed they do, but they can be made safer or less safe, and can have a little more or less legroom. Today's internet protocols (think about Hypertext Transfer Protocol Secure, which most readers would know by its abbreviation HTTPS) that have set the rules of data-sharing among billions of people for decades came from people making decisions sometime between the 1970s and the 2000s. All of this is to say: The producers and users of AI technologies can expect tools that serve collective interests and resist developing and using such tools when they fall short.

Wholesale rejection, as the oft-misunderstood Luddites of the nineteenth century opted for, is one among many options. In fact, there is value in not making every single tool just because it can be made.[2] For example, the campaign to ban lethal autonomous weapons systems wants to reclaim the power of saying 'no.' Some proposed

[1] Kevin De Liban, "Inescapable AI: The Ways AI Decides How Low-Income People Work, Live, Learn, and Survive," *TechTonic Justice*, November 2024 (www.techtonicjustice.org/reports/inescapable-ai).

[2] Sadowski, *The Mechanic and the Luddite: A Ruthless Criticism of Technology and Capitalism*.

AI tools have already faced stiff resistance. Emotion recognition software has time and again been found to produce lots of errors and lack a basis in scientific research. Likewise, growing concern around military AI applications – especially those automating the selection of hit targets – has prompted the mobilization of a social movement that lobbies various national governments and international organizations to get lethal autonomous weapon systems banned. Most other forms of organized resistance demand guardrails and useful applications, rather than an outright ban. For example, school teachers and university professors, who face immense pressure to adopt AI tools for education, often resist the temptation to experiment with their students and instead seek guidelines on meaningful, effective, and safe AI adoption.

CONCLUSION

The pace of technological change is truly astounding. AI-powered social transformations may reshape the world as we know it in a few years. Everyone is well-advised to adapt to change or risk getting swept by it. Yet, change may not change much if those affected by it cannot take part in it. The change we want from AI should get us closer to eradicating poverty, discrimination, authoritarianism, disinformation, war, and other social and political problems rather than continue or aggravate the ones we already have.

What we need is a *both/and* approach. We should embrace AI *and* mitigate its risks and harms, reap the benefits of expertise *and* empower non-experts to make moral and political decisions, and give businesses space to develop useful products *and* protect ourselves from their harmful actions. Ultimately, we should admire the human ingenuity that manifests itself in technological innovation *and* admire the human wisdom that gives direction to it.

"We must all learn to live together as brothers or we will perish together as fools," is one of the repeated warnings in Martin Luther King, Jr.'s sermons. His commencement address at Oberlin College connects this famous warning to scientific and technological progress: "What we are facing today is the fact that through our scientific and technological genius we've made of this world a neighborhood. And now through our moral and ethical commitment we must make of it a brotherhood."[3] His vision should guide our path more than ever in the age of AI. We need to rebuild the relationship between technology and society one line of code, one piece of advice, one piece of legislation, one refusal, one strike, and one class session at a time. If this book argues for the maximalist position that everyone should take part in governing AI with whatever power and leverage they have, that's because the challenge in front of us requires such maximalism. Let's build better AI, and through it, a better society.

3 "Remaining Awake Through a Great Revolution," Commencement Address for Oberlin College by Rev. Dr. Martin Luther King, Jr., June 1965, Oberlin, Ohio (www2.oberlin.edu/external/EOG/BlackHistoryMonth/MLK/CommAddress.html).

Bibliography

Abebe, Rediet, Solon Barocas, Jon Kleinberg, Karen Levy, Manish Raghavan, and David G. Robinson. "Roles for Computing in Social Change." In *Proceedings of the 2020 Conference on Fairness, Accountability, and Transparency*, 252–60. Barcelona, Spain: ACM, 2020. https://doi.org/10.1145/3351095.3372871.

Abu-Elyounes, Doaa. "Contextual Fairness: A Legal and Policy Analysis of Algorithmic Fairness." *Journal of Law, Technology & Policy* 2020, no. 1 (2020). https://doi.org/10.2139/ssrn.3478296.

Aguirre, Anthony, Gaia Dempsey, Harry Surden, and Peter B. Reiner. "AI Loyalty: A New Paradigm for Aligning Stakeholder Interests." *IEEE Transactions on Technology and Society* 1, no. 3 (September 2020): 128–37. https://doi.org/10.1109/TTS.2020.3013490.

Alpsancar, Suzana. "What Is AI Ethics? Ethics as Means of Self-Regulation and the Need for Critical Reflection." In International Conference on Computer Ethics, 1 no. 1, 2023.

Alter, Adam. *Irresistible: The Rise of Addictive Technology and the Business of Keeping Us Hooked*. New York City: Penguin Books, 2017.

Andrus, McKane, Elena Spitzer, Jeffrey Brown, and Alice Xiang. "What We Can't Measure, We Can't Understand: Challenges to Demographic Data Procurement in the Pursuit of Fairness." In *Proceedings of the 2021 ACM Conference on Fairness, Accountability, and Transparency*, 249–60. Virtual Event Canada: ACM, 2021. https://doi.org/10.1145/3442188.3445888.

Aral, Sinan. "The Problem with Online Ratings." *MIT Sloan Management Review* 55, no. 2 (2014): 47–52. www.learning.oreilly.com/library/view/the-problem-with/53863MIT55224/chapter001.html#h1-1.

Arendt, Hannah. *The Human Condition (with an Introduction by Margaret Canovan)*. 2nd ed. Chicago: University of Chicago Press, 1998.

Asaro, Peter M. "AI Ethics in Predictive Policing: From Models of Threat to an Ethics of Care." *IEEE Technology and Society Magazine* 38, no. 2 (2019): 40–53.

Asaro, Peter M. "Politicizing Data: AI Ethics as a Social Critique of Algorithms." *Social Research: An International Quarterly* 90, no. 4 (December 2023): 675–703. https://doi.org/10.1353/sor.2023.a916350.

Ashurst, Carolyn, Emmie Hine, Paul Sedille, and Alexis Carlier. "AI Ethics Statements – Analysis and Lessons Learnt from NeurIPS Broader Impact Statements." *arXiv* (November 2, 2021). http://arxiv.org/abs/2111.01705.

Attard-Frost, Blair, Andrés De los Ríos, and Deneille R. Walters. "The Ethics of AI Business Practices: A Review of 47 AI Ethics Guidelines." *AI and Ethics* (April 13, 2022). https://doi.org/10.1007/s43681-022-00156-6.

Awad, Edmond, Sohan Dsouza, Richard Kim, Jonathan Schulz, Joseph Henrich, Azim Shariff, Jean-François Bonnefon, and Iyad Rahwan. "The Moral Machine Experiment." *Nature* 563, no. 7729 (November 2018): 59–64. https://doi.org/10.1038/s41586-018-0637-6.

Bail, Christopher A., Lisa P. Argyle, Taylor W. Brown, John P. Bumpus, Haohan Chen, M. B. Fallin Hunzaker, Jaemin Lee, Marcus Mann, Friedolin Merhout, and Alexander Volfovsky. "Exposure to Opposing Views on Social Media Can Increase Political Polarization." *Proceedings of the National Academy of Sciences* 115, no. 37 (September 11, 2018): 9216–21. https://doi.org/10.1073/pnas.1804840115.

Bailey, Diane E., and Stephen R. Barley. "Beyond Design and Use: How Scholars Should Study Intelligent Technologies." *Information and Organization* 30, no. 2 (June 2020): 100286. https://doi.org/10.1016/j.infoandorg.2019.100286.

Baird, Alice, and Björn Schuller. "Considerations for a More Ethical Approach to Data in AI: On Data Representation and Infrastructure." *Frontiers in Big Data* 3 (September 2, 2020): 25. https://doi.org/10.3389/fdata.2020.00025.

Bakiner, Onur. "What Do Academics Say about Artificial Intelligence Ethics? An Overview of the Scholarship." *AI and Ethics* 3, no. 2 (May 2023): 513–25. https://doi.org/10.1007/s43681-022-00182-4.

Ball, Philip. *The Book of Minds: How to Understand Ourselves and Other Beings, from Animals to AI to Aliens*. Chicago: The University of Chicago Press, 2022.

Barberá, Pablo. "Social Media, Echo Chambers, and Political Polarization." In *Social Media and Democracy: The State of the Field, Prospects for Reform*, edited by Nathaniel Persily and Joshua A. Tucker, 1st ed., 34–55. Cambridge: Cambridge University Press, 2020. https://doi.org/10.1017/9781108890960.004.

Baria, Alexis T., and Keith Cross. "The Brain Is a Computer Is a Brain: Neuroscience's Internal Debate and the Social Significance of the Computational Metaphor." *arXiv Preprint*, 2021, 14.

Barocas, Solon, and Andrew D. Selbst. "Big Data's Disparate Impact." *California Law Review* 104, no. 3 (2016): 671–732. https://doi.org/10.2139/ssrn.2477899.

Barredo Arrieta, Alejandro, Natalia Díaz-Rodríguez, Javier Del Ser, Adrien Bennetot, Siham Tabik, Alberto Barbado, Salvador Garcia, et al. "Explainable Artificial Intelligence (XAI): Concepts, Taxonomies, Opportunities and Challenges toward Responsible AI." *Information Fusion* 58 (June 2020): 82–115. https://doi.org/10.1016/j.inffus.2019.12.012.

Basl, John, Ronald Sandler, and Steven Tiell. *Getting from Commitment to Content in AI and Data Ethics: Justice and Explainability*. Washington, DC: Atlantic Council, 2021.

Batool, Amna, Didar Zowghi, and Muneera Bano. "AI Governance: A Systematic Literature Review." *AI and Ethics*, January 14, 2025. https://doi.org/10.1007/s43681-024-00653-w.

Bauer, Greta R., and Daniel J. Lizotte. "Artificial Intelligence, Intersectionality, and the Future of Public Health." *American Journal of Public Health* 111, no. 1 (January 2021): 98–100. https://doi.org/10.2105/AJPH.2020.306006.

Baum, Seth D. "Social Choice Ethics in Artificial Intelligence." *AI & Society* 35, no. 1 (March 2020): 165–76. https://doi.org/10.1007/s00146-017-0760-1.

Baxter, Kathy, Yoav Schlesinger, Sarah Aerni, Lewis Baker, Julie Dawson, Krishnaram Kenthapadi, Isabel Kloumann, and Hanna Wallach. "Bridging the Gap from AI Ethics Research to Practice." In *Proceedings of the 2020 Conference on Fairness, Accountability, and Transparency*, 682–82. Barcelona, Spain: ACM, 2020. https://doi.org/10.1145/3351095.3375680.

Belenguer, Lorenzo. "AI Bias: Exploring Discriminatory Algorithmic Decision-Making Models and the Application of Possible Machine-Centric Solutions Adapted from the Pharmaceutical Industry." *AI and Ethics*, February 10, 2022. https://doi.org/10.1007/s43681-022-00138-8.

Belfield, Haydn. "Activism by the AI Community: Analysing Recent Achievements and Future Prospects." In *Proceedings of the AAAI/ACM Conference on AI, Ethics, and Society*, 15–21. New York, NY: ACM, 2020. https://doi.org/10.1145/3375627.3375814.

Bender, Emily M., Timnit Gebru, Angelina McMillan-Major, and Shmargaret Shmitchell. "On the Dangers of Stochastic Parrots: Can Language Models Be Too Big?" In *Proceedings of the 2021 ACM Conference on Fairness, Accountability, and Transparency*, 610–23. Virtual Event Canada: ACM, 2021. https://doi.org/10.1145/3442188.3445922.

Benjamin, Ruha. *Viral Justice: How We Grow the World We Want*. Princeton: Princeton University Press, 2022.

Benjamins, Richard, Alberto Barbado, and Daniel Sierra. "Responsible AI by Design in Practice." *arXiv E-Prints*, 2019.

Bergstrom, Carl T., and Jevin D. West. *Calling Bullshit: The Art of Skepticism in a Data-Driven World. Random House*, 2020.

Bernstein, Gaia. *Unwired: Gaining Control over Addictive Technologies*. Cambridge: Cambridge University Press, 2023.

Bietti, Elettra. "From Ethics Washing to Ethics Bashing: A Moral Philosophy View on Tech Ethics." *Journal of Social Computing* 2, no. 3 (September 2021): 266–83. https://doi.org/10.23919/JSC.2021.0031.

Birhane, Abeba, Ryan Steed, Victor Ojewale, Briana Vecchione, and Inioluwa Deborah Raji. "AI Auditing: The Broken Bus on the Road to AI Accountability." *arXiv*, January 25, 2024. https://doi.org/10.48550/arXiv.2401.14462.

Bolukbasi, Tolga, Kai-Wei Chang, James Zou, Venkatesh Saligrama, and Adam Kalai. "Man Is to Computer Programmer as Woman Is to Homemaker? Debiasing Word Embeddings." *arXiv*, July 21, 2016. http://arxiv.org/abs/1607.06520.

Brady, William J., Killian McLoughlin, Tuan N. Doan, and Molly J. Crockett. "How Social Learning Amplifies Moral Outrage Expression in Online Social Networks." *Science Advances* 7, no. 33 (2021). https://doi.org/10.1126/sciadv.abe5641.

Breaugh, Martin, and Dean Caivano. "A Living Critique of Domination: Exemplars of Radical Democracy from Black Lives Matter to #MeToo." *Philosophy & Social Criticism*, May 4 (2022): 019145372210937. https://doi.org/10.1177/01914537221093726.

Bruns, Axel. *Are Filter Bubbles Real?* Cambridge: Polity Press, 2019.

Bullock, Justin B., Yu-Che Chen, Johannes Himmelreich, Valerie M. Hudson, Anton Korinek, Matthew M. Young, and Baobao Zhang, eds. *The Oxford Handbook of AI Governance (Oxford Handbooks)*. New York: Oxford University Press, 2024.

Bundy, Professor Alan. "Artificial Intelligence: Art or Science?" *RSA Journal* 136 (1988): 557–69.

Buolamwini, Joy, and Timnit Gebru. "Gender Shades: Intersectional Accuracy Disparities in Commercial Gender Classification." *Proceedings of Machine Learning Research* 81 (2018): 1–15.

Calo, Ryan. "Artificial Intelligence and the Carousel of Soft Law." *IEEE Transactions on Technology and Society* 2, no. 4 (December 2021): 171–74. https://doi.org/10.1109/TTS.2021.3113288.

Cammaerts, Bart, and Robin Mansell. "Digital Platform Policy and Regulation: Toward a Radical Democratic Turn." *International Journal of Communication* 14 (2020): 135–54.

Celis, Elisa. "Debiasing the Algorithm." In *From Bias to Feminist AI*. <A>Alliance, 2021. www.feministai.pubpub.org/pub/debiasing-the-algorithm.

Cercone, Nick, and Carole Murchison. "Integrating Artificial Intelligence into Literary Research: An Invitation to Discuss Design Specifications." *Computers and the Humanities* 19, no. 4 (October 1985): 235–43. https://doi.org/10.1007/BF02259577.

Chen, Lingjiao, Matei Zaharia, and James Zou. "How Is ChatGPT's Behavior Changing over Time?" arXiv, August 1, 2023. http://arxiv.org/abs/2307.09009.

Cheng, Lu, Kush R. Varshney, and Huan Liu. "Socially Responsible AI Algorithms: Issues, Purposes, and Challenges." *Journal of Artificial Intelligence Research* 71 (August 28, 2021): 1137–81. https://doi.org/10.1613/jair.1.12814.

Church, Peter, and Richard Cumbley. "Data and Data Protection." In *Artificial Intelligence: Law and Regulation*, edited by Charles Kerrigan, 163–96. Cheltenham, UK; Northampton, MA: Edward Elgar Publishing, 2022.

Cihon, Peter, Jonas Schuett, and Seth D. Baum. "Corporate Governance of Artificial Intelligence in the Public Interest." *Information* 12, no. 7 (July 5, 2021): 275. https://doi.org/10.3390/info12070275.

Coleman, Flynn. *A Human Algorithm: How Artificial Intelligence Is Redefining Who We Are. Melville House UK*, 2020. www.read.amazon.com/?asin=B07N8YYRVK.

Colonna, Liane. "Artificial Intelligence in Higher Education: Towards a More Relational Approach," 2022.

Cowls, Josh, Andreas Tsamados, Mariarosaria Taddeo, and Luciano Floridi. "The AI Gambit: Leveraging Artificial Intelligence to Combat Climate Change – Opportunities, Challenges, and Recommendations." *AI & Society* 38, no. 1 (February 2023): 283–307. https://doi.org/10.1007/s00146-021-01294-x.

Crawford, Kate. "Artificial Intelligence's White Guy Problem." *The New York Times*, June 25, 2016.

Crawford, Kate. *Atlas of AI*. Yale University Press, 2021.

Cressman, Darryl. *The Necessity of Critique: Andrew Feenberg and the Philosophy of Technology*. Cham, Switzerland: Springer Nature, 2022.

Dahlgren, Peter. "Civic Identity and Net Activism: The Frame of Radical Democracy." In *Radical Democracy and the Internet*, edited by L. Dahlberg and E. Siapera. London: Palgrave Macmillan, 2007.

Dancy, Christopher L., and P. Khalil Saucier. "AI and Blackness: Toward Moving Beyond Bias and Representation." *IEEE Transactions on Technology and Society* 3, no. 1 (March 2022): 31–40. https://doi.org/10.1109/TTS.2021.3125998.

De Almeida, Patricia Gomes Rêgo, Carlos Denner Dos Santos, and Josivania Silva Farias. "Artificial Intelligence Regulation: A Framework for Governance." *Ethics and Information Technology* 23, no. 3 (September 2021): 505–25. https://doi.org/10.1007/s10676-021-09593-z.

De Laat, Paul B. "Companies Committed to Responsible AI: From Principles towards Implementation and Regulation?" *Philosophy & Technology* 34, no. 4 (December 2021): 1135–93. https://doi.org/10.1007/s13347-021-00474-3.

De Vries-Gao, Alex. "Artificial Intelligence: Supply Chain Constraints and Energy Implications." *Joule* 9 (May 2025): 101961. https://doi.org/10.1016/j.joule.2025.101961.

DeLong, Lauren Nicole, Ramon Fernández Mir, and Jacques D. Fleuriot. "Neurosymbolic AI for Reasoning over Knowledge Graphs: A Survey." *IEEE Transactions on Neural Networks and Learning Systems*, 2024, 1–21. https://doi.org/10.1109/TNNLS.2024.3420218.

Deranty, Jean-Philippe, and Thomas Corbin. "Artificial Intelligence and Work: A Critical Review of Recent Research from the Social Sciences." *AI & Society* 39, no. 2 (April 2024): 675–91. https://doi.org/10.1007/s00146-022-01496-x.

DiResta, Renée. *Invisible Rulers: The People Who Turn Lies into Reality*. New York, NY: PublicAffairs, 2024.

Douek, Evelyn. "What Kind of Oversight Board Have You Given Us?" *University of Chicago Law Review Online* 1 (2020): 1–11.

Downey, Laura J. "Emerging Legal Concepts at the Nexus of Law, Technology and Society: A Case Study in Identity." PhD in Law, University of Edinburgh, 2017.

Dressel, Julia, and Hany Farid. "The Accuracy, Fairness, and Limits of Predicting Recidivism." *Science Advances* 4, no. 1 (January 2018): eaao5580. https://doi.org/10.1126/sciadv.aao5580.

Ebert, Isabel, Isabelle Wildhaber, and Jeremias Adams-Prassl. "Big Data in the Workplace: Privacy Due Diligence as a Human Rights-Based Approach to Employee Privacy Protection." *Big Data & Society* 8, no. 1 (January 2021): 205395172110130. https://doi .org/10.1177/20539517211013051.

Edelman, Benjamin, Michael Luca, and Dan Svirsky. "Racial Discrimination in the Sharing Economy: Evidence from a Field Experiment." *American Economic Journal: Applied Economics* 9, no. 2 (April 1, 2017): 1–22. https://doi.org/10.1257/app.20160213.

Ehret, Soenke. "Public Preferences for Governing AI Technology: Comparative Evidence." *Journal of European Public Policy* 29, no. 11 (November 2, 2022): 1779–98. https://doi.org/1 0.1080/13501763.2022.2094988.

Etienne, Hubert. "The Dark Side of the 'Moral Machine' and the Fallacy of Computational Ethical Decision-Making for Autonomous Vehicles." *Law, Innovation and Technology* 13, no. 1 (January 2, 2021): 85–107. https://doi.org/10.1080/17579961.2021.1898310.

Eubanks, Virginia. *Automating Inequality: How High-Tech Tools Profile, Police, and Punish the Poor*. New York: St. Martin's Press, 2018.

EUNIC DX / AI Week: The Geopolitics of AI Technologies, 2020.www.youtube.com/ watch?v=3Fh6lO1w_zo.

European Commission Joint Research Centre. *The EU Digital Markets Act: A Report from a Panel of Economic Experts. LU: Publications Office*, 2021. www.data.europa.eu/doi/10.2760/139337.

Fabbri, Matteo. "Social Influence for Societal Interest: A pro-Ethical Framework for Improving Human Decision Making through Multi-Stakeholder Recommender Systems." *AI & Society* 38, no. 2 (April 2023): 995–1002. https://doi.org/10.1007/s00146-022-01467-2.

Feenberg, Andrew. *Between Reason and Experience: Essays in Technology and Modernity*. Cambridge, MA, and London, England: MIT Press, 2010.

Feenberg, Andrew. *Critical Theory of Technology*. New York: Oxford University Press, 1991.

Feenberg, Andrew. "Marcuse's Critique of Technology Today." *Philosophy & Social Criticism* 49, no. 6 (July 2023): 672–85. https://doi.org/10.1177/01914537231164657.

Feenberg, Andrew. *Technosystem: The Social Life of Reason*. Cambridge, MA: Harvard University Press, 2017.

Feenberg, Andrew. *Transforming Technology: A Critical Theory Revisited*. New York: Oxford University Press, 2002.

Floridi, Luciano, Josh Cowls, Monica Beltrametti, Raja Chatila, Patrice Chazerand, Virginia Dignum, Christoph Luetge, et al. "AI4People – An Ethical Framework for a Good AI Society: Opportunities, Risks, Principles, and Recommendations." *Minds and Machines* 28, no. 4 (December 2018): 689–707. https://doi.org/10.1007/s11023-018-9482-5.

Floridi, Luciano, Josh Cowls, Thomas C. King, and Mariarosaria Taddeo. "How to Design AI for Social Good: Seven Essential Factors." *Science and Engineering Ethics* 26, no. 3 (June 2020): 1771–96. https://doi.org/10.1007/s11948-020-00213-5.

Frey, Carl Benedikt. *The Technology Trap: Capital, Labor, and Power in the Age of Automation*. Princeton & Oxford: Princeton University Press, 2019.

Fuchs, Christian. *Digital Humanism: A Philosophy for 21st Century Digital Society*. Bingley: Emerald, 2022.

Gabriel, Iason. "Artificial Intelligence, Values, and Alignment." *Minds and Machines* 30, no. 3 (September 2020): 411–37. https://doi.org/10.1007/s11023-020-09539-2.

Garcez, Artur d'Avila, and Luís C. Lamb. "Neurosymbolic AI: The 3rd Wave." *Artificial Intelligence Review* 56, no. 11 (November 2023): 12387–406. https://doi.org/10.1007/ s10462-023-10448-w.

Ghosh, Dipayan. "It's All in the Business Model: The Internet's Economic Logic and the Instigation of Disinformation, Hate, and Discrimination." *Georgetown Journal of International Affairs* 21, no. 1 (2020): 129–35. https://doi.org/10.1353/gia.2020.0012.

Gillespie, Nicole, Steve Lockey, Caitlin Curtis, Javad Pool, and Ali Akbari. "Trust in Artificial Intelligence: A Global Study." The University of Queensland and KPMG Australia, 2023.

González-Bailón, Sandra, David Lazer, Pablo Barberá, Meiqing Zhang, Hunt Allcott, Taylor Brown, Adriana Crespo-Tenorio, et al. "Asymmetric Ideological Segregation in Exposure to Political News on Facebook." *Science* 381, no. 6656 (July 28, 2023): 392–98. https://doi .org/10.1126/science.ade7138.

Green, Ben. "The Contestation of Tech Ethics: A Sociotechnical Approach to Technology Ethics in Practice." *Journal of Social Computing* 2, no. 3 (September 2021): 209–25. https:// doi.org/10.23919/JSC.2021.0018.

Green, Ben, and Amba Kak. "The False Comfort of Human Oversight as an Antidote to A.I. Harm." *Future Tense*, June 15, 2021. www.slate.com/technology/2021/06/human-oversight-artificial-intelligence-laws.html.

Greene, Daniel, Anna Lauren Hoffmann, and Luke Stark. "Better, Nicer, Clearer, Fairer: A Critical Assessment of the Movement for Ethical Artificial Intelligence and Machine Learning." In *Proceedings of the 52nd Hawaii International Conference on System Sciences*, 2122–31, 2019.

Guess, Andrew M., Neil Malhotra, Jennifer Pan, Pablo Barberá, Hunt Allcott, Taylor Brown, Adriana Crespo-Tenorio, et al. "How Do Social Media Feed Algorithms Affect Attitudes and Behavior in an Election Campaign?" *Science* 381, no. 6656 (2023): 398–404.

Guess, Andrew M., Neil Malhotra, Jennifer Pan, Pablo Barberá, Hunt Allcott, Taylor Brown, Adriana Crespo-Tenorio, et al. "Reshares on Social Media Amplify Political News but Do Not Detectably Affect Beliefs or Opinions." *Science* 381, no. 6656 (2023): 404–8.

Guihot, Michael. "Coherence in Technology Law." *Law, Innovation and Technology* 11, no. 2 (July 3, 2019): 311–42. https://doi.org/10.1080/17579961.2019.1665792.

Gundersen, Torbjørn, and Kristine Bærøe. "The Future Ethics of Artificial Intelligence in Medicine: Making Sense of Collaborative Models." *Science and Engineering Ethics* 28, no. 2 (April 2022): 17. https://doi.org/10.1007/s11948-022-00369-2.

Gupta, Abhishek. "The Imperative for Sustainable AI Systems." *The Gradient* (blog), September 18, 2021. www.thegradient.pub/sustainable-ai/.

Gutierrez, Carlos Ignacio. "Transitioning from Ideas to Action: Trends in the Enforcement of Soft Law for the Governance of Artificial Intelligence." *IEEE Transactions on Technology and Society* 2, no. 4 (December 2021): 210–16. https://doi.org/10.1109/TTS.2021.3113590.

Gutierrez, Carlos Ignacio, and Gary Marchant. "Soft Law 2.0: Incorporating Incentives and Implementation Mechanisms into the Governance of Artificial Intelligence." *OECD.AI Policy Observatory* (blog), July 13, 2021. www.oecd.ai/en/wonk/soft-law-2-0.

Haan, James P. de. "Preventing #MeToo: Artificial Intelligence, the Law, and Prophylactics." *Minnesota Journal of Law & Inequality* 38, no. 2 (2020): 69–105.

Hacker, Philipp, Johann Cordes, and Janina Rochon. "Regulating Gatekeeper AI and Data: Transparency, Access, and Fairness under the DMA, the GDPR, and Beyond." *SSRN Electronic Journal*, 2022. https://doi.org/10.2139/ssrn.4316944.

Hadfield, Gillian K., and Jack Clark. "Regulatory Markets: The Future of AI Governance." *arXiv*, April 2023. https://arxiv.org/pdf/2304.04914.pdf.

Harari, Yuval Noah. "Why Technology Favors Tyranny." *The Atlantic*, October 24, 2018, 16.

Heilinger, Jan-Christoph. "The Ethics of AI Ethics. A Constructive Critique." *Philosophy & Technology* 35, no. 3 (September 2022): 61. https://doi.org/10.1007/s13347-022-00557-9.

Hicks, Marie. *Programmed Inequality: How Britain Discarded Women Technologists and Lost Its Edge in Computing*. Cambridge: MIT Press, 2017.

Hicks, Michael Townsen, James Humphries, and Joe Slater. "ChatGPT Is Bullshit." *Ethics and Information Technology* 26, no. 2 (June 2024): 38. https://doi.org/10.1007/ s10676-024-09775-5.

Hirsch, Dennis, Timothy Bartley, Arvind Chandrasekaran, Davon Norris, Srinivasan Parthasarathy, and Piers Norris Turner. *Business Data Ethics: Emerging Models for Governing AI and Advanced Analytics*. Cham, Switzerland: Springer, 2024.

Hirsch, Professor Dennis, Jared Ott, and Angie Westover-Munoz. "Responsible AI Management: Evolving Practice, Growing Value." International Association of Privacy Professionals & The Ohio State University Program on Data and Governance, 2024.

Hoffmann, Anna Lauren. "Terms of Inclusion: Data, Discourse, Violence." *New Media & Society* 23, no. 12 (2021): 3539–56. https://doi.org/10.1177/1461444820958725.

Hooker, Sara. "Moving beyond 'Algorithmic Bias Is a Data Problem.'" *Patterns* 2, no. 4 (April 2021): 100241. https://doi.org/10.1016/j.patter.2021.100241.

Hosseinmardi, Homa, Amir Ghasemian, Aaron Clauset, Markus Mobius, David M. Rothschild, and Duncan J. Watts. "Examining the Consumption of Radical Content on YouTube." *Proceedings of the National Academy of Sciences* 118, no. 32 (August 10, 2021): e2101967118. https://doi.org/10.1073/pnas.2101967118.

Hu, Shu, Yuezun Li, and Siwei Lyu. "Exposing GAN-Generated Faces Using Inconsistent Corneal Specular Highlights." *arXiv*, October 12, 2020. http://arxiv.org/abs/2009.11924.

Ihde, Don. "Technology and Prognostic Predicaments." *AI & Society* 13, no. 1–2 (March 1999): 44–51. https://doi.org/10.1007/BF01205256.

Jobin, Anna, Licinia Güttel, Laura Liebig, and Christian Katzenbach. "AI Federalism: Shaping AI Policy within States in Germany." Shaping AI. Alexander von Humboldt Institute for Internet and Society; University of Bremen, 2021. www.osf.io/dc9f8.

Jobin, Anna, Marcello Ienca, and Effy Vayena. "Artificial Intelligence: The Global Landscape of Ethics Guidelines." *Nature Machine Intelligence* 1, no. 9 (2019): 389–99.

Joerges, Bernward. "Do Politics Have Artefacts?" *Social Studies of Science* 29, no. 3 (1999): 411–31.

John-Mathews, Jean-Marie, Dominique Cardon, and Christine Balagué. "From Reality to World. A Critical Perspective on AI Fairness." *Journal of Business Ethics* (February 25, 2022). https://doi.org/10.1007/s10551-022-05055-8.

Karell, Daniel, Andrew Linke, Edward Holland, and Edward Hendrickson. "'Born for a Storm': Hard-Right Social Media and Civil Unrest." *American Sociological Review* 88, no. 2 (April 2023): 322–49. https://doi.org/10.1177/00031224231156190.

Kasirzadeh, Atoosa. "Algorithmic Fairness and Structural Injustice: Insights from Feminist Political Philosophy." In AIES'22: Proceedings of the AAAI/ACM Conference on AI, Ethics, and Society. Association for Computing Machinery (ACM), New York, pp. 349–56. Oxford, UK; New York, NY, 2022. https://doi.org/10.1145/3514094.3534188.

Kellner, Douglas. "Schoolman on Marcuse." *New German Critique*, no. 26 (1982): 185–201. https://doi.org/10.2307/488031.

Kelly, Kevin. *The Inevitable: Understanding the 12 Technological Forces That Will Shape Our Future*. New York: Viking Press, 2016.

Kerr, Aphra, Marguerite Barry, and John D. Kelleher. "Expectations of Artificial Intelligence and the Performativity of Ethics: Implications for Communication Governance." *Big Data & Society* 7, no. 1 (January 2020): 1–12. https://doi.org/10.1177/2053951720915939.

Kieslich, Kimon, Birte Keller, and Christopher Starke. "Artificial Intelligence Ethics by Design. Evaluating Public Perception on the Importance of Ethical Design Principles of Artificial Intelligence." *Big Data & Society* 9, no. 1 (January 2022): 205395172210929. https://doi.org/10.1177/20539517221092956.

Klonick, Kate. "The Facebook Oversight Board: Creating an Independent Institution to Adjudicate Online Free Expression." *The Yale Law Journal* 129, no. 8 (2020): 2418–99.

Kooiman, Jan. "Social-Political Governance: Overview, Reflections and Design." *Public Management: An International Journal of Research and Theory* 1, no. 1 (1999): 67–92.

Laclau, Ernesto, and Chantal Mouffe. *Hegemony and Socialist Strategy: Towards a Radical Democratic Politics*. London, UK: Verso, 1985.

Lavista Ferres, Juan M., and William B. Weeks. *AI for Good: Applications in Sustainability, Humanitarian Action, and Health*. John Wiley & Sons, 2024.

Leenders, Gijs. "The Regulation of Artificial Intelligence – A Case Study of the Partnership on AI." *Becoming Human: Artificial Intelligence Magazine (Medium Blog)* (blog), April 13, 2019. www.becominghuman.ai/the-regulation-of-artificial-intelligence-a-case-study-of-the-partnership-on-ai-c1c22526c19f.

Leibowicz, Claire R., and Christian H. Cardona. "From Principles to Practices: Lessons Learned from Applying Partnership on AI's (PAI) Synthetic Media Framework to 11 Use Cases." *arXiv*, 2024.

Liang, Weixin, Mert Yuksekgonul, Yining Mao, Eric Wu, and James Zou. "GPT Detectors Are Biased against Non-Native English Writers." *Patterns* 4, no. 7 (July 2023): 100779. https://doi.org/10.1016/j.patter.2023.100779.

Lin, Zhiyuan "Jerry," Jongbin Jung, Sharad Goel, and Jennifer Skeem. "The Limits of Human Predictions of Recidivism." *Science Advances* 6, no. 7 (2020): 1–8. https://doi.org/10.1126/sciadv.aaz0652.

Liu, David, Priyanka Nanayakkara, Sarah Ariyan Sakha, Grace Abuhamad, Su Lin Blodgett, Nicholas Diakopoulos, Jessica R. Hullman, and Tina Eliassi-Rad. "Examining Responsibility and Deliberation in AI Impact Statements and Ethics Reviews." In *Proceedings of the 2022 AAAI/ACM Conference on AI, Ethics, and Society*, 424–35. Oxford, UK: ACM, 2022. https://doi.org/10.1145/3514094.3534155.

Lobel, Orly. *The Equality Machine: Harnessing Digital Technology for a Brighter, More Inclusive Future*. New York: PublicAffairs, 2022.

Luccioni, Alexandra Sasha, and Joseph D. Viviano. "What's in the Box? A Preliminary Analysis of Undesirable Content in the Common Crawl Corpus." *arXiv*, May 31, 2021. http://arxiv.org/abs/2105.02732.

Luccioni, Sasha. "The Mounting Human and Environmental Costs of Generative AI." *ArsTechnica*, April 12, 2023. www.arstechnica.com/gadgets/2023/04/generative-ai-is-cool-but-lets-not-forget-its-human-and-environmental-costs/.

MacCarthy, Mark, and Kenneth Propp. "Machines Learn That Brussels Writes the Rules: The EU's New AI Regulation." *Lawfare Blog* (blog), April 28, 2021. www.lawfareblog.com/machines-learn-brussels-writes-rules-eus-new-ai-regulation.

Madaio, Michael, Lisa Egede, Hariharan Subramonyam, Jennifer Wortman Vaughan, and Hanna Wallach. "Assessing the Fairness of AI Systems: AI Practitioners' Processes, Challenges, and Needs for Support." *Proceedings of the ACM on Human-Computer Interaction* 6, no. CSCW1 (March 30, 2022): 1–26. https://doi.org/10.1145/3512899.

Mantelero, Alessandro. *Beyond Data: Human Rights, Ethical and Social Impact Assessment in AI*. Information Technology and Law Series, IT&Law 36. The Hague: Asser Press, 2022. https://doi.org/10.1007/978-94-6265-531-7.

Marchant, Gary. "'Soft Law' Governance of Artificial Intelligence." AI Pulse January 25, 2019. Retrieved from www.escholarship.org/uc/item/0jq252ks.

Marchant, Gary, Braden R. Allenby, and Joseph Herkert, eds. *The Growing Gap Between Emerging Technologies and Legal-Ethical Oversight: The Pacing Problem*. The International Library of Ethics, Law and Technology 7. Dordrecht, Heidelberg, London, New York: Springer, 2011.

Marchant, Gary E. "Professional Societies as Adopters and Enforcers of AI Soft Law." *IEEE Transactions on Technology and Society* 2, no. 4 (December 2021): 183–91. https://doi.org/10.1109/TTS.2021.3116524.

Marcus, Gary. "The Next Decade in AI: Four Steps Towards Robust Artificial Intelligence." *arXiv Preprint*, 2020.

Marcuse, Herbert. "From Ontology to Technology: Fundamental Tendencies of Industrial Society." In *Critical Theory and Society: A Reader*, edited by Stephen Eric Bronner and Douglas MacKay Kellner, 119–27. New York: Routledge, 1989.

Marcuse, Herbert. *One-Dimensional Man: Studies in the Ideology of Advanced Industrial Society*. Boston: Beacon Press, 1991.

Marcuse, Herbert. "Some Social Implications of Modern Technology." In *Technology, War and Fascism: Collected Papers of Herbert Marcuse Volume One*, edited by Douglas Kellner. London and New York: Routledge, 1998.

Martin, Kirsten, and Carolina Villegas-Galaviz. "AI and Corporate Responsibility: How and Why Firms Are Responsible for AI." In *Encyclopedia of Business and Professional Ethics*, edited by Deborah C. Poff and Alex C. Michalos, 1–5. Cham: Springer International Publishing, 2022. https://doi.org/10.1007/978-3-319-23514-1_1297-1.

Marwick, Alice, Benjamin Clancy, and Katherine Furl. "Far-Right Online Radicalization: A Review of the Literature." The Bulletin of Technology and Public Life. Center for Information, Technology, and Public Life, 2022.

Maslej, Nestor, Loredana Fattorini, Raymond Perrault, Yolanda Gil, Vanessa Parli, Njenga Kariuki, Emily Capstick, et al. "*Artificial Intelligence Index Report 2025*." Stanford, California: AI Index Steering Committee, Institute for Human-Centered AI, Stanford University, 2025.

Mayor, Adrienne. *Gods and Robots: Myths, Machines, and Ancient Dreams of Technology*. Princeton & Oxford: Princeton University Press, 2018.

Mehrabi, Ninareh, Fred Morstatter, Nripsuta Saxena, Kristina Lerman, and Aram Galstyan. "A Survey on Bias and Fairness in Machine Learning." *ACM Computing Surveys* 54, no. 6 (July 31, 2022): 1–35. https://doi.org/10.1145/3457607.

Metcalf, Jacob. "Owning Ethics: Corporate Logics, Silicon Valley, and the Institutionalization of Ethics." *Social Research: An International Quarterly* 86, no. 2 (2019): 449–76.

Meyer, Mikaela, Aaron Horowitz, Erica Marshall, and Kristian Lum. "Flipping the Script on Criminal Justice Risk Assessment: An Actuarial Model for Assessing the Risk the Federal Sentencing System Poses to Defendants." Seoul, Republic of Korea, 2022. www.dl.acm .org/doi/fullHtml/10.1145/3531146.3533104.

Mikalef, Patrick, Kieran Conboy, Jenny Eriksson Lundström, and Aleš Popovič. "Thinking Responsibly about Responsible AI and 'the Dark Side' of AI." *European Journal of Information Systems* 31, no. 3 (May 4, 2022): 257–68. https://doi.org/10.1080/0960085X.2022.2026621.

Mökander, Jakob. "Auditing of AI: Legal, Ethical and Technical Approaches." *Digital Society* 2, no. 3 (December 2023): 49. https://doi.org/10.1007/s44206-023-00074-y.

Molnar, Petra. "Technology on the Margins: AI and Global Migration Management from a Human Rights Perspective." *Cambridge International Law Journal* 8, no. 2 (December 2019): 305–30. https://doi.org/10.4337/cilj.2019.02.07.

Morales-Forero, Andres, Samuel Bassetto, and Eric Coatanea. "Toward Safe AI." *AI & Society* 38, no. 2 (April 2023): 685–96. https://doi.org/10.1007/s00146-022-01591-z.

Morley, Jessica, Luciano Floridi, Libby Kinsey, and Anat Elhalal. "From What to How: An Initial Review of Publicly Available AI Ethics Tools, Methods and Research to Translate Principles into Practices." *Science and Engineering Ethics* 26, no. 4 (August 2020): 2141–68. https://doi.org/10.1007/s11948-019-00165-5.

Mouffe, Chantal. *The Return of the Political*. London and New York: Verso, 1993.

Mügge, Daniel. "The Securitization of the EU's Digital Tech Regulation." *Journal of European Public Policy* (January 30, 2023): 1–16. https://doi.org/10.1080/13501763.2023 .2171090.

Murgia, Madhumita. *Code Dependent: Living in the Shadow of AI*. New York: Henry Holt and Company, 2024.

Narayanan, Arvind, and Sayash Kapoor. *AI Snake Oil: What Artificial Intelligence Can Do, What It Can't, and How to Tell the Difference*. Princeton: Princeton University Press, 2024.

Narayanan Venkit, Pranav, Mukund Srinath, and Shomir Wilson. "Automated Ableism: An Exploration of Explicit Disability Biases in Sentiment and Toxicity Analysis Models." In *Proceedings of the 3rd Workshop on Trustworthy Natural Language Processing (TrustNLP 2023)*, 26–34. Toronto, Canada: Association for Computational Linguistics, 2023. https://doi.org/10.18653/v1/2023.trustnlp-1.3.

Neff, Gina. *Venture Labor Work and the Burden of Risk in Innovative Industries*. Cambridge, MA: MIT Press, 2012.

Nilsson, Nils J. *The Quest for Artificial Intelligence: A History of Ideas and Achievements*. 1st ed. Cambridge University Press, 2009. https://doi.org/10.1017/CBO9780511819346.

Nkonde, Mutale. "Automated Anti-Blackness: Facial Recognition in Brooklyn, New York." *Harvard Journal of African American Public Policy* 20 (2019): 30–36.

Noble, Safiya Umoja. *Algorithms of Oppression: How Search Engines Reinforce Racism*. New York: NYU Press, 2018.

Nyhan, Brendan, Jaime Settle, Emily Thorson, Magdalena Wojcieszak, Pablo Barberá, Annie Y. Chen, Hunt Allcott, et al. "Like-Minded Sources on Facebook Are Prevalent but Not Polarizing." *Nature* 620, no. 7972 (August 3, 2023): 137–44. https://doi.org/10.1038/s41586-023-06297-w.

Obafemi-Ajayi, Tayo, Andy Perkins, Bindu Nanduri, Donald C. Wunsch II, James A. Foster, and Joan Peckham. "No-Boundary Thinking: A Viable Solution to Ethical Data-Driven AI in Precision Medicine." *AI and Ethics* (November 29, 2021): 1–9. https://doi.org/10.1007/s43681-021-00118-4.

O'Neil, Cathy. *Weapons of Math Destruction: How Big Data Increases Inequality and Threatens Democracy*. New York: Broadway Books, 2016.

Pariser, Eli. *The Filter Bubble: What the Internet Is Hiding from You*. London: Penguin, 2011.

Pasquale, Frank. "Data-Informed Duties in AI Development." *Columbia Law Review* 119, no. 7 (2019): 1917–40.

Pasquinelli, Matteo. *The Eye of the Master: A Social History of Artificial Intelligence*. New York and London: Verso Books, 2023.

Pei, Kexin, Yinzhi Cao, Junfeng Yang, and Suman Jana. "DeepXplore: Automated Whitebox Testing of Deep Learning Systems." In *Proceedings of the 26th Symposium on Operating Systems Principles*, 1–18, 2017. https://doi.org/10.1145/3132747.3132785.

Peters, Dorian, Karina Vold, Diana Robinson, and Rafael A. Calvo. "Responsible AI – Two Frameworks for Ethical Design Practice." *IEEE Transactions on Technology and Society* 1, no. 1 (March 2020): 34–47. https://doi.org/10.1109/TTS.2020.2974991.

Phillips, P. Jonathon, Carina A. Hahn, Peter C. Fontana, Amy N. Yates, Kristen Greene, David A. Broniatowski, and Mark A. Przybocki. *Four Principles of Explainable Artificial Intelligence*. Gaithersburg, MD: National Institute of Standards and Technology (U.S.), September 29, 2021. https://doi.org/10.6028/NIST.IR.8312.

Quinn, Michael J. *Ethics for the Information Age*. Boston, MA: Pearson, 2014.

Raji, Inioluwa Deborah, and Joy Buolamwini. "Actionable Auditing Revisited – Investigating the Impact of Publicly Naming Biased Performance Results of Commercial AI Products." *Communications of the ACM* 66, no. 1 (2023): 101–8.

Renda, Andrea. *Artificial Intelligence: Ethics, Governance and Policy Challenges: Report of a CEPS Task Force*. Brussels: Centre for European Policy Studies, 2019.

Ribeiro, Manoel Horta, Raphael Ottoni, Robert West, Virgílio A. F. Almeida, and Wagner Meira. "Auditing Radicalization Pathways on YouTube." In *Proceedings of the 2020*

Conference on Fairness, Accountability, and Transparency, 131–41. Barcelona, Spain: ACM, 2020. https://doi.org/10.1145/3351095.3372879.

Rijmenam, Mark van. "Building a Greener Future: The Importance of Sustainable AI." *The Digital Speaker* (blog), February 23, 2023. www.thedigitalspeaker.com/greener-future-importance-sustainable-ai/.

Robertson, Ronald E., Shan Jiang, Kenneth Joseph, Lisa Friedland, David Lazer, and Christo Wilson. "Auditing Partisan Audience Bias within Google Search." *Proceedings of the ACM on Human-Computer Interaction* 2, no. CSCW (November 1, 2018): 1–22. https://doi.org/10.1145/3274417.

Rochel, Johan, and Florian Evéquoz. "Getting into the Engine Room: A Blueprint to Investigate the Shadowy Steps of AI Ethics." *AI & Society* 36 (2021): 609–22.

Russell, Stuart J., and Peter Norvig. *Artificial Intelligence: A Modern Approach*. Upper Saddle River, NJ: Pearson Education Limited, 2013.

Ryan, Mark. "In AI We Trust: Ethics, Artificial Intelligence, and Reliability." *Science and Engineering Ethics* 26, no. 5 (October 2020): 2749–67. https://doi.org/10.1007/s11948-020-00228-y.

Sadowski, Jathan. *The Mechanic and the Luddite: A Ruthless Criticism of Technology and Capitalism*. Oakland: University of California Press, 2025.

Schaake, Marietje. *The Tech Coup: How to Save Democracy from Silicon Valley*. Princeton: Princeton University Press, 2024.

Schellmann, Hilke. *The Algorithm: How AI Decides Who Gets Hired, Monitored, Promoted & Fired & Why We Need to Fight Back Now*. New York City, NY: Hachette Books, 2024.

Schiff, Daniel, Jason Borenstein, Justin Biddle, and Kelly Laas. "AI Ethics in the Public, Private, and NGO Sectors: A Review of a Global Document Collection." *IEEE Transactions on Technology and Society* 2, no. 1 (March 2021): 31–42. https://doi.org/10.1109/TTS.2021.3052127.

Schiff, Daniel, Bogdana Rakova, Aladdin Ayesh, Anat Fanti, and Michael Lennon. "Principles to Practices for Responsible AI: Closing the Gap." *arXiv*, June 8, 2020. http://arxiv.org/abs/2006.04707.

Schuett, Jonas, Anka Reuel, and Alexis Carlier. "How to Design an AI Ethics Board." *arXiv*, April 14, 2023. http://arxiv.org/abs/2304.07249.

Schultz, Mario D., and Peter Seele. "Towards AI Ethics' Institutionalization: Knowledge Bridges from Business Ethics to Advance Organizational AI Ethics." *AI and Ethics*, 2022. https://doi.org/10.1007/s43681-022-00150-y.

Schulze, Heidi, Julian Hohner, Simon Greipl, Maximilian Girgnhuber, Isabell Desta, and Diana Rieger. "Far-Right Conspiracy Groups on Fringe Platforms: A Longitudinal Analysis of Radicalization Dynamics on Telegram." *Convergence: The International Journal of Research into New Media Technologies* 28, no. 4 (August 2022): 1103–26. https://doi.org/10.1177/13548565221104977.

Schwartz, Reva, Apostol Vassilev, Kristen Greene, Lori Perine, Andrew Burt, and Patrick Hall. "Towards a Standard for Identifying and Managing Bias in Artificial Intelligence." Gaithersburg, MD: National Institute of Standards and Technology (U.S.), March 15, 2022. https://doi.org/10.6028/NIST.SP.1270.

Scientific Foresight Unit. "The Impact of the General Data Protection Regulation on Artificial Intelligence." LU: Publications Office, European Parliament Directorate General for Parliamentary Research Services, 2020. www.data.europa.eu/doi/10.2861/293.

Seah, Josephine, and Mark James Findlay. "Communicating Ethics across the AI Ecosystem." SMU Centre for AI & Data Governance Research Paper, 2021. www.ssrn.com/abstract=3895522.

Selbst, Andrew D., Danah Boyd, Sorelle A. Friedler, Suresh Venkatasubramanian, and Janet Vertesi. "Fairness and Abstraction in Sociotechnical Systems." In *Proceedings of the*

Conference on Fairness, Accountability, and Transparency, 59–68. Atlanta, GA: ACM, 2019. https://doi.org/10.1145/3287560.3287598.

Shin, Donghee. "The Effects of Explainability and Causability on Perception, Trust, and Acceptance: Implications for Explainable AI." *International Journal of Human-Computer Studies* 146 (February 2021): 102551. https://doi.org/10.1016/j.ijhcs.2020.102551.

Shneiderman, Ben. "Responsible AI: Bridging from Ethics to Practice." *Communications of the ACM* 64, no. 8 (August 2021): 32–35. https://doi.org/10.1145/3445973.

Smuha, Nathalie A. "From a 'Race to AI' to a 'Race to AI Regulation': Regulatory Competition for Artificial Intelligence." *Law, Innovation and Technology* 13, no. 1 (January 2, 2021): 57–84. https://doi.org/10.1080/17579961.2021.1898300.

Smuha, Nathalie A. "The EU Approach to Ethics Guidelines for Trustworthy Artificial Intelligence." *Computer Law Review International* 20, no. 4 (August 1, 2019): 97–106. https://doi.org/10.9785/cri-2019-200402.

So, Wonyoung, Pranay Lohia, Rakesh Pimplikar, A. E. Hosoi, and Catherine D'Ignazio. "Beyond Fairness: Reparative Algorithms to Address Historical Injustices of Housing Discrimination in the US." In *2022 ACM Conference on Fairness, Accountability, and Transparency*, 988–1004. Seoul, Republic of Korea: ACM, 2022. https://doi.org/10.1145/3531146.3533160.

Spier, Shaked. "The Politics of Platform Technologies: A Critical Conceptualization of the Platform and Sharing Economy." *Philosophy & Technology* 38, no. 1 (March 2025): 12. https://doi.org/10.1007/s13347-025-00840-5.

Stahl, B. C., A. Andreou, P. Brey, T. Hatzakis, A. Kirichenko, K. Macnish, S. Laulhé Shaelou, A. Patel, M. Ryan, and D. Wright. "Artificial Intelligence for Human Flourishing – Beyond Principles for Machine Learning." *Journal of Business Research* 124 (January 2021): 374–88. https://doi.org/10.1016/j.jbusres.2020.11.030.

Stahl, Bernd Carsten, Doris Schroeder, and Rowena Rodrigues. *Ethics of Artificial Intelligence: Case Studies and Options for Addressing Ethical Challenges*. SpringerBriefs in Research and Innovation Governance. Cham: Springer International Publishing, 2023. https://doi.org/10.1007/978-3-031-17040-9.

Steels, Luc, and Ramon Lopez de Mantaras. "The Barcelona Declaration for the Proper Development and Usage of Artificial Intelligence in Europe." *AI Communications* 31, no. 6 (December 21, 2018): 485–94. https://doi.org/10.3233/AIC-180607.

Strubell, Emma, Ananya Ganesh, and Andrew McCallum. "Energy and Policy Considerations for Deep Learning in NLP." *arXiv*, June 5, 2019. http://arxiv.org/abs/1906.02243.

Sunstein, Cass R. *Going to Extremes: How Like Minds Unite and Divide*. New York, NY: Oxford University Press, 2009.

Tang, Brian W. "Independent AI Ethics Committees and ESG Corporate Reporting on AI as Emerging Corporate and AI Governance Trends." In *The AI Book: The Artificial Intelligence Handbook for Investors, Entrepreneurs and FinTech Visionaries*, edited by Ivana Bartoletti, Anne Leslie, and Shân M. Millie, 180–85. John Wiley & Sons, 2020.

Tanweer, Anissa. "Tradeoffs All the Way down: Ethical Abduction as a Decision-Making Process for Data-Intensive Technology Development." *Big Data & Society* 9, no. 1 (January 2022): 205395172211013. https://doi.org/10.1177/20539517221101351.

Tarnoff, Ben. *Internet for the People: The Fight for Our Digital Future*. London and New York: Verso Books, 2022.

Tavani, Herman T. "Expanding the Standard ICT-Ethics Framework in an Era of AI." *Journal of Information Ethics* 29, no. 2 (2020): 11–35.

The High-Level Expert Group on AI. *Ethics Guidelines for Trustworthy AI*. Brussels: European Commission, April 8, 2019.

Thiebes, Scott, Sebastian Lins, and Ali Sunyaev. "Trustworthy Artificial Intelligence." *Electronic Markets* 31, no. 2 (June 2021): 447–64. https://doi.org/10.1007/s12525-020-00441-4.

Tigard, Daniel W. "Responsible AI and Moral Responsibility: A Common Appreciation." *AI and Ethics* 1, no. 2 (May 2021): 113–17. https://doi.org/10.1007/s43681-020-00009-0.

Timcke, Scott. *Algorithms and the End of Politics: How Technology Shapes 21st-Century American Life*. Bristol: Bristol University Press, 2021.

Turnbull, Neil. "At Modernity's Limit: Technology as World and Idea." *Theory, Culture & Society* 23, no. 5 (September 2006): 135–50. https://doi.org/10.1177/0263276406067103.

Turner Lee, Nicol. *Digitally Invisible: How the Internet Is Creating the New Underclass*. Washington, DC: Brookings Institution Press, 2024.

Vaidhyanathan, Siva. *Antisocial Media: How Facebook Disconnects and Undermines Democracy*. New York: Oxford University Press, 2018.

Vallor, Shannon. *The AI Mirror: How to Reclaim Our Humanity in an Age of Machine Thinking*. New York City, NY: Oxford University Press, 2024.

Vallor, Shannon, and George A. Bekey. "Artificial Intelligence and the Ethics of Self-Learning Robots." In *Robot Ethics 2.0: From Autonomous Cars to Artificial Intelligence*, edited by Patrick Lin, Keith Abney, and Ryan Jenkins. New York: Oxford University Press, 2017.

Van Bekkum, Marvin, and Frederik Zuiderveen Borgesius. "Using Sensitive Data to Prevent Discrimination by Artificial Intelligence: Does the GDPR Need a New Exception?" *Computer Law & Security Review* 48 (April 2023): 105770. https://doi.org/10.1016/j.clsr.2022.105770.

Vaswani, Ashish, Noam Shazeer, Niki Parmar, Jakob Uszkoreit, Llion Jones, Aidan N. Gomez, Łukasz Kaiser, and Illia Polosukhin. *Attention Is All You Need*. 31st Conference on Neural Information Processing Systems (NIPS 2017), Long Beach, CA, 2017.

Veale, Michael, and Frederik Zuiderveen Borgesius. "Demystifying the Draft EU Artificial Intelligence Act – Analysing the Good, the Bad, and the Unclear Elements of the Proposed Approach." *Computer Law Review International* 22, no. 4 (2021): 97–112.

Veale, Michael, Kira Matus, and Robert Gorwa. "AI and Global Governance: Modalities, Rationales, Tensions." *Annual Review of Law and Social Science* 19 (2023): 255–75.

Villasenor, John. "Soft Law as a Complement to AI Regulation." *Brookings* (blog), July 31, 2020. www.brookings.edu/research/soft-law-as-a-complement-to-ai-regulation/.

Vöneky, Silja. "Key Elements of Responsible Artificial Intelligence – Disruptive Technologies, Dynamic Law." *Ordnung Der Wissenschaft*, 1 (2020): 9–22.

Wachter, Sandra. *Artificial Intelligence: GDPR and Beyond*. The Alan Turing Institute, 2018. www.youtube.com/watch?v=7pibisWRncY.

Wachter, Sandra, Brent Mittelstadt, and Luciano Floridi. "Transparent, Explainable, and Accountable AI for Robotics." *Science Robotics* 2, no. 6 (May 31, 2017): 1–2. https://doi .org/10.1126/scirobotics.aan6080.

Waelen, Rosalie. "Why AI Ethics Is a Critical Theory." *Philosophy & Technology* 35, no. 1 (March 2022): 9. https://doi.org/10.1007/s13347-022-00507-5.

Waldman, Ari Ezra. "Challenging Technology Expertise." *SSRN*, 2025.

Walters, William H. "The Effectiveness of Software Designed to Detect AI-Generated Writing: A Comparison of 16 AI Text Detectors." *Open Information Science* 7, no. 1 (October 6, 2023): 20220158. https://doi.org/10.1515/opis-2022-0158.

Walters, William H., and Esther Isabelle Wilder. "Fabrication and Errors in the Bibliographic Citations Generated by ChatGPT." *Scientific Reports* 13, no. 1 (September 7, 2023): 14045. https://doi.org/10.1038/s41598-023-41032-5.

Weizenbaum, Joseph. *Computer Power and Human Reason: From Judgment to Calculation*. San Francisco, CA: W. H. Freeman and Co., 1976.

Welbl, Johannes, Amelia Glaese, Jonathan Uesato, Sumanth Dathathri, John Mellor, Lisa Anne Hendricks, Kirsty Anderson, Pushmeet Kohli, Ben Coppin, and Po-Sen Huang. "Challenges in Detoxifying Language Models." *arXiv:2109.07445* [Cs], September 15, 2021. http://arxiv.org/abs/2109.07445.

Wernick, Alina. "Impact Assessment as a Legal Design Pattern – A 'Timeless Way' of Managing Future Risks?" *Digital Society* 3, no. 2 (August 2024): 29. https://doi.org/10.1007/s44206-024-00111-4.

Wiener, Norbert. *Invention*. MIT Press, 1993.

Winner, Langdon. "Do Artifacts Have Politics?" *Daedalus* 109, no. 1 (1980): 121–36.

Winner, Langdon. "The Democratic Shaping of Technology: Its Rise, Fall and Possible Rebirth." *Engaging Science, Technology, and Society* 7, no. 1 (October 5, 2021): 95–103. https://doi.org/10.17351/ests2021.825.

Winner, Langdon. "Where Technological Determinism Went." In *Visions of STS: Counterpoints in Science, Technology, and Society Studies*, edited by Stephen H. Cutcliffe and Carl Mitcham. Albany: State University of New York Press, 2001.

Wong, David, and Luciano Floridi. "Meta's Oversight Board: A Review and Critical Assessment." *Minds and Machines* 33, no. 2 (2023): 261–84. https://doi.org/10.1007/s11023-022-09613-x.

World Economic Forum. "Global Gender Gap Report 2023." *Insight Report*, June 2023.

World Economic Forum, In collaboration with the Markkula Center for Applied Ethics at Santa Clara University, USA. "Responsible Use of Technology: The Microsoft Case Study." White paper, February 2021.

Wu, Carole-Jean, Ramya Raghavendra, Udit Gupta, Bilge Acun, Newsha Ardalani, Kiwan Maeng, Gloria Chang, et al. "Sustainable AI: Environmental Implications, Challenges and Opportunities." *arXiv*, January 9, 2022. http://arxiv.org/abs/2111.00364.

Wynsberghe, Aimee van. "Sustainable AI: AI for Sustainability and the Sustainability of AI." *AI and Ethics* 1, no. 3 (August 2021): 213–18. https://doi.org/10.1007/s43681-021-00043-6.

Young, Iris Marion. *Responsibility for Justice*. Oxford: Oxford University Press, 2011.

Yu, Bowen, Ye Yuan, Loren Terveen, Zhiwei Steven Wu, Jodi Forlizzi, and Haiyi Zhu. "Keeping Designers in the Loop: Communicating Inherent Algorithmic Trade-Offs Across Multiple Objectives." *arXiv:1910.03061 [Cs]*, July 5, 2020. http://arxiv.org/abs/1910.03061.

Zhao, Jieyu, Tianlu Wang, Mark Yatskar, Vicente Ordonez, and Kai-Wei Chang. "Men Also Like Shopping: Reducing Gender Bias Amplification Using Corpus-Level Constraints." *arXiv*, July 28, 2017. http://arxiv.org/abs/1707.09457.

Zuiderveen Borgesius, Frederik J. "Strengthening Legal Protection against Discrimination by Algorithms and Artificial Intelligence." *The International Journal of Human Rights* 24, no. 10 (November 25, 2020): 1572–93. https://doi.org/10.1080/13642987.2020.1743976.

Index

Printed by Integrated Books International,
United States of America